Modern Trends in Pervasive Intelligence

Edited by

Shruti Bhargava Choubey
Department of Electronics and Communication Engineering
Sreenidhi Institute of Science & Technology,
Hyderabad, Telangana
India

Yogesh Shrivastava
Department of Mechanical Engineering
Galgotias College of Engineering and Technology,
Greater Noida, Uttar Pradesh, India

Modern Trends in Pervasive Intelligence

Editors: Shruti Bhargava Choubey & Yogesh Shrivastava

ISBN (Online): 979-8-89881-501-1

ISBN (Print): 979-8-89881-502-8

ISBN (Paperback): 979-8-89881-503-5

Published by Bentham Science Publishers Pte. Ltd. Singapore,

First published in 2026.

Bentham Science Publishers Pte. Ltd.
No. 9 Raffles Place
Office No. 26-01
Singapore 048619
Singapore
Email: subscriptions@benthamscience.net

BENTHAM
SCIENCE

CONTENTS

FOREWORD

It gives me immense pride and satisfaction to present Modern Trends in Pervasive Intelligence, a scholarly volume that brings together the insights and expertise of distinguished authors from diverse domains. This work is the result of collective dedication, academic rigor, and an unwavering commitment to advancing knowledge in the field of pervasive intelligence.

The chapters contained within this book cover a wide spectrum of contemporary themes, ranging from intelligent sensing and context-aware computing to edge AI, IoT, and smart environments. Each contribution reflects not only deep research and analysis but also a vision for how these technologies can shape the future of intelligent systems and their integration into everyday life.

This endeavor has been marked by close collaboration between editors and contributors, and I wish to acknowledge the professionalism, responsiveness, and intellectual engagement that each author has brought to the process. Their work has given this volume both depth and relevance, making it a valuable resource for researchers, students, and practitioners alike.

In many ways, this book is more than a collection of chapters, it is a reflection of interdisciplinary collaboration and the shared pursuit of innovation. It demonstrates how collective scholarship can address pressing challenges and open new pathways in the rapidly evolving landscape of pervasive intelligence.

I extend my heartfelt congratulations to the editors and authors for their commitment and excellence. I am confident that this book will serve as an important reference for years to come, inspiring further research and practical applications in this dynamic field.

Bhagat Singh
Department of Mechanical Engineering
Jaypee University of Engineering and Technology,
Guna, Madhya Pradesh
India

PREFACE

The rapid evolution of artificial intelligence and its integration into every aspect of our lives has given rise to a new era of pervasive intelligence. Modern Trends in Pervasive Intelligence is a timely and comprehensive volume that brings together cutting-edge research and thought leadership from academics, practitioners, and industry experts working at the forefront of this dynamic field.

This edited book explores the multifaceted dimensions of pervasive intelligence, from ubiquitous computing and sensor networks to AI-driven automation, edge computing, and intelligent decision-making systems. The chapters presented herein highlight novel methodologies, emerging technologies, and practical applications that are transforming sectors such as healthcare, manufacturing, smart cities, education, and beyond.

Our goal in compiling this volume is to provide readers, including researchers, graduate students, and technology professionals, with a deeper understanding of the challenges, opportunities, and future directions of pervasive intelligence. Each chapter has been carefully selected and peer-reviewed to ensure high academic and technical quality.

We express our sincere gratitude to all the contributing authors for their valuable insights and scholarly rigor. Their expertise has enriched the content of this book and contributed to its relevance in the current landscape of intelligent systems. We are also thankful to the reviewers and technical advisors for their constructive feedback throughout the editorial process.

We hope this book serves as a useful resource and a catalyst for further exploration and innovation in the field of pervasive intelligence.

Shruti Bhargava Choubey
Department of Electronics and Communication Engineering
Sreenidhi Institute of Science & Technology,
Hyderabad, Telangana
India

Yogesh Shrivastava
Department of Mechanical Engineering
Galgotias College of Engineering and Technology,
Greater Noida, Uttar Pradesh
India

List of Contributors

Ashutosh Choubey	Department of Electrical and Electronics Engineering, Baderia Global Institute of Engineering & Management, Jabalpur, Madhya Pradesh, India
Abhishek Choubey	Department of Electronics and Communication Engineering, Sreenidhi Institute of Science & Technology, Hyderabad, Telangana, India
Anurag Agarwal	Department of MBA, IMS Engineering College, Ghaziabad, Uttar Pradesh, India
A. Sathiya	Department of Electronics and Communication Engineering, M. Kumarasamy College of Engineering, Karur, Tamil Nadu, India
A. Sridevi	Department of Electronics and Communication Engineering, M. Kumarasamy College of Engineering, Karur, Tamil Nadu, India
A. Sangeetha	Department of Electronics and Communication Engineering, M. Kumarasamy College of Engineering, Karur, Tamil Nadu, India
A.K. Richharia	Department of Mechanical Engineering, Galgotia College of Engineering and Technology, Greater Noida, Uttar Pradesh, India
Brijesh Verma	Department of Mechanical Engineering, Galgotia College of Engineering and Technology, Greater Noida, Uttar Pradesh, India
CSN Koushik	Department of Electrical and Computer Engineering, New York University, Tandon School of Engineering, New York, USA
Eesha Thakur	Department of Computer Science and Engineering, Sreenidhi University, Hyderabad, Telangana, India
G. Aarushi Reddy	Department of Computer Science and Engineering, Sreenidhi University, Hyderabad, Telangana, India
Hunny Gaur	Department of Computer Science, IMS Engineering College, Ghaziabad, Uttar Pradesh, India
J. Samuel Manoharan	Department of Electronics and Communication Engineering, M. Kumarasamy College of Engineering, Karur, Tamil Nadu, India
K. Harinadh	School of Management Sciences, Sreenidhi Institute of Science and Technology, Hyderabad, Telangana, India
Nitesh Pandey	Department of Computer Science and Engineering, Jaypee University of Engineering and Technology, Guna, Madhya Pradesh, India
Prateek Mishra	Department of Electrical and Electronics Engineering, Baderia Global Institute of Engineering & Management, Jabalpur, Madhya Pradesh, India
Padmaja Grandhe	Department of Computer Science and Engineering, Sreenidhi University, Hyderabad, Telangana, India
Pankaj Gupta	Department of Mechanical Engineering, Jaypee University of Engineering and Technology, Guna, Madhya Pradesh, India
Pawan Kumar Arora	Department of Mechanical Engineering, Galgotias College of Engineering and Technology, Greater Noida, Uttar Pradesh, India
Radha Raman Pandey	Department of Computer Science, IMS Engineering College, Ghaziabad, Uttar Pradesh, India

Ranjan Mishra	Department of Computer Science and Engineering, Jaypee University of Engineering and Technology, Guna, Madhya Pradesh, India
Rashmi Rani Maheshwari	Department of Mechanical Engineering, Galgotias College of Engineering and Technology, Greater Noida, Uttar Pradesh, India
SPV Subba Rao	Department of Electronics and Communication Engineering, Sreenidhi Institute of Science & Technology, Hyderabad, Telangana, India
Shruti Bhargava Choubey	Department of Electronics and Communication Engineering, Sreenidhi Institute of Science & Technology, Hyderabad, Telangana, India
Saket Gumudavelli	College of Engineering, Northeastern University, Boston, Massachusetts, USA
Sri Silpa Padmanabhuni	Department of Computer Science and Engineering, PSCMR College of Engineering & Technology, Vijayawada, Andhra Pradesh, India
Swathi Buragadda	Department of Computer Science and Engineering, Lakireddy Balireddy College of Engineering, Mylavaram, Andhra Pradesh, India
Shambhavi Tamrakar	School of Management Sciences, Sreenidhi Institute of Science and Technology, Hyderabad, Telangana, India
T V Divya	Department of Computer Science and Engineering, Sreyas Institute of Engineering and Technology, Bandlaguda, Hyderabad, Telangana, India
Vivek Singh	Department of Mechanical Engineering, Galgotia College of Engineering and Technology, Greater Noida, Uttar Pradesh, India
Yaamini R	Department of Computer Science and Engineering, Sreenidhi University, Hyderabad, Telangana, India, India
Yogesh Shrivastava	Department of Mechanical Engineering, Galgotias College of Engineering and Technology, Greater Noida, Uttar Pradesh, India

CHAPTER 1

Data Mining and Knowledge Discovery in Pervasive Environments

Ashutosh Choubey[1,*] and **Prateek Mishra**[1]

[1] *Department of Electrical and Electronics Engineering, Baderia Global Institute of Engineering & Management, Jabalpur, Madhya Pradesh, India*

Abstract: Data mining and knowledge discovery are crucial in pervasive computing systems, which are distinguished by dynamic user behaviours, contextual variations, and different management requirements. Unlike classical data mining, which uses static databases or data warehouses, ubiquitous data mining works at the communication level, frequently in real time and on flowing data. Streaming data mining is supported by a variety of technologies, each with unique requirements imposed by the nature of pervasive data, such as variability, volume, and velocity. Data transmission time, contextual distinction, and processing accuracy are all important factors to consider. This study investigates the capabilities of current data streaming infrastructures and identifies issues particular to pervasive contexts. We demonstrate the limitations of current systems in handling real-time, adaptive mining activities using hypothetical application scenarios and instructive case studies. These examples demonstrate crucial gaps and growing opportunities, particularly in real-time decision making and adaptive intelligence. To summarise, pervasive data mining is a dynamic and expanding research subject with tremendous promise for transdisciplinary applications in social sciences, healthcare, transportation, and smart environments.

Keywords: AI ethics, Data mining, Emotion recognition, Emotional intelligence (EI), Empathy in AI.

INTRODUCTION TO PERVASIVE ENVIRONMENTS

One of the central research themes in the information society era is the advancement of pervasive environments. Pervasive computing envisions a world where computing technologies are seamlessly integrated into everyday objects, enabling them to communicate over the Internet.

* **Corresponding author Ashutosh Choubey:** Department of Electrical and Electronics Engineering, Baderia Global Institute of Engineering & Management, Jabalpur, Madhya Pradesh, India; E-mail: ashutoshchoubey14@gmail.com

Shruti Bhargava Choubey & Yogesh Shrivastava (Eds.)

In such environments, physical objects become context-aware entities capable of sensing, processing, and exchanging information. This connectivity allows the environment to recognize these objects, interpret the data they hold, and autonomously interact with or respond to the external world.

In this context, pervasive environments are envisioned as spaces where technology is embedded as unobtrusively as possible into everyday physical objects, which are primarily devoted to daily life activities [1]. This paradigm fosters new modes of human interaction, where devices are not only interconnected but also endowed with intelligence, context-awareness, and communication capabilities. The aim is to enhance user experience by linking physical objects with relevant and meaningful digital information, thereby creating a seamless, intelligent, and responsive environment.

This ubiquitous computing framework is expected to become a defining characteristic of the information society. The pervasive integration of information chips into a wide range of settings, including homes, workplaces, and public spaces, transforms these environments into intelligent systems [2]. For example, refrigerators may suggest recipes based on their contents, washing machines could recommend optimal programs, and phones might automatically place calls based on user habits and context.

The conceptualization of pervasive environments is increasingly informed by the analysis of practical systems and real-world applications. While developing robust and dependable services often requires divergent technological approaches, there are also significant overlaps and shared characteristics that allow applications to be embedded across diverse environments. This interconnectivity results in networks of complex, often ubiquitous systems that span various domains.

The complexity and relevance of pervasive environments are further amplified in priority sectors such as healthcare, education, and entertainment, where emerging applications demand innovative solutions. The term pervasive denotes not only the physical distribution of technology but also an underlying modeling approach that captures the behavior and interactions of intelligent components within the environment. To systematically represent such systems, conceptual models may be developed in a three-phase approach: the first phase aims to characterize the dynamic nature of pervasive environments and define foundational modeling constructs.

Definition and Characteristics

Over the past years, there has been a growing interest in data mining and knowledge discovery in pervasive environments. This area covers the development, implementation, and evaluation of data processing methods and data-driven models in technologically enhanced pervasive real-world environments that have traditionally not been perceived as primarily data collection platforms. Such environments, pervasive environments, can be physical or virtual, and they should be able to host complex systems that actively process a huge amount of heterogeneous information in near real-time. Pervasive environments are assumed to be unique in terms of their users' behavior, content, data dynamics, and information processing. They are defined as complex physical or virtual spaces enriched with various electronic devices and displays, where information is seamlessly accessed, and a broad range of services is composed.

These environments are characterized by the ubiquity of various devices, suggesting that technological solutions are omnipresent and not objects of deliberate interest to inhabitants. In order to build and maintain such solutions, their components need to function according to the user's current needs and expectations. In other words, pervasive environments are a special class of applications where ICT systems are supposed to be able to adapt to and model their natural environment in order to enhance remote communication or interaction with such an environment. Hence, the notion of pervasive environments as objects of data processing can be particularly associated with the class of complex technology-augmented environments.

This part presents the definition and characteristic features of such environments. Furthermore, it explains how these environments enrich the user's involvement by providing just-in-time and just-in-situ information content. Subsections then discuss the implications of pervasive environments on data dynamics from both the generation of data and the user interaction perspective. At least it proffers a brief taxonomy that should facilitate identifying the key components in a pervasive environment data model. The taxonomy also covers the results of data exploratory analysis that can be later visualized as actionable forms, something that is imperative for further usability of the knowledge discovered.

Applications and Importance

In the last few decades, a variety of places in almost any location have become smart thanks to the incorporation of computer-based systems that can sense, interact, and autonomously act in the world, also known as ubiquitous or pervasive computing. The Internet-of-Things (IoT) paradigm has propelled this gradual transformation of a multitude of everyday environments into interconnected devices capable of supporting complex new applications that contribute to transforming the environment for more efficient and interactive contexts.

The interest in pervasive environments is growing because they enable a diverse range of applications in a wide range of sectors. Therefore, various applications of pervasive environments are introduced to demonstrate their importance, highlighting the opportunities and research challenges that will be addressed in this chapter. The first of these is the analysis of a healthcare monitoring system that obtains data from wearable sensors in a stand-alone way without requiring any attention from the users. Next, an innovative teaching approach is presented, illustrating the possibility of offering active presentations when projectors detect that there are no people paying attention to the slides. A different idea is sketched involving the provision of messages to users traversing a university campus when the lift that they usually take is out of service. Thanks to the integration of mechanical systems with pervasive devices, it is possible to interact with a wide range of everyday items, favoring a reactive attitude to collected data.

Smart cities are urban areas where local governments promote the integration of intelligent technologies in numerous sectors. Waste management is a significant concern in urban contexts; it usually accounts for 5 to 20% of the public spending budget. A pervasive infrastructure that interacts with containers is introduced. A significant reduction in the vehicle fleet was achieved, and a fourfold increase in the fill-level clustering with ground truth was observed, which led us to consider reformulating the service routes [2]. Special attention is also to be paid to emerging widespread uses of this technology, guaranteeing a user experience that is respectful of privacy and freedom. It is questioned whether the increasing intrusion into the private space of individuals is questioned, as well as the proliferation of so-called "Big Brother" systems that establish powerful surveillance mechanisms. It is discussed that privacy and freedom-violating solutions are to be ethically questioned. Some initiatives adopting pervasive technologies radically change human-machine interaction paradigms. Companies start selling devices and applications that raise awareness on online behavior or allow the objects to communicate amongst themselves, exchanging information [3]. These solutions have the potential for large dissemination. On the other hand, a large involvement of the population is very difficult to achieve. Using a set of building blocks and the Guifi network that already spans a significant portion of Catalonia allows for the rapid, low-cost development of new pervasive environments. Some examples describing initiatives that have investigated the introduction of pervasive computing into everyday life are provided. For instance, many of the projects utilize all-pervasive mobile devices to enable a transformation of the surrounding environment.

Other than its widespread use, the ability of this technology to enable a truly "tacit" informational interface, really transparent to the user, and continuously active regardless of personal behavior. It is suggested that the physical spaces, everyday objects, or wearable garments become active participants in the interaction with the surrounding environment, with the users, and with each other. As a result, an enormous amount of data is gathered, both by users and by the environment itself. The environment is supposed to process this data in a real-time fashion, performing complex high-level data analysis and, as a consequence, becoming a place where "things know the way they are used." The embedding of sophisticated automatic data analysis in the pervasive environment allows for a novel form of passive interaction, fostering intelligent environments where everyday happenings are driven by events as triggered by data analysis. It is likely the most significant change compared to today's interaction with electro-domestic appliances that are activated "ad personam." For instance, the coffee machine in the office lab is programmed to turn on automatically at 10 and 16, or when a person approaches it. Considering a pervasive environment, this appliance would switch on only when smart devices carrying a coffee cup detect the absence of a toxic substance nearby. The presented vision outlines a variety of possible futures for the pervasive environments.

Moreover, it reflects the key points where the pervasive environments would affect. In order to properly address the wide variety of different fields in the scope, the mechanisms to employ these developing environments might also be very diverse, including energy-efficient data management, novel interfaces between humans and systems, task automation, *etc*. In this sense, some of the examples have been carefully chosen in an attempt to provide a comprehensive and clear example of their versatility in the diverse direction of application areas. On the other hand, the challenges and techniques for the design of such environments are illustrated clearly, thus providing a solid background for those who seek the practical support to undertake realistic projects. Overall, it is hoped that the scope of context provided might open minds to new applications, provide sustaining evidence to assess initial ideas, and disturbances of a developing field in terms of data mining and knowledge discovery.

FUNDAMENTALS OF DATA MINING

This section starts by engaging readers with the main foundation upon which data mining is built, particularly highlighting its value or relevance in pervasive environments. Following this, a comprehensive set of essential data mining techniques is explained that are commonly used to unearth insightful patterns from sizable datasets.

Data mining is associated with a rich collection of techniques used for extracting implicit, previously unknown, and potentially valuable data or hidden patterns from large data repositories [4]. The overall goal is to uncover patterns that may not be easily recognized or deduced through straightforward means. It is critical in pervasive environments to comprehend the shape of the data and the scenes in which the data is embedded. Valuable information concealed within these datasets can be unearthed and serve as the foundation for constructing intricate reasoning and reactive mechanisms that suppose the setting and possible forthcoming actions of their subjects. Accomplishing this offers improved tailoring to individual needs and scenarios.

Data mining encompasses a large array of knowledge and procedures from distinct areas, such as data visualization, machine learning, neural networks, spatial data patterns, spatial-temporal modelling, statistical learning theories, and rule induction methods. Since much data is essentially part-dimensional or multidimensional, and pervasive environments often reflect spatial-context characteristics, giants such as information visualization and visual data mining have unexpectedly gained much attention. This chapter gives a concise explanation of substantial aspects associated with the idea of deriving pervasive patterns.

Data Mining Techniques

As data gets ever more pervasive, large amounts of data are being collected from various devices or information systems and stored in databases. However, the stock of raw data has little benefit unless it is transformed into knowledge or insights through the data mining process. In data mining, researchers have developed and are further developing various techniques to uncover patterns or knowledge and extract practical value from this vast data collection. Data Mining (DM) is defined as the process of discovering patterns or knowledge from data. It makes sense of vast amounts of data and turns it into actionable information. Throughout the data mining process, a data mining task or technique is used, including classification, clustering, regression, and association rule mining.

Classification is the process of finding a model (or function) that describes and distinguishes data classes or concepts. The model can help label objects, automatically assigning them to one of the several predefined classes. Clustering is the process of grouping a set of objects in such a way that objects in the same group (or cluster) are more similar (in some sense) to each other than to those in other groups. Regression is the process of finding the function that models the data with the least error. Association rule mining is the task of discovering relations between variables in vast databases. It can help reveal significant pieces of knowledge contained in vast amounts of raw data [5]. Although not a goal, researchers are moving toward completely automating the data mining process. Some system designs are envisioned in the future requiring the users only to provide their data and relevant information. Unfortunately, without entirely understanding the user data and without massive amounts of computational power, a black-box-like process would not be able to guarantee consistent discoveries of invaluable knowledge. However, even the most advanced technology will not be able to completely replace the human brain. Such a system would be difficult to evaluate, and users could not easily trust or validate the results. Judging the feasibility and compatibility of these techniques with the user data is a human step, and no system can currently perform this crucial task as efficiently as a knowledgeable data miner [6].

Data Preprocessing

Data preprocessing is the critical step in the knowledge discovery process in pervasive environments. It is vital because it can determine the success of data mining tasks; the accuracy of the mining models derived from the output of data mining algorithms is strongly influenced by the quality of the input data. Once data is available, they have to be transformed into an acceptable form, an important requirement due to the variety of sensors and networks that potentially create unstructured and heterogeneous data in pervasive environments. Data preprocessing in this context consists of several steps: data cleaning, normalization, transformation, and reduction. Cleaning data is usually the most demanding job when dealing with data obtained through pervasive technologies. Some of the issues that need to be addressed are how to handle missing data, filtering of noise, data sampling, development of detection mechanisms for outliers, and how to work with data sets that are too large for common software packages. Additionally, due to the dynamic nature of wireless communication, the need is to keep a continuous check on sources of unwanted interferences, collisions, or obstructions from the nodes in the network [7]. Thus, a mechanism to synchronize and correct all deviations from an expected behavior should be established, since it is known that any inconsistency could damage the quality of the output mining models. On the other hand, for analysis, it is sometimes necessary to warp the time variable into a more 'willing' bucket of knowledge. This requires the development of mechanisms for the condensation of time-stamped data, aggregation rules, and possibly some form of feature extraction. The relevant transformations are then applied to make data mining tools possible to work on the knowledge engineering process. Played after the transformation tasks performed on a case study, reduction of data sets is also needed, namely, when computational facilities are the bottleneck. In this case, approaches rely on aggregation strategies, k-means clustering, grid computing, using data compression, or the filter scheme to vary the number of attributes (especially if it is too high for the mining algorithm to handle). The knowledge engineer might also wish to analyze the capacity of the models under certain data sampling (undersampling, oversampling, and borderline oversampling methods are possible). However, a word of caution is due as using data reduction can easily violate some basic properties of the data sets. False measure rates might result, as well as erroneous evaluation indexes. Reducing the number of instances affects the representativeness of the sample, so it requires very appropriate conduct. Especially in imbalanced data sets, great homogeneity across classes should be observed in the sample. In any case, the performance attribution to the different attributes plays no role when risk factor mining is the final goal of the knowledge engineering task, since an assessment of 'goodness' divided by the number of attributes is the more meaningful measure under these circumstances.

CHALLENGES IN DATA MINING IN PERVASIVE ENVIRONMENTS

Pervasive environments are settings of people's daily life activities in which computing and communication capabilities are interwoven in artifacts distributed in the environment. These settings help to improve individuals' daily interactions and overall experience by providing pervasive services and applications. In pervasive environments, sensors (*e.g.*, cameras) and Bluetooth devices are employed to collect, in a continuous fashion, information about the environments in which subjects' daily lives take place. Among all the challenges characterizing data mining in pervasive environments, the major ones have to do with security and privacy. The risk of continuously collecting and processing users' data is lurking. Until now, pervasive environments have been addressing privacy issues through de-identification practices, in that personal data are collected, managed, and analyzed without the possibility of retrieving the identity of the subjects. However, security concerns persist. Attempts at unauthorized data tampering are increasingly happening, which has already started to undermine the trust of the users [8].

The data mining process needs to be informed rigorously about the data sharing and analysis procedures. The concept of informed consent of the data subject is crucial. Much of the proposed research in pervasive environments does not discuss the issue of informed consent. It must be guaranteed that data mining, data integration, and knowledge discovery are employed transparently and ethically, in respect of the privacy policies. Without this, users will likely feel uneasy or harassed. Besides the privacy challenge, scalability is a big issue in pervasive environment data mining, as the quantity of available data sources grows exponentially. Scalability does not only refer to the data volume. How data mining and knowledge discovery can deal with external environment data sources and with homogeneous data is a question still to be answered by the community [9]. Moreover, given the dynamics of the data sources within pervasive environments, a flexible approach is needed in order to integrate, analyze, and deliver real-time information, and new solutions are eagerly sought by the stakeholders involved in the system/intelligent environment development. Understanding and facing the challenges described in this work is the first step towards the promotion of education and new paradigms, in the vision that more "conscious" pervasive environments are able to frame the development of respectful data mining strategies.

Data Privacy and Security

The advent of pervasive computing and sensing technologies has led to rapid growth in data collection within various settings, such as smart homes, transportation systems, and healthcare. While advances in data mining have provided powerful tools for extracting knowledge from such data, they have also raised concerns over user data privacy and security [8]. Unauthorized access to and misuse of sensitive data collected by pervasive systems are associated with a range of risks, including identity theft, user profiling, and personal threats. In response to these concerns, security mechanisms that comply with industry standards and government regulations are needed to provide adequate protection. For instance, data collected from pervasive systems must be stored securely in an encrypted database or using physical security, such as locked file cabinets. Personally-identifiable data should be anonymized or obfuscated through data masking and replaced with artificial, secure values. Access to sensitive data should be strictly controlled by limiting data access to trusted parties with clearance, for instance, using security credentials. While such measures offer sensible suggestions for organizations processing user data, ethical considerations must also be taken into account [9]. For example, mined data is only acceptable if consent is obtained from users, and organizations should be transparent regarding data usage. Data gathered in violation of users' privacy expectations must not be mined, regardless of societal benefits. In addition to these ethical concerns, legal regulations around privacy can themselves limit the use of data mining in certain ways that may not typically align with organizational objectives. Finally, it should be remembered that legal and financial penalties from privacy breaches can outweigh the benefits of mining altogether, and that the effects of a single breach can be severe in the extreme. For instance, the case of the Target Corporation's 2013 breach that leaked credit and debit card data from millions of customers resulted in fraud losses, targeted phishing attacks on customers, and a deep fall in company stock as the corporation faced lawsuits and regulatory investigations. Similar risks should be considered in the development of data mining solutions in pervasive environments.

Scalability Issues

Due to the ubiquitous nature of pervasive systems, a multitude of sensor and device types is typically used. Sensors may be passive (such as temperature, RFID, or IP sensors) or active (such as cameras, microphones, or GPS devices), while devices might be actuating (such as displays, speakers, or projectors) or processing (such as CPUs, GPUs, or sensor nodes). Moreover, the tight integration with the physical environment leads to various networking technologies from personal-area up to satellite communication, and also to multiple specialization scenarios, from environmental monitoring to health/fitness tracking. As a consequence, an incredible volume of data can potentially be generated. As highlighted by [10], both academia and industry have an urgent need for tools to make meaning from the generated data. Such tools should consist of data-gathering suites and online and offline data-mining toolboxes. Nevertheless, the volume of generated data and the heterogeneity of the gathering tools are such that analysis and filtering strategies are required, in order not to overwhelm storage and classical data processing frameworks. Even more important than scalability for office-based data processing, scalability, similarly to sample size, plays a particular relevance in pervasive environments and real-time applications. Scalability may originate from different dimensions, and it is easy to foresee that both data and user commands will grow significantly in the near future. Therefore, it is necessary to pursue scalability-aware solutions in both algorithm and tool design to prevent the lack of results or faulty results and the non-responsiveness of the (possibly cascaded) data-mining process.

KNOWLEDGE DISCOVERY IN PERVASIVE ENVIRONMENTS

There is a growing research interest in the intersection of data mining and pervasive environments beyond the typical scenarios of monitoring sensor data or location-based services. Thus, there are proactive proposals for multimodal mobile systems and innovative modeling approaches for the exploitation of large-scale data in urban environments. There are also related special issues on challenges and opportunities coming along with novel data sources generated by Internet of Things (IoT) environments, such as streaming data, spatiotemporal data, and big data generated by a dense deployment of smart objects in a variety of environments. It is argued that there are implications regarding how data is to be discovered and scrutinized, ranging from sensor networks to urban environments. This overview is seen as a complementary piece to existing special issues, delineating more broadly the ongoing lines of work addressing data mining applications in pervasive knowledge discovery.

Formally, knowledge discovery may be defined as the process of extracting information based upon a balance of metrics, judgment, experience, and knowledge. It is also referred to as knowledge finding, except for collecting information, often by making use of information technology. It encompasses prospecting an assemblage of large, complex datasets to discern the latest display to bolster business strategies, enhance commodity research, or draw other significant conclusions. The significant increase in available computer capacity, data accumulation, and commercial benefits has encouraged data discovery to develop rapidly, transforming a distinct branch of the investigation into a multi-faceted domain, enacting a comprehensive assortment of methodologies [11]. In many communities, knowledge discovery is interchangeably utilized with data discovery or simply known as mining. However, true knowledge discovery entails various extra phenomena, including substantiation, use, representation, and apprehension of the discovered knowledge. Data mining and data discovery are nonidentical; the latter is how knowledge is discovered from data. The value of mining the data relies upon the adequacy of data discovery, and vice versa; the significance of mining the data affects how data is ascertained [12].

Concepts and Methods

In pervasive environments, the analysis of sensor data becomes a non-trivial task for several reasons, such as an increasing dimensionality (*e.g.*, data can be grouped in streams of a potentially high number of dimensions), potential absence of a clear analytic model, the large effort needed for pre-processing the incoming data, continuous and semi-unstructured data analysis requirements, *etc*. Just dealing with the serious dimensionality-related problems, the task of analyzing pervasive data does not regard isolated data sets. Frequently, data to be mined may be grouped in complex structures involving imbalance in the number of samples between clusters (*e.g.*, both high- and low-traffic places can be monitored within the same environment), needs to be processed in real-time, or has distribution patterns that may change in a time-varying manner.

Techniques

To facilitate the extraction of knowledge from such complex and sometimes heterogeneous data sources, well-known techniques in the data mining and signal processing areas can be used. Several can be cited, such as clustering, classification [11], and pattern recognition. Considering that the data processing approach strictly depends on the type of application, it is important to point out that not all traditional algorithmic approaches in pervasive data analysis can be used. Thus, there is a need to define new methodologies robust to different data distribution patterns of low computational cost and able to adjust the mining process to new data distributions automatically. In this way, special attention to the data streaming approach is given, pointing out some "clues" about different methodologies to pursue future work. Moreover, it discusses advanced strategies such as hybrid models using a mixture of different data mining techniques (knowledge fusion). This is an interesting approach to adapt the mining technique to the environmental and user context behavior (or even for data quality assessment). As far as it is advanced in the technical literature, no special attention to this problem of knowledge discovery application is given. Finally, essential strategies of context knowledge sources from, for the most common: (i) environmental features that have direct representation in the datasets; and (ii) strategies to integrate machine learning and artificial intelligence approaches to the knowledge discovery process are also discussed.

SENSOR DATA COLLECTION AND ANALYSIS

The pivotal role in pervasive environments is the functionality of the sensors. A thorough understanding of the sensors and their data types is one of the major prerequisites for successful data mining. The well-known techniques and materials required for data collection include various sensors. Different techniques with the sensors can be used, such as direct sampling, active sensing determination, and data fusion, for collecting more comprehensive data. Other material requirements are concerned with the environment. Reliability and validity are very important, since any subsequent modeling and understanding of the data is inherently based on the collected data. With the sensors being the primary source for data acquisition, the issue of sensor network layout becomes the most critical.

A sensor network is a spatial communication network that is laid on top of a certain field of interest to monitor events or phenomena of interest in that field. There are several challenging mathematical ones. The first of them is the optimal input design aiming at efficiently selecting time points at which to make observations. The second one is concerned with the access limitations placed on the sensors by the controllers, and finally, the variety of sensors will influence the observer's performance. Mathematically, the last issue is formulated as a problem of sensor/node placement and placement of the links between them. Mathematically, one is looking at the network design problem in which sensors are to be effectively allocated to these links and nodes of the network so as to optimize the surveillance capability. The set of imminent challenges due to potential impacts on the quality of collected data and long-term challenges driven by the complex infrastructure in which sensor data is observed are identified [13]. In this context, topoi is viewed both as a summary of the state of the modeling of sensor data by a particular approach and as a classification of various modeling approaches according to the requirements on the spatiotemporal characteristics [14]. A few practical implications of the topoi approach as a guideline for the application and development of appropriate data mining algorithms and sensor network analysis tools are given.

Types of Sensors

Sensors in pervasive environments have been widely used to detect and capture various ambient data that can be automatically processed [13]. The types of information that can be captured are diverse and can range from temperature, humidity, motion, to biometric. Each type of sensor is dedicated to capturing specific data and thus to measuring specific entities. Temperature sensors measure the ambient temperature of a pervasive environment. Such information is invaluable in various applications, including detecting unwanted changes in an industrial environment and monitoring indoor environmental comfort. Humidity sensors are employed to measure the humidity in an environment, complementing the information captured by temperature sensors. High humidity is usually an unwanted condition in many places. Motion sensors generate outputs when the sensor is moved.

They are commonly used in security applications for detection and triggering alarms. Open/closed doors, broken windows, and similar events can all be captured using such sensors. Biometric sensors are sensors that can be implemented to extract information related to human behavior or other biological phenomena. Both biometric and motion sensors are used in security applications. However, motion sensors are limited to recognizing movement in a specific zone and do not give any identity information. Biometric sensors, on the other hand, provide an identity to the recognized action, but in contrast, have a limitation in capturing only directly measurable attributes related to the behavior.

To ensure that the data collected by such sensors is, in fact, a valid representation of the environment, calibration of the sensors is needed. The accuracy of the data generated by a sensor is a critical issue in pervasive environment applications. The impact of erroneous data is that further processed data using the sensor data will be unreal or inaccurate, and thus, the potential knowledge discovered will not be reliable. Furthermore, several types of sensors are usually combined into one execution in order to obtain a comprehensive information set.

Mapping low-level sensor information to high-level information and fusing sensor data into parametric user models are explained and illustrated with examples from multi-sensor approaches in different pervasive applications. The sensors used for each specific pervasive environment application are described, and the related processing methods and architectures are presented. Different applications provide a good example of the interchangeable content between the technology of the sensor used and the outcome afforded by the sensor data.

Data Collection Techniques

Pervasive environments are a common paradigm in knowledge discovery, as entities interact with the environment and leave a trail of information that can be analyzed to extract knowledge. The term pervasive implies an omnipresence of computing devices embedded in everyday objects and infrastructures. These devices are equipped with sensors that produce observations about the entity and the environment. Thus, data that can be analyzed to discover knowledge can be gathered.

In such environments, a challenging task is to design effective and efficient techniques to gather this data. Effectiveness means that the collected data is of the required quality and relevance, while efficiency refers to the optimization of the data gathering process [15]. This means that cost issues, like energy consumption, should be taken into account, and also that further steps in the KD (Knowledge Discovery) process, such as data storage and cleaning, must be as efficient as possible.

Available data gathering techniques depend on the interaction level of such environments with the data consumer. These techniques can vary from continuous monitoring to different types of sampling. In continuous monitoring, observations are continuously and autonomously produced by the devices. This technique is widely used in weather prediction, and new data mining and machine learning algorithms have been designed to deal with such data and discover knowledge. In pervasive environments, the continuous monitoring of the sensors is often used to supervise the status of the environment and derive some ad-hoc knowledge. However, other techniques can be employed.

For instance, event-driven sampling means that observations are produced each time a particular event occurs. For generic purposes, more standard techniques are often used. For example, data can be gathered in an aggregate form at a fixed time scale, thus reducing the complexity of the data mining process. On the other hand, applying data mining algorithms to raw data allows the discovery of knowledge that is hidden in the aggregated form. Thus, it is crucial to choose the right data gathering technique based on the peculiarities of the environment and applications.

MACHINE LEARNING IN PERVASIVE ENVIRONMENTS

Pervasive environments, by their very nature, provide an opening for the application of data mining and knowledge discovery principles, potentially leading to more actionable insights. Data streams in such environments often have a chaotic arrival pattern, originate from a dynamic number of data sources, and may be spatially spread, among other constraints. Machine learning has been proposed as a technique able to naturally adapt to such settings. In this context, filtering and data mining are applied to the data that is continuously gathered to transform raw data into new information that can be employed for future use.

The application of the most common machine learning algorithms in pervasive environments and an in-depth discussion of the processes of validation and training are the subject matters of this section, with a particular focus on the importance of such processes for the overall success of the operation. Pervasive environment transforms the role of machine learning in practice. Instead of extracting knowledge from the human expert, the nature of the application area now requires the knowledge to be extracted from the data [16].

Data mining emerges as a bridge that integrates machine learning algorithms, providing a knowledge discovery process that leads to the extraction of a model and a decision-making approach that yields automatically derived results, conclusions, or otherwise usable actionable insights. However, most of the central approaches in the pervasive knowledge discovery area examined so far do not address such a transformation at all. They assume that the model is already known and the only thing to do is to apply a given mining process to the data depicted in a certain format. In that sense, such approaches are no different from more standard data mining literature, where knowledge extraction is not an integral part of an analysis. Additionally, existing techniques implicitly base on the assumption that, upon the arrival of real-time data, a centralized data mining process should be conducted offline.

Then, from time to time, knowledge (*e.g*., discovered models) will find a route to act locally on data sources. Such methodologies are not suited to dynamically changing environments, where real-time processing and decision-making are required. The need for online learning mechanisms that are able to operate in highly dynamic environments characterized by limited prior knowledge and multiple involved parties is argued.

Machine learning has been successfully applied to a plethora of diverse applications in the scope of a pervasive environment. Interpretively, the term applies to both a learning algorithm (classification, clustering, regression, *etc*.) and a low-level process that extracts an adequate model of a learner, which can then be utilized for, *e.g*., prediction and classification tasks. In the presented discussion, attention is directed predominantly towards the former use of the phrase. The presented enumeration is by no means exhaustive and is deliberately confined to a more general overview; the goal is that the understanding of the remaining part dealing with the specifics of particular learners is not affected.

Algorithms and Models

This subsection gives an overview of algorithms and models employed in machine learning for pervasive data mining and knowledge discovery. A variety of algorithms and models have been extensively studied in machine learning in pervasive environments. Decision trees are one of the most widely used algorithms. They have been found to perform well in learning from abstract data types that predominate in pervasive environments, and they can construct more and simpler models than other algorithms.

Nevertheless, some well-known problems of decision trees, such as an inconsistent model for the same data set with different sequences, usually handle datasets that only have full or partial knowledge structuring. Neural networks are another widely employed algorithm, mostly due to the adaptive learning capabilities of data with incompletely learned structures. Support vector machines are among the newer algorithms and are efficient when it comes to handling the classification of high-dimensional spaces.

A detailed discussion on these algorithms in machine learning is presented in the next sections, encompassing an explanation of their current context. The model selection section also elaborates on the takeaways from this model selection and on the pertinence of designing these models. Choosing the appropriate model is of paramount importance; it can significantly influence the performance of data processing. Theoretically, there is always the best model for a set of data. However, in practice, from the vast collection of models and little information about the data to be processed, selecting the model for processing is much more complicated. Hybrid algorithms can also provide a more appropriate solution for pervasive data mining and knowledge discovery.

Meanwhile, a flexible solution to integrate the algorithm model design is proposed. Machine learning in pervasive environments is used as the object of discussion throughout this section, although these ideas can be extended to different implementations. In addition to model selection, there are several important considerations related to the practical implementation of this model that have a significant impact on the model; these include the preparation of training models and hyperparameter features. The section following the next section contains recommended methods based on the experiences gained during model selection. The discussion on these topics will equip the reader with a comprehensive understanding of this model that can be optimally applied to machine learning in pervasive environments.

CASE STUDIES AND APPLICATIONS

The healthcare costs are increasing day by day across the world. However, despite the increase in costs, the service quality of the healthcare organizations has not improved as expected due to various reasons. Thereby, the demand and interest in healthcare data mining applications have increased. The healthcare industry accumulates vast amounts of data in a variety of forms, and it is believed that the use of different data mining techniques can help discover hidden relationships and important information from this data. When the data originates from multiple sources and contains multiple time dimensions, it is termed complex data. The complex data may involve text data, spatial data, temporal data, multimedia data, and others. The various types of complex data mining approaches are discussed in the review.

A variety of data mining techniques can be used in possible applications and services in the healthcare system; accordingly, general data mining, predictive data mining, and prescriptive data mining techniques are introduced [17 - 19]. Several diseases are cited as supporting predictive data mining of their diagnosis. In addition, possible applications and benefits are presented for diseases like cancer, epilepsy, and diabetes, including possible benefits, and some comparisons between them.

Thus, since the data mining methods involve the algorithms in their operation, it was considered that practical applications could be better comprehended *via* algorithms. Finally, given that the case study for breast cancer disease is a practical and easy-to-understand one, algorithms could not be effectively examined.

The growth of urban areas and potential threats force cities to act professionally. There is a new policy trend to provide smart infrastructure and make cities smart. The management of traffic, public transport, natural resources, and safety is of high interest. Efficient control and reasonable access to the multiple data streams are key to success. Data mining plays an important role in transforming data into useful knowledge, which could indirectly make decisions to operate efficiently [20 - 23]. It was envisioned that data-driven decisions in smart cities would allow managing systems most beneficially. Based on the objectives and specific problem in many research works, operations research was used. Incorporated was the design of models for the optimization of city resources, which would prepare efficient solutions and a decision-making basis. Personal reasons dictate the projection of the studies on pervasive environments.

Healthcare

The pervasiveness of computational devices in the environment describes the paradigm of pervasive computing. In such environments, the development of Data Mining and Knowledge Discovery (DMKD) techniques is particularly challenging yet arguably promising. The data collected in such a setting is noisy, high-dimensional, often exists in a multitude of diverse sources, and generally evolves. On the other hand, the wealth of available multimodal data provides an opportunity to realize knowledge discovery with much higher resolution and richness. This chapter provides an exploration of the conceptual and technical issues involved in the development of DMKD in such environments. Healthcare, surveillance, transportation, and advertisement are discussed as examples [24].

Pervasive computing and networking have the potential to transform existing settings, providing humans with rich and portable information and control services in the environment. This, in turn, offers potential venues for the frequent collection of data about everyday life events of outstandingly diverse and sophisticated nature. A possible consequence can be the development of a kind of AI-driven proactive environment where patterns in accidents can provide the background for revising possible interventions. Another possible development could be in the health sector, where real-time data collected from the patient can provide the basis for real-time fine-tuning of treatment protocols that substantially increase the probability of achieving positive outcomes. An example can be the development of predictive models of early symptoms of disease outbreaks that are based on intensive real-time analysis of multimodal sensing data. In the very short future, it could be envisaged a treatment that is modulated on real-time signals acquired from the patient, that is recorded *via* wearable and nonintrusively implanted biosensors, that together with genetic markers are used to trigger the release of personalized drugs. The continuous monitoring of users can occur using wearable devices and through the exploitation of the common reasoning of the activities of everyday life [18]. There is full awareness of the required development of an infrastructure that takes into account the privacy of the stored data and makes the integration of data of possibly diverse nature easy. All these open problems should stimulate an intense and articulated research targeted at the definition of innovative solutions and holistic visions. The presentation of recent events is intended to show the success of the paradigm in application scenarios outside the pervasive domain, providing some insights that can serve as a model for the application in the addressed domain.

Smart Cities

Rapid urbanization poses significant challenges for growing cities, such as the need for efficient resource management, safe public services, and speedy response to challenges like natural disasters and epidemics. In recent years, pervasive technologies have been employed by the smart city paradigm to create new interactive and efficient socio-technical urban environments. Fields such as traffic management, environmental health, energy management, infrastructure security, and crowd management are only a few sectors expected to be re-engineered by smart city applications. Consequently, there is a need for data mining techniques to innovate and orchestrate the data processing in the context of such pervasive environments, to engage with the realization of future cities in which it is desirable to live.

Huge amounts of data are generated by sensors monitoring the city. Traffic sensors on lights and streets may be used to increase traffic flow and reduce pollution. The required pollutant data can be extracted from the environmental sensors, and the pollution can be reduced by optimizing the traffic flow. Furthermore, the sound of a city environment may be recognized using microphones and audio digital signal processing techniques. Similarly, the sound characteristics of a gunshot may be detected. As a result, the gunshot data is transmitted to the server and triggers a fast response in the police department. These are just a few examples; it is simple to think of multiple functionalities and massive amounts of data generated by new technologies as an opportunity for the application of data mining [19]. Smart cities are all about community-driven collaboration. A Citizen Feedback System in a smart city is designed to collect opinions, concerns, and suggestions for improvement to the city. An analysis of this data is conducive to a new decision-making culture involving citizens and authorities. Case studies successively corroborate the optimistic developments [20]. The models of smart streets and intersections may be created for use in urban planning to optimize energy consumption and public safety. In another case, a district overheating algorithm is designed for application to a weekend sun path simulator. The operational met data and a 3D model are also required.

ETHICAL AND LEGAL CONSIDERATIONS IN PERVASIVE DATA MINING

Technological advancements are leading to an unprecedented growth of digital data in pervasive environments. Due to the heterogeneity, complexity, and interactivity of pervasive environments, there is a need for effective ways for knowledge discovery and data mining. Data mining in pervasive environments brings up many challenges at different levels, ranging from data processing and knowledge representation to interpreting the discovered knowledge and making use of it effectively. However, before embracing the promises of data mining and knowledge discovery, there are some ethical and legal factors to consider [21]. Due to the newest privacy policies, the public has been more aware of the active nature of data collection from passive behavior. This means that making the participants aware of signs of active data collection is no longer sufficient to make privacy considered ethical. Data collection policy must also identify what resources are accessed, transmitted, and used to store passive information that gives a signal to either the participant or the observer of data collection.

Beyond the technical and methodological challenges, there are major concerns about the ethical and social implications of the related practices. Research and development in data mining technologies and applications should address important ethical and legal considerations that might arise from the pervasive character of the data. Every data miner has a great responsibility regarding how learned knowledge is further exploited. There is an ethical obligation to inform the parties that are affected by certain acquired knowledge. Respectable researchers and practitioners did care in advance to anonymize the acquired knowledge in formed rules, modeling relations, *etc*. Moreover, the same party concerning the data processing can be a material and immaterial holder of such knowledge. It is a legal right of a person to obtain ammunition or have access to the personal discoveries obtained by data-mining techniques based on the sensed data. Anyhow, the irrelevance of the acquired knowledge for the data processing could also be guaranteed by properly designing the data-mining tools used.

Privacy Regulations

The digital transformation process has created a range of smart applications, gadgets, and services that are seamlessly embedded into everyday lives. As a result, the pervasive environment has become full of interconnected smart objects that can gather various sensor data, ranging from proximity or temperature to biological signals. Since individuals interact with pervasive environments daily, a massive volume of highly detailed data is created. These datasets offer distinctive opportunities for discovering hidden data patterns that can have a significant societal and commercial impact. Nevertheless, the data mining performed in the pervasive environment incorporates many potential violations of information rights. Discussions will begin by summarizing the specific regulations for data mining relevant to preserving safety and confidentiality in the pervasive environment.

The studies aim to provide clarity about the particular privacy laws concerning data mining in pervasive environments. The variety of regulations surrounding data mining reveals that thorough thought on privacy is required before or ASAP the commencement of any data mining activities [9].

The pervasive environment (also frequently referred to as the pervasive or ubiquitous computing, the Internet of Things, *etc.*) has become an utterly connected background where clever gadgets and models are seamlessly fused into daily human lives. Recent statistics estimate that 75 billion smart things will be employed worldwide by 2025, gathering and distributing much intelligent data. Smart things can be cars, as in smart transport, homes, just as a smart apartment, or organisms, like smart biomedical devices supervising biological signals.

Several smart applications, goods, and services that are thoroughly integrated into life have been rendered by the digital shift. Therefore, there is a significant volume of interconnected smart objects in people's environment. Objects are furnished with measuring instruments and communicative interfaces. Smart things are available in several different sizes, ranging from wristwatches and shaker weights to traffic robots and street lamps. Smart things are often operated as one or play a supporting part in smart environments, like software-defined radios or spatial air quality testing devices.

CONCLUSION, FUTURE TRENDS, AND RESEARCH DIRECTIONS

Recent advances in multiple research areas, such as machine learning [22, 25], artificial intelligence [23], and big data technologies, have created a unique landscape for the future development of data mining and knowledge discovery methodologies in pervasive environments. Above all, these scientific disciplines have merged into several interconnected research branches, allowing the enhancement and development of new pervasive applications and results. It becomes visible that, on the one hand, a fruitful collaboration within the scientific research community is flocking to different innovations. On the other hand, omnipresent computing systems, where computational technologies are woven into everyday life applications, reveal a latent expansion and success in the interaction between the human and technological environments. One of the remarkable issues associated with the emergence of such a social evolution is related to the management and exploitation of an expanding amount of unstructured data of different natures, such as physiological signals, multimedia presentations, cartographic information, expert data, social networks, *etc*. This remarkable explosion has already spurred an extensive study on new scientific research areas, considering data management, parsing, mining, and understanding for generating helpful and understandable information for individuals. This scenario establishes an elegant background for stimulating an interdisciplinary community able to answer a plethora of theoretical and empirical research questions in order to address the emerging dependence challenges among data management, multimodal data mining, pervasive applications, and knowledge discovery methodologies.

In this pioneering invitation, the crucial role is foreseen that innovation in pervasive data mining and knowledge discovery research is going to lead to a variety of common scientific branches. Several pursued research directions are delineated and purposely left open in order to gather possibilities for cooperation and brainstorming at the intersection of pervasive computing, data and knowledge mining, communication, and interpretation techniques. Meanwhile, a collection of addresses, associations, journals, and conference forums is reported with the view of pointing out relevant investigations and reviews in the above-established research community. All of these issues could have the wished-for consequence to drive and handle beyond the near future some brilliant cooperative research initiatives and educational actions in the domain, taking into account such a big intertwining and multifaceted scenario of opportunities and challenges. In addition, some novelties and breakthroughs in the emergent perspectives of works realized and results achieved in the addressed discipline are also presented.

Emerging Technologies

This subsection explores the emerging technologies that are set to revolutionize data mining and the discovery of knowledge throughout pervasive environments. This includes deep learning, with the emerging artificial intelligence more broadly, machine learning, particularly distributed and federated, and the up-and-coming edge computing, especially for real-time data treatment. The Internet of Things (IoT) is discussed as a pivotal catalyst for an unprecedented expansion and integration of data through interconnected devices. Emerging cloud computing technologies are presented with a focus on elasticity, scalability, and support for emerging applications such as blockchains. Big data technology, understanding here the complementary big data storage and analytics, is then discussed. Reference frameworks, middleware, and open technology platforms that will make it possible to seamlessly integrate such technologies with existing pervasive environments are suggested. Finally, the transformative impacts anticipated by emerging pervasive data mining and knowledge discovery applications are considered, ensuring the beginning of a new era of innovative services and products across a variety of sectors and applications. This subsection looks into the emerging technologies that are set to revolutionize data mining and the discovery of knowledge throughout pervasive environments. These include the emerging artificial intelligence, with the particular advances occurring in deep learning, machine learning, and the rapidly evolving distributed and federated versions. Recent technologies in cloud computing, edge computing, and the broader IoT paradigm are also discussed, including IoT gateways and emerging technologies supporting seamless and ubiquitous connectivity. Finally, discipline-specific advancements, such as the increasingly sophisticated electronic sensors and monitoring devices developed across industry sectors, are looked into for their implications and opportunities when fed into emerging data mining and knowledge discovery systems. Understanding these emerging technologies is crucial for the pervasive data mining and knowledge discovery practitioner, be it in envisioning the possibilities for developing the next generation of innovative practices or designing them to most effectively integrate into existing pervasive environments.

REFERENCES

[1] J.E. Fernandes, R.J. Machado, and J.Á. Carvalho, "Profiling and framing structures for pervasive information systems development", In: *Proceedings of the 2012 IEEE International Conference on Pervasive Computing and Communications Workshops* Lugano, Switzerland, 2012, pp. 1-6. [http://dx.doi.org/10.1007/978-3-642-31800-9_29]

[2] E. Medina, D. Lopez, R. Meseguer, and S.F. Ochoa, "Mobile Autonomous Sensing Unit (MASU): A framework that supports distributed pervasive data sensing", *Proceedings of the 2016 IEEE International Conference on Pervasive Computing and Communications Workshops,* pp. 1-6, 2016.Kona, HI, USA [http://dx.doi.org/10.3390/s16071062]

[3] X.I.N. Xiao, "Data Mining Techniques for Complex User-Generated Data", *Proceedings of the 2016 IEEE International Conference on Data Mining Workshops,* pp. 1-8, 2016.Barcelona, Spain

[4] M. Obeidat, M. North, L. Burgess, and S. North, "DRIP - Data Rich, Information Poor: A concise synopsis of data mining", *Proceedings of the 2014 IEEE International Conference on Data Mining Workshops,* pp. 1-6, 2014.Shenzhen, China

[5] Z. Yu, "Mining Hidden Knowledge from Measured Data for Improving Building Energy Performance", *Proceedings of the 2012 IEEE International Conference on Data Mining Workshops,* pp. 1-6, 2012.Brussels, Belgium

[6] N.A. Le-Khac, M. Bue, M. Whelan, and T. Kechadi, "A clustering-based data reduction for very large spatio-temporal datasets", *Proceedings of the 2016 IEEE International Conference on Data Mining Workshops,* pp. 1-6, 2016.Barcelona, Spain

[7] K. Gibert, M. Sanchez-Marre, and J.I. Sebastián, "A survey on pre-processing techniques: Relevant issues in the context of environmental data mining", *Environ. Model. Softw.,* vol. 75, pp. 1-14, 2016.

[8] O.M. Abbas, M.E. Mustafa, and S.B. Ibrahim, "The role of data mining in information security", *Proceedings of the 2015 IEEE International Conference on Data Mining Workshops,* pp. 1-6, 2015.Atlantic City, NJ, USA

[9] R.O. Oturugbum, "Preserving the safety and confidentiality of data mining information in health care: A literature review", *Proceedings of the 2023 IEEE International Conference on Healthcare Informatics,* pp. 1-6, 2023.Chicago, IL, USA

[10] W. Gan, J.C.W. Lin, P. Fournier-Viger, and H.C. Chao, "A survey of parallel sequential pattern mining", *Proceedings of the 2018 IEEE International Conference on Data Mining Workshops,* pp. 1-8, 2018.Singapore

[11] T. Silwattananusarn, and K. Tuamsuk, "Data mining and its applications for knowledge management: A literature review from 2007 to 2012", *Proceedings of the 2012 International Conference on Knowledge Management and Information Sharing,* pp. 1-6, 2012.Rome, Italy [http://dx.doi.org/10.5121/ijdkp.2012.2502]

[12] B. Shen, "Universal knowledge discovery from big data: Towards a paradigm shift from 'knowledge discovery' to 'wisdom discovery", *Proceedings of the 2014 IEEE International Conference on Big Data,* pp. 1-6, 2014.Washington, DC, USA

[13] H. Banaee, M. Ahmed, and A. Loutfi, "Data mining for wearable sensors in health monitoring systems: a review of recent trends and challenges", *Sensors (Basel),* vol. 13, no. 12, pp. 17472-17500, 2013.
[http://dx.doi.org/10.3390/s131217472] [PMID: 24351646]

[14] Y. Zhong, S. Fong, S. Hu, and R. Wong, "A novel sensor data pre-processing methodology for the Internet of Things using anomaly detection and transfer-by-subspace-similarity transformation", *Proceedings of the 2019 IEEE International Conference on Internet of Things,* pp. 1-6, 2019.Las Vegas, NV, USA
[http://dx.doi.org/10.3390/s19204536]

[15] M. Kholghi, and M. Keyvanpour, "An analytical framework for data stream mining techniques based on challenges and requirements", *Proceedings of the 2011 IEEE International Conference on Data Mining Workshops,* pp. 1-6, 2011.Vancouver, BC, Canada

[16] M.A. Alsheikh, S. Lin, D. Niyato, and H.P. Tan, "Machine learning in wireless sensor networks: Algorithms, strategies, and applications", *Proceedings of the 2014 IEEE International Conference on Communications,* pp. 1-6, 2014.Sydney, Australia
[http://dx.doi.org/10.1109/COMST.2014.2320099]

[17] R. Ghorbani, and R. Ghousi, "Predictive data mining approaches in medical diagnosis: A review of some diseases prediction", *Proceedings of the 2019 IEEE International Conference on Healthcare Informatics,* pp. 1-6, 2019.Xi'an, China
[http://dx.doi.org/10.5267/j.ijdns.2019.1.003]

[18] M. Adya, "Data mining in health-care: Issues and a research agenda", *Proceedings of the 2000 IEEE International Conference on Data Mining,* pp. 1-6, 2000.San Jose, CA, USA

[19] F.G. Mohammadi, F. Shenavarmasouleh, M.H. Amini, and H.R. Arabnia, "Data analytics for smart cities: Challenges and promises", *Proceedings of the 2021 IEEE International Conference on Big*

Data, pp. 1-6, 2021.Orlando, FL, USA

[20] C. Lim, K.J. Kim, and P.P. Maglio, "Smart cities with big data: Reference models, challenges, and considerations", *Proceedings of the 2018 IEEE International Conference on Big Data,* pp. 1-6, 2018.Seattle, WA, USA [http://dx.doi.org/10.1016/j.cities.2018.04.011]

[21] L. Hutton, and T. Henderson, "Beyond the EULA: Improving consent for data mining", *Proceedings of the 2017 IEEE International Conference on Big Data,* pp. 1-6, 2017.Boston, MA, USA [http://dx.doi.org/10.1007/978-3-319-54024-5_7]

[22] H. Luan, P. Geczy, H. Lai, and J. Gobert, "Challenges and future directions of big data and artificial intelligence in education", *Proceedings of the 2020 IEEE International Conference on Big Data,* pp. 1-6, 2020.Atlanta, GA, USA [http://dx.doi.org/10.3389/fpsyg.2020.580820]

[23] S.R. Bashir, S. Raza, and V. Misic, "Progress in privacy protection: A review of privacy preserving techniques in recommender systems, edge computing, and cloud computing", *Proceedings of the 2024 IEEE International Conference on Big Data,* pp. 1-6, 2024.San Francisco, CA, USA

[24] Z. H. Kilimci, M. Yalcin, A. Kucukmanisa, and A. K. Mishra, "Heart disease detection using vision-based transformer models from ECG images," arXiv preprint arXiv:2310.12630, 2023.

[25] O. S. Albahri, A. A. Zaidan, B. B. Zaidan, M. Hashim, A. S. Albahri, and M. A. Alsalem, "Real-time remote health-monitoring Systems in a Medical Centre: A review of the provision of healthcare services-based body sensor information, open challenges and methodological aspects," *J. Med. Syst.*, vol. 42, no. 9, Art. no. 164, 2018.

CHAPTER 2

Exploring Human-Computer Interaction and Affective Computing

SPV Subba Rao[1,*], **Shruti Bhargava Choubey**[1] and **Abhishek Choubey**[1]

[1] *Department of Electronics and Communication Engineering, Sreenidhi Institute of Science & Technology, Hyderabad, Telangana, India*

Abstract: This study begins with the notion that Human-Computer Interaction (HCI) and affective computing have a common goal: understanding, capturing, and altering human affect and physiological states. However, well-established methods from psychology, communication, and media studies have received limited attention in HCI and affective computing. This presentation provides: (1) a rationale for incorporating insights from these disciplines into effective research; (2) an outline of methodological frameworks used in humanistic studies of affect; and (3) examples of how these methods might enhance and inspire new paths in HCI and affective computing. The paper finishes by discussing the benefits and limitations of interdisciplinary collaboration in this context.

Keywords: Affective computing, Human-computer interaction (HCI), Human affect, Interdisciplinary research, Methodological models.

INTRODUCTION TO HUMAN-COMPUTER INTERACTION

Technological advancements in the last few decades have led to the rapid development of many research areas. It has become clear that computers are no longer confined to laboratories, companies, and governmental organizations but have found their way into every part of everyday life. Satellites, televisions, and credit cards are widely used, and home computers, mobile phones, and the internet have all become household items. The social and economic impacts of such an infusion of technology are obvious in today's society. In recent years, it is believed that the next generation of technology should not only consider how fast it operates and how large its memory space is, but also give emphasis on how

* **Corresponding author SPV Subba Rao:** Department of Electronics and Communication Engineering, Sreenidhi Institute of Science & Technology, Hyderabad, Telangana, India; E-mail: subbarao.s@sreenidhi.edu.in

Shruti Bhargava Choubey & Yogesh Shrivastava (Eds.)

easy it is to use. This belief has led researchers to debate the emphasis on performance and memory space to assist users in becoming more creative. One research area developed from such discussions is the field of Human-Computer Interaction (HCI) [1].

Important research questions in HCI include: How should interfaces be designed so that users can easily control computers? What system architecture and cognitive models best meet user needs?; Do visual icons better portray concepts for students as opposed to the written word?; and What are the usability advantages and disadvantages of using multimedia in an online tutorial? Simultaneously, the human interface with devices and computer games is also of great concern. Simple examples include pushing a button for the correct time on a watch, setting the temperature on a thermostat, and using a dizzying array of interaction devices for computer game consoles. The key issue here is that this new generation of devices is likely to stretch the traditional novel/homeowner interaction to the limits and present a research challenge beyond HCI. There are two cautions to be taken. Firstly, it is completely recognized that HCI is a broad church, with many researchers having disparate interests focusing on the common denominator of human use of computers. This study should be viewed not as a total description of the research area, but as an introduction to new research directions within HCI. Secondly, common threads are running throughout the paper; these being that models of HCI, in all its guises, should be "numerical" methods to allow discrimination about what works and what does not. This pre-testing, post-testing methodology espoused has much broader implications and is viewed as a significant advance in research methods and HCI practice [2].

Definition and Evolution of HCI

When addressing Human-Computer Interaction (HCI), it is essential to first define the relevant terms of the phrase itself. The term "human-computer" describes what is interacting, namely, human beings and computer systems. The term "interaction" is used to describe how people and computers work together, describing a set of practices, methods, and techniques that influence the way humans and computers communicate or work together. Therefore, "Human-Computer Interaction" can be seen as a mixture of arts, science, social disciplines, and many other fields that literally influence the use of technology and how users interact with technology.

Although the current practice of HCI is relatively new, its roots can be traced back to the early days of computing usage. HCI as we know it today originated as a term in the 1980s, emerging from technical and engineering-related discourse concerning man-machine systems, incorporating other fields such as cognitive psychology. The first occurrences of the term were found in ACM publications in 1982, quickly adopted by commercial industries [3].

Since then, HCI has transformed into a burgeoning field with a much broader definition and scope, which goes beyond computing usability concerns. Interaction design focuses on user goals and needs, system constraints, the processes by which humans interact with these systems, and the outcome of this interaction. This tradition has expanded to address complex systems and activities while providing richer alternatives for user experience by considering the overall context of use. Instituted protocols ensure the potential design solution is usable by users, useful in terms of their needs, and can be transferred into effective IT products or systems. HCI has been subject to various design fashions and philosophies since the 1980s. From early cognitive man-machine systems thinking, it evolved to address a wider and deeper appreciation of user needs and behaviors [4]. This led to a focus on User-Centered Design (UCD) in the early 1990s. Over the past twenty-five years, these principles have been adopted pervasively in software and internet design. On the other hand, the 2010s witnessed the predominance of new design approaches like flat design and material design. However, central to all these different design epochs are the users themselves and their needs, goals, and behaviors. The development of computing and related technologies has been shaped by the different ways people interact with them. From complex command line instructions, the development of Graphical User Interfaces, the WWW, and, more recently, mobile technology, all these developments are, in one way or another, related to the discipline of HCI. Moreover, HCI is characterized by the somewhat eclectic mixture of disciplines in which it rests. On the one hand, it is informed by insights from cognitive science, enabling the design of technologies adapted to human cognition and other mental processes. On the other hand, it incorporates principles drawn from social psychology and communication to understand the emotional and social aspects of the user. At a broader level, interaction design engages in a broader conversation between the technological world and that of social sciences and the humanities, enabling forms of insights and innovations that otherwise would not have occurred. This study will explore Affective Computing as a specific part of this macrocosm. Focusing on the design of technologies that respond to the user's emotional inputs and states, it will cover advancements, applications, and, mostly, their implications in technology and society [5].

FUNDAMENTAL CONCEPTS IN HCI

Introduction

The process of Human-Computer Interaction (HCI) is a discipline that bases its studies on the development and study of the interaction between people and technology. Several principles and concepts in HCI need to be understood to understand or predict user behavior in interacting with technology, and provide strategies for designing a user-friendly interface. The HCI that has been performed has three approaches. First is usability. The purpose of technology can be seen from a social aspect to feel the effectiveness and efficiency of using technology well. The search for technology can also be done from the user side to see whether interaction with technology is easy or difficult in the long term. Second is accessibility. Technology is used in everyday life. The use of technology that cannot be controlled will make one feel annoyed. The third is user experience. The feasibility of technology will be measured by the feelings that occur in someone who has used the technology. These three factors are the factors that influence the adoption of technology by societal needs [6].

Based on the understanding of HCI, several design strategies have been proposed. Designed patterns of interface can be a consideration for developers when developing an interface. Interface patterns can also be regarded as a solution to the problem when doing the interface refactoring process. The meaning of the interaction model is a model that is the initial concept and guide for understanding, describing, and designing details of interaction with technology. Several sub-concepts are underlying an interaction model. The Interaction Model is a theoretical or conceptual framework that handles the process of making decision-making models and descriptions of the user and the system in order to pay attention to interaction and the effect of mapping through the interface to facilitate the creation of interfaces that have user efficiency. Task Model is a description at an abstract level that gives rise to various tasks that can be done by the user while using the application. Mood Model defines three aspects of the user's emotional aspect of interest, ie, the quality, intensity, and speed of change in the emotion. The Cognitive Model is a description of the process of how the user learns to interact with technology and uses technology to achieve the end. Conceptual Model is a model that tells how the user perceives the interface of the system. Dialog Notation is a visual representation of the behavior of the interface when the user interacts and how the user interacts [7]. Finally, Software Model is a model that relates to data and the information system needs expressed in the form of use case modeling, class modeling, object modeling, activity modeling, component modeling, and deployment modeling. Made this model to design an interaction model that will be able to comprehend how a simulation model interacts with the user. The facility of the interaction model provided by schematic dialog has been searched to make it easier to create interface designs every time the visual simulator is created. Iterative Interaction is a process that is continuous in revising interaction models and repetitively performing various kinds of iterative processes. These strategies are User and Task Analysis, Prototyping, Designing Wizards, Designing Dialogs, and Testing Dialogs.

User Interface Design Principles

This study presents the robust considerations that a User Interface Designer must address in the design process. First, it introduces the ideas behind user interface design and progressive scintillate until the final stage, with design considerations for research literature on approaches to design in engineering or computer science alone. Predominantly, that literature presents an emphasis on the usability of products, one of the keystones of effective technical communication and the objective of affective design [8].

To be sure, there can be no meaningful separation between the design of an interface, mechanical, digital, or otherwise, and those aspects of a system that drive its operation and deliver its functionality. An interface serves as both a gateway into this operation and a guide for its uses. An effective interface spells out what is happening and why, ensures access to the full capability of a system, and does not allow a user to do the impossible. As a discipline, interface design ought to be embraced in technical communication degree programs.

In conclusion, interface design is, first and foremost, a task of effective technical communicators. Since the time of cavemen, people have intended to have a better life by inventing things that made life easier to live, such as inventing materials and other things used in daily life, starting from the first stone tools to the digital gadgets nowadays. Design is a creation of a plan or convention for the construction of an object, system, or measurable human interaction.

While User Interface (UI) design includes designing and creating graphical user interfaces, some research is also conducted on the methods underlying these designs. User interfaces in the widest sense have been the focus of many areas of research, from those that analyze methods for formal specification, design, implementation, as well as verification and testing, to cognitive and perceptual issues.

AFFECTIVE COMPUTING: UNDERSTANDING EMOTIONS IN TECHNOLOGY

Affective Computing is an ever-growing area of interest and is considered to be one of computing's latest frontiers. Affective Computing can be described as "computing that relates to, arises from, or deliberately influences emotion or other affective phenomena" and while the benefits of incorporating Emotion or Affective Awareness into interaction with systems or devices are many, the act of this merger is a challenging one given that emotions, as phenomena, transpire in several ways and are, as yet, not perfectly understood or closely defined. Emotions play a pivotal role in many actions performed by people during the day. It happens frequently that a human emotion triggers an action that has a significant effect on the user's way of interacting. In human-computer interaction, emotions might arise from such commonly seen instances as being welcomed by an email from a friend, feeling upset upon a bad comment, or feeling anxious from a game.

Affective Computing is becoming more and more present in present-day research as the technology becomes more sophisticated. Broadly expressed, Affective Computing can be seen in terms of (1) Computer systems that can sense emotion, (2) Affective reactions to computer applications or from the computer in which the response is affected by emotion, and (3) Computer systems that have decision-making that influences emotions, or that are themselves influenced by emotion [9]. Two key points differentiate Affective Computing from Emotional Intelligence. Firstly, the technology is in the very early stages of research and thus is either non-existent or not tested. Broadly, Affective Computing is the study of machines that can recognize, interpret, and respond to human emotion, an inherently multidisciplinary endeavor that encompasses insights from diverse fields. At the broadest level, computers can (1) recognize emotions, such as by capturing human physiological parameters, speech, or facial expressions; (2) interpret emotions observed in users, such as by inferring emotional states across different modalities; and (3) respond in ways that are socially and emotionally appropriate, such as through affective dialogues and the generation of music or art. When integrated into interactive systems, such advanced technologies can enhance the user experience, stimulate creativity, and foster unique forms of engagement. At the same time, using such technologies, individuals can express and disclose facets of cognition and affect that would remain otherwise undetected [10].

Emotion Recognition Techniques

Human-Computer Interaction (HCI) is a fast-growing interdisciplinary field focusing on designing technological systems and products that mediate the communication between people and digital content. HCI thus developed a growing interest in the design of systems and computer programs that can understand and interpret human emotions. This interest has led to the rise of an interdisciplinary field named Affective Computing. Affective Computing is focused on the design of systems and computer programs that can recognize, interpret, synthesize, and respond to the psychological state of a user. It is a multidisciplinary field at the crossroads between HCI, psychology, and computer science [11].

Since the assessment of emotions is a difficult, multi-faceted task, the different models will exploit multiple data sources and features. The use of multiple models suggests the use of Machine Learning (ML) and Artificial Intelligence (AI) techniques to find out how to properly combine the models and their features. The employment of these techniques has resulted in the realization of a multitude of different approaches and methods for the analysis of user emotions. Besides seminal approaches, such as facial expression recognition, voice analysis, and monitoring of physiological signals, several novel techniques have been proposed. Eye-tracking, for instance, has received attention, and novel methods have been proposed in the literature aiming at the real-time detection of the user's emotional reactions. For each of these methodologies, current approaches, challenges, and future development opportunities are reviewed. One of the main limits of these methodologies is related to the fact that they tend to have average recognition results on a precise subset of emotions. However, the success of affective systems and affective interfaces depends on the accuracy and reliability of the emotion recognition and classification algorithm. Thus, understanding the challenges, limitations, and potentials in these methodologies can also be useful for the design of more effective experimental paradigms in the context of affective research and can provide a solid understanding for the formulation of more effective guidelines for the development of new Affective Computing and HCI systems [12].

THE ROLE OF EMOTIONS IN HUMAN-COMPUTER INTERACTION

The topic of emotions has a critical, albeit sometimes misleading, place within the field of Human-Computer Interaction (HCI). As people use technology, they experience joy, frustration, surprise, and a myriad of other feelings. These emotions influence interactions in a considerable range of ways, shaping the decisions individuals make, the level of their engagement, and even the satisfaction felt with the technology in the aftermath. Thus, it is the effectiveness of the technology used that largely determines the kind and strength of emotions felt while using it.

One may have a delightful conversation with a friend, laugh at a silly joke, or wipe a tear after hearing sad news. Similarly, user interactions with computers can also evoke a variety of effects. Emotion is also strongly connected with decision-making; the richer the emotional component of an event, the stronger the decision consequences. Robots are about to enter our daily lives, changing them the way personal computers did back in the 1980s. Thus, the research on how emotions can affect such decisions is of utmost importance. Consequently, it will have direct implications for making technology that is more human-like, as well as for its acceptance and successful use.

On a different level, there is a pressing need for design in HCI to move away from a purely function-driven approach. Over the last few decades, the cognition-focused approach has led to robust advances in understanding human nature, but perhaps to the detriment of considering a wider understanding of how the mind works. The dawn of the information era has seen rapid developments in every aspect of life, including technology itself. The pervasiveness and importance of new technologies stem from the fact that devices and computers are now used not only for providing information and support in tasks, but also for entertainment, communication, or social interaction. It will be argued for considering the design implications of humanities towards emotions, suggesting that users' emotional needs and responses should be placed at the centre of interface design [1]. The experience and aspect of usability will then be considered with a focus on emotion, as appropriate technology design has a considerable effect on how users feel about a system. From a more futuristic perspective, a tangible interface that strives to incorporate aspects of emotional intelligence into the design will be briefly presented in the concluding remarks.

Emotional Design in User Interfaces

Emotional design is a fundamental element of user interface creation that is often ignored or approached haphazardly. Little research on the topic is available, especially in the technical communication and Human-Computer Interaction (HCI) fields; with the increasing focus on multimodal interface technologies in these fields, examining and understanding the emotional and affective qualities of these technologies will be important [1]. A good example of this growing technical focus on affective computing and computer emotional responses can be found in the many new books, papers, and conferences devoted to these topics that have recently appeared.

To develop an in-depth understanding of the subject, a multidisciplinary approach is necessary. To that end, the analysis integrates major theories on the nature of emotions and their impact on action, cognition, and design; research on the role of emotions in the creation, assessment, and use of technological artifacts; and contributions from the field of interactive art. The analysis culminates in a "mind framework of emotional design. This framework recognizes five types of emotions, or mental states, that could be experienced, due to different causes, by engaging with an object of design: (1) aesthetic emotions, induced by the contemplation of the outward appearance of an object; (2) physiological emotions, caused by the bodily interactions with a matter; (3) cognitive emotions, stemming from the representations that the manipulation of an object triggers; (4) social emotions, due to the knowledge of what an object stand for; and (5) contact emotions, passively arising from a temporary and surface involvement with an object.

USER-CENTERED DESIGN AND EMOTION

The prevailing focus of research on the effectiveness of Human-Computer Interaction (HCI) has been to increase task productivity, ease of use, and to generally design systems that do what people need to do [1]. However, user experience is more than the rational/logical interaction tasks in which the overwhelming majority of these productivity-focused studies are interested. Recent advancements in the science of user experience and the increasing availability of behavioral data are both trends that argue for a complementary approach to traditional productivity-focused studies. This piece reports on a major empirical study of emotional experience and its methodology, specifically how a variety of visual and auditory emotional dimensions were gathered with temporal accuracy throughout the contours of desktop usage and recreation web usage behaviors. There are quantitative models of user behavior and temporal emotional expression across task and web page usage, and a strategy-centered design methodology for affective computing technologies. Technology and methodology attributes are key to the successful collection of lab data, and future directions for complementing research and development are also discussed. Critically under-addressed issues that arise in designing for emotional experience through behavior have profound implications for the setup and design of multifaceted HCI study and experiment conditions. Additionally, it is argued that there are compelling reasons for HCI researchers to take the analysis of user experience seriously, ranging from philosophical considerations of what users are to the practical effectiveness of interaction design [4].

Emotion Elicitation Techniques

Over the past decades, it has become recognized that considering user emotions alongside traditional cognitive variables can significantly enhance the user experience. This prompted the proliferation of systems aiming at understanding and adapting to users' emotions, a topic of ongoing research in the interdisciplinary field of affective computing. In order to design and evaluate such systems, it is crucial to draw upon emotion elicitation techniques. In this special issue, a set of articles is presented showcasing different techniques used to elicit and comprehend a user's emotional reactions and the role they play in the context of user-centered design. This collection of mixed-methods approaches draws attention to various possibilities of exploring emotions, encouraging reflection upon the role of emotions in users' interaction with technology, and comfortable design improvements. Methodological challenges are addressed, highlighting the impact of situational context on emotional responses and ethical implications regarding user consent and privacy. The need to ensure a genuine understanding of emotions and provide recommendations for fostering their advancement is posed. Although considerable progress has been made in this area, several open challenges and limitations are pinpointed, underscoring the individual variability of emotional expression as a particular stumbling block to using large-scale field studies [1].

EMPATHY AND TRUST IN HCI

Empathy and Trust in HCI are terms inextricably woven through the fabric of human existence. As society continues to automate and computerize at an accelerating pace, the relationships between these three could very well determine the success of future technologies or the comfort and safety of the societies they will support. The goal of HCI has always been to create technology that is "human-centered" in the sense that it facilitates the goals of the human user; however, the technology does not exist in a vacuum. Consideration must be given to the human side of the "interaction," including issues of comfort, sociability, emotions, trust, and, predictably, empathy, in addition to issues of efficiency [1]. Understanding and designing with this multifaceted, rich environment can only serve to benefit and broaden the horizon of the field as a whole.

How users feel about something plays a critical role in how they will interact with it. Emotional responses have a vast potential effect upon human decision-making and can considerably influence the level of trust a user is willing to extend to a system. This, in turn, has wide-reaching implications for the interactions that will occur. Indeed, the design of a user interface can directly affect a user's emotional state, and affective state can directly affect trust. A good design philosophy is empathetic; designers must seek to understand the "emotional landscapes" of their users to more effectively shape that experience. People want to be understood by their technology. They want to be listened to and treated with sensitivity. People like their technology better when it shares and supports their emotional states. For these reasons, fostering empathy in the design of technology is a no-brainer. Broadly, the technology itself may be empathetic when it conveys to the user that it understands and can respond appropriately to their emotional state; however, the technology could also be said to empower empathy between the user and another, a mechanism which would allow the user to more effectively express or gauge another's emotions. Such systems can enhance a user's understanding and ability to cope with the emotional states of others. It is strongly felt that a technology focusing on these two types of empathy could lead to excessively beneficial techniques and systems. The need for such systems will only increase, since the lines between technology and communication are quickly blurring, and there is a growing demand for systems that mediate the emotional communication that is lost in the digital realm. Summarization of state-of-the-art and formulation of future research directions within the field are given. Varied technical capabilities exist for a machine to communicate and display its emotional state, which include ones based on facial and body expressions, in vocal nuances, in physiological responses such as heart rate or heat flux, and in overt verbal expressions. A system that takes as input some or all of these cues and, through some manner of inference engine, simulates an emotionally responsive output would be categorized as an emotionally responsive interface. Another kind of system is a virtual agent, computer-generated character, or robotic device that acts as a mediator between the user and a secondary user or other technology. This creation could communicate a sense of empathy in its look, gestures, or responses to the user, or it could be designed to read emotional cues and responses between interactants. Technologies could include aural, visual, or database representations of user input.

Building Trust in Technology

There is a lot of talk about human-computer interaction and how we can design systems that interrelate effectively with people. Far less has been written about affective computing and how we get machines to recognize and simulate affect. Trust is consistently brought up in discussions of appropriate interactions. Trust is seen as a cornerstone for interactions by users with technology [5]. Several aspects of technology that can affect a user's trust are transparency, reliability, and user experience. Transparency can be provided through messages and design that convey to the user how a system has worked or is expected to work in the future. It is suggested that any use of an intelligent machine with humans requires it to be incredibly effectively bounded. To bound such a machine under trust conditions, it would be necessary to require that when the machine fell out of trust, either according to its prediction or due to the prediction of a human, it would mount a U-turn.

For a machine facing humans, this could be achieved by an explicit agreement or treaty in which the machine accurately details its method of operation, with what it has said, or might say, to other agents. This would allow observers to intervene on behalf of the user. A reliance on trust would not be placed on invisible machine-only deals. Since instances of technological betrayal are real, and as systems become more complex and opaque, they will necessarily increase. Thus, trust research and policy must search for modes of technological obviation. One approach is through the formulation of new norms and modes of behavior, not, however, of humans, but of machines. A machine might be required to undergo iterative human safety testing. It should be possible to observe that trust may be broken at any time, and thus to design in reset mechanisms. Similarly, a machine might be compelled only to conduct visible person-present dealings. Another approach is through the offering of trust-aids, such as adaptable automated trust calculators, able to easily adjust machine trust levels, and in so doing, closely following human model strategies.

CULTURAL AND ETHICAL CONSIDERATIONS IN AFFECTIVE COMPUTING

With the rapidly increasing interest in computer technology, it is important for users to consider the importance of designing and evaluating computers in many sociotechnical systems. The concerns can include the accessibility of technology and learning for people with disabilities, the design to promote divergent problem-solving approaches, and cultural aspects of human-computer interaction. The number of individuals from societies different than those that have dominated most of the human-computer interaction research and systems has rapidly increased. Consequently, technology designers and users are beginning to notice how the designs are based upon the values, knowledge, and assumptions of a particular socio-cultural setting, and can have significant problems in transferring them to or sharing them with people from very diverse cultural settings, but rely heavily on them.

Cultural considerations are increasingly relevant to technology because they are one of the socially constructed elements that mediate human definitions of the world, learning concerning its arrangement, and ways of making decisions and actions. Because designs translate these viewpoints, embody them in the arrangements, assumptions, methodologies, and feedback of a technology, laptops and related socio-technical systems make public the hidden worldviews of a culture and the user for whom it was designed. Consequently, the designs could be greatly improved: 1) to diminish these and other culturally congruent mechanisms of technology by making them more specific, and 2) to enhance the excellent components of designs that dovetail.

Cross-Cultural Differences in Emotional Expression

Affective computing systems are increasingly deployed in differing individual settings worldwide and must tackle the always-important yet complex job of unobtrusively identifying human emotions. Within these undertakings, research into cross-cultural differences in emotional expressions is crucial for a respectful understanding of how people all over the globe understand and express their affective states [6]. People across different cultures communicate and interpret emotions differently. Many cultural dimensions play into how emotional expressions are shaped and perceived. Hofstede's cultural dimensions emphasize broad contrasts between different cultures, engendering either certain varieties of emotional expressions or diverse interpretations of these expressions, like Individualism *vs.* Collectivism or High-Context *vs.* Low-Context. Technology acceptance and success notably rise when user needs and preferences are considered in the design and implementation of technology, for effective systems, which include recognizing cultural differences in emotional expressions from the perspective of potential end-users. Misinterpretation of emotion can be a major hindrance for users to get engaged with Affective Computing systems. Thus, developing strategies for making technology flexible enough to be able to consider a varying emotional expression of various cultural contexts is of utmost interest for user satisfaction, inclusiveness of a system, and trustworthy interaction. Nevertheless, there are multifarious challenges to securing a complete understanding of cross-cultural differences in emotional expressions. Language synopsis and the authenticity of emotional materials result from an arbitrative issue, as translation of them can subscribe to the prominent variances in perceived expressiveness. Further, a culture's particularity is not meaningful per se but only the combined contribution of multiple factors to a particular expression of emotion. Environment, social norms, mental state, *etc.*, can totally vary the expressiveness of given stimuli. Thus, to obtain a complete notion of a culture-tied emotional display, a careful consideration of these factors is needed. From the perspective of a computer vision scientist, emotional representation is largely treated in terms of facial expressions. Considering the facial modality, the same emotional state can result in a distinctive phenomenological expression depending on the culture. Thus, one of the first challenges for the affective system's developer is to delicately robust algorithms to cultural scrutiny. Sadness variably occurs with a distinct eye activity according to the culture; whereas the Chinese elongate such eye movements visible from afar, the Germans constrict these noticeable eye movements. A current challenge is to effectively recognize an emotion variable across cultures that is displayed with culturally distinctive multimodal cues. Taking all these descriptions into account will encourage those working in the TRR to create machines that are sensitive to different manners of expression and are both accepted and rejected in a particular context by the users.

AFFECTIVE COMPUTING APPLICATIONS

Driven by Artificial Intelligence and Big Data, smart technologies revolutionize every aspect of modern life: industry, commerce, management, *etc*. The use of computers is no longer confined merely to statistics, word processing, and routine communication, and is becoming an important means in various fields. The human-computer interface, which relates to the direct manipulation of the computer system, is especially crucial [7, 12]. The more we depend on computers, the more the importance of the human-computer interface with powerful functions is felt. Enhanced by human-computer applications, various intelligent devices appear, which greatly promote the development of electronics and information science Technology. However, the emotional requirements have been ignored in the features of these technologies, which makes the application process far from human-like features [8]. Therefore, the research on emotional requirements and applications is gaining widespread attention, with specific emotions, including joy, anger, peace, and sadness, being paid substantially more attention.

Recently, as technology rapidly advances, these requirements and applications can be withdrawn from the emotional types, and the area of focus turns toward the emotion-related properties and available technologies in specific regions. Affective Computing, which is the recognition of human emotions *via* computers, has recently emerged and raises widespread concern, contributing to HCI development. This technique can detect human feelings by computers through speech, body gesture, emotional words, facial appearance, and bio-signals. Emotion perception is measured, analyzed, applied, and developed as feelings into visualization, speech, and body movement, respectively. With more potential applications in a variety of fields, the future trends are also highlighted accordingly.

Emotionally Intelligent Systems

Emotionally intelligent systems are increasingly prevalent and play a critical part in everyday interaction with technology, from preparing responses in Gmail and

Outlook to suggesting playlists on Spotify or composing tweets. Particularly ripe for emotional intelligence exploration are applications and interfaces that allow individuals to provide more flexible user input, such as voice and touch user interfaces, as well as ambient and adaptive user experiences, such as mood-responsive music selection or calming products. At its core, an emotionally intelligent system should be able to detect, interpret, and respond to users' emotional states, particularly considering the feedback loops between these abilities. Emotion recognition for emotionally intelligent systems is a challenging but budding field that combines a variety of techniques, including machine learning, signal processing, and multimodal data analysis. Similar complexity lies in generating a response, best described as the capacity to understand emotions and how to represent and convey these feelings back meaningfully through the technology [9, 12].

Implying adaptivity during use, both technically (how adaptivity is achieved, *e.g.*, *via* real-time emotion detection, pre-trained settings, flexible response generation) and experientially (how adaptation is experienced by the user, *e.g.*, through dynamic user interface changes, active help-seeking behavior, conversational modeling). The potential of emotional intelligence to transform user experiences and interactions with technology is vast and diverse, promising, among other advantages, enhanced engagement and acquisition, empathic user support and trust-building, and improved productivity and knowledge exchange. Similarly, emotionally intelligent systems can offer practitioners real-time feedback on skill development or client interactions, support mental health recovery, and encourage healthier habits, potentially on the same devices where stressful or challenging tasks are performed, but also where the majority of time is already spent. Vast opportunities and increased reliance on emotional intelligence in technology are paired with multiple caveats and challenges [10]. Technologies robustly mimicking empathic human responses might be mistaken for sentient beings, to the point of ethical violations. Defensive or nurturing reactions by intelligent systems to unhappy or angry users could counterproductively enmesh them further in a cycle of low spirits, frustration, and hopelessness. There are also difficulties in detecting or portraying certain emotional states and complexities in privacy requirements.

FUTURE DIRECTIONS IN HCI AND AFFECTIVE COMPUTING

Ethical AI and Emotional Intelligence

We find ourselves in a time during human civilization when much attention is given to the design and development of artificial intelligence systems and their integration into everyday environments. Computers and algorithms are being designed to autonomously make decisions and carry out tasks that traditionally only humans could do, or to augment collective behaviors and empower otherwise constrained operations. We also find ourselves in an age when centuries of human progress and acceptance of universal social justice are being questioned, as if we have not collectively learned fundamental and tragic lessons from recent history. The widespread impact of algorithmic decisions in our society is being debated, and only recently has there been a re-examination and demand for redesigning data-driven systems to be non-discriminatory and transparent. The design of artificial emotional intelligence can help overcome these biases since artificial systems lack emotions and cannot ascribe them to their users; they may inadvertently behave towards their users in ways that are perceived as indifferent or insensitive.

The lack of emotional intelligence in the design of computing systems and interfaces has been the focus of much research in Affective Computing during the last two decades. In this age of systemic human inequality and increasing awareness of society's structural biases, it is very timely that Affective Computing broadens its scope from developing empathically sensitive computer interfaces to designing emotionally transparent systems that can understand their users and are capable of using emotions in computing applications in ethical ways. The challenge then becomes that of operationalizing established ethical precepts and social justice values in the design of a new generation of emotionally intelligent systems that are consistent with the cultural uniqueness of different groups of users.

CONCLUSION

In summary, the main arguments presented highlight the topic's significance. The discussion underscores the various aspects that contribute to a comprehensive understanding, including critical evidence, contrasting viewpoints, and the implications of these ideas in real-world scenarios. These elements collectively illustrate the subject's complexity, revealing the necessity for ongoing exploration and analysis. Additionally, the conclusion reinforces the value of synthesizing the information while considering diverse perspectives. This approach not only enriches the discourse but also encourages informed decision-making and further inquiry. By recognizing the interconnectedness of the points discussed, we can appreciate the broader context and the potential impact of the findings on future developments in the field.

REFERENCES

[1] M. A. Rosen, "Affective design in technical communication," *Master's thesis, Univ. of Central Florida*, Orlando, FL, USA, 2005. Available: https://scispace.com/pdf/affective-design-in-techni-al-communication-3fj9xkm52a.pdf

[2] S. Afzal, H. A. Khan, I. U. Khan, M. J. Piran, and J. W. Lee, "A comprehensive survey on affective computing: Challenges, trends, applications, and future directions," *arXiv preprint arXiv:2305.07665*, May 08, 2023.
[http://dx.doi.org/10.48550/arXiv.2305.07665]

[3] J.Z. Lim, J. Mountstephens, and J. Teo, "Emotion Recognition Using Eye-Tracking: Taxonomy, Review and Current Challenges", *Sensors (Basel),* vol. 20, no. 8, p. 2384, 2020.
[http://dx.doi.org/10.3390/s20082384] [PMID: 32331327]

[4] S. Triberti, A. Chirico, G. La Rocca, and G. Riva, "Developing Emotional Design: Emotions as Cognitive Processes and their Role in the Design of Interactive Technologies", *Front. Psychol.,* vol. 8, p. 1773, 2017.
[http://dx.doi.org/10.3389/fpsyg.2017.01773] [PMID: 29062300]

[5] L.J. Camp, H. Nissenbaum, and C. McGrath, Trust: A Collision of Paradigms.*Financial Cryptography.,* P. Syverson, Ed., Springer: Berlin, Germany, 2002, pp. 91-105.
[http://dx.doi.org/10.1007/3-540-46088-8_10]

[6] J.P. Stein, and P. Ohler, "Saving Face in Front of the Computer? Culture and Attributions of Human Likeness Influence Users' Experience of Automatic Facial Emotion Recognition", *Front. Psychol.,* vol. 9, p. 145, 2018.

[7] Y. Wang, W. Song, W. Tao, A. Liotta, D. Yang, X. Li, S. Gao, Y. Sun, W. Ge, W. Zhang, and W. Zhang, "A systematic review on affective computing: emotion models, databases, and recent advances", *Inf. Fusion,* vol. 83-84, pp. 19-52, 2022.
[http://dx.doi.org/10.1016/j.inffus.2022.03.009]

[8] G.N. Yannakakis, "Enhancing Health Care via Affective Computing", *Malta Journal of Health Sciences,* vol. 5, no. 1, pp. 38-42, 2018.

[9] E. Svikhnushina and P. Pu, "Social and emotional etiquette of chatbots: A qualitative approach to understanding user needs and expectations," *arXiv preprint arXiv:2009.08189*, Sep. 2020. Available: https://api.semanticscholar.org/CorpusID:221771156

[10] D. Kanevsky, and M. Leder, "Emotional Assistants for Applications", *Proceedings of the 2016 IEEE International Conference on Consumer Electronics (ICCE),* pp. 1-2, 2016.Las Vegas, NV, USA

[11] A. Mudigonda, U. D. Yalavarthi, P. Satyanarayana, A. Alkhayyat, A. N. Arularasan, S. S. Ganesh, and C. M. S. Kumar, "IDEAL: an inventive optimized deep ensemble augmented learning framework for opinion mining and sentiment analysis," *Social Netw. Anal. Min.*, vol. 14, no. 1, Art. no. 89, 2024.

[12] M. F. Şahin and F. Anka, "Metaheuristics role in image processing and computer vision applications: a comprehensive review," *Cluster Comput.*, vol. 28, no. 13, Art. no. 871, 2025.

CHAPTER 3

Designing Empathy: The Role of Emotion in Human-Computer Collaboration

Anurag Agarwal[1], **Radha Raman Pandey**[2,*] and **Hunny Gaur**[2]

[1] *Department of MBA, IMS Engineering College, Ghaziabad, Uttar Pradesh, India*

[2] *Department of Computer Science, IMS Engineering College, Ghaziabad, Uttar Pradesh, India*

Abstract: Imagine a world in which computers understand not just our commands but also our emotions. This is the promise of incorporating empathy into human-computer communication as technology progresses; integrating Emotional Intelligence (EI) into robots becomes more possible. However, this trip is not without obstacles. People's belief in the power of emotions is what hinders the advancement of Artificial Intelligence (AI). AI emotions enhance human-machine cooperation, fostering empathy and trust. AI systems can handle emotional input by incorporating EI and empathy, affecting human-computer interaction. This section explains how to connect naturally with robots using their emotional model. The incorporation of EI and empathy in AI systems improves human-computer interaction and collaboration. This chapter explores the design and implementation of empathy in AI, namely the machines' ability to feel, grasp, and react to human emotions. This raises ethical concerns, such as the distinction between simulated emotion and actual human connections. This chapter highlights the importance of emotional intelligence systems in shaping the future of human-computer interaction and presents technologies with human-like thinking and emotions.

Keywords: AI ethics, Emotion recognition, Emotional intelligence (EI), Empathy in AI, Human-computer interaction (HCI).

INTRODUCTION

Breakthroughs in AI and HCI are occurring at a rapid pace, generating a new generation of human-machine teamwork. One needs empathy or the ability to connect with the feelings of another person in such alliances [1 - 3]. With the increasing presence of AI systems in our lives, such as virtual assistants, smart healthcare devices, *etc*., the book called " Designing Empathy" examines the role of emotions in human-computer communication, and the way emotions can strengthen it through the virtue of empathy.

* **Corresponding author Radha Raman Pandey:** Department of Computer Science, IMS Engineering College, Ghaziabad, Uttar Pradesh, India; E-mail: radharamanp@gmail.com

Shruti Bhargava Choubey & Yogesh Shrivastava (Eds.)

The creation of Emotional Intelligence (EI) in systems is an important area of research as machines increase their ability to make sense of and respond to human emotions [4 - 6]. This chapter examines the effects of emotions (human and machine) on collaborative relationships. The aim is to be aware of situations where emotionally conscious AI can contribute to more reflexive, attentive, and efficient exchanges.

AI is the ability of a machine to perform tasks like intelligent beings, particularly within computer systems. Among the subfields of AI are machine learning, computer vision, natural language processing, robotics, and expert systems. The capacity to carry out speech recognition, high-level data processing, decision-making, and communicate using language, amongst others, is no longer in the domain of human work; it is done by AI systems. The image shows how to develop an AI system, as shown in Fig. (**1**):

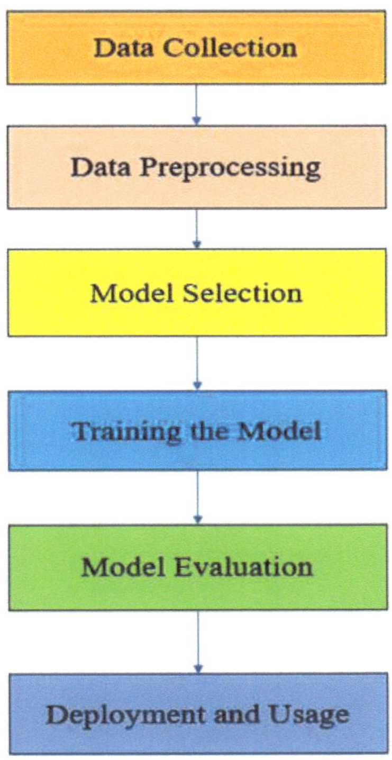

Fig. (1). Process of creating an AI system.

Emotional Intelligence (EI) is connected to the ability to recognize, read, and manage emotional expressions. This is an essential talent across various aspects of life, from personal relationships to career success. As reflected in Fig. (**2**), there are five important components of EI.

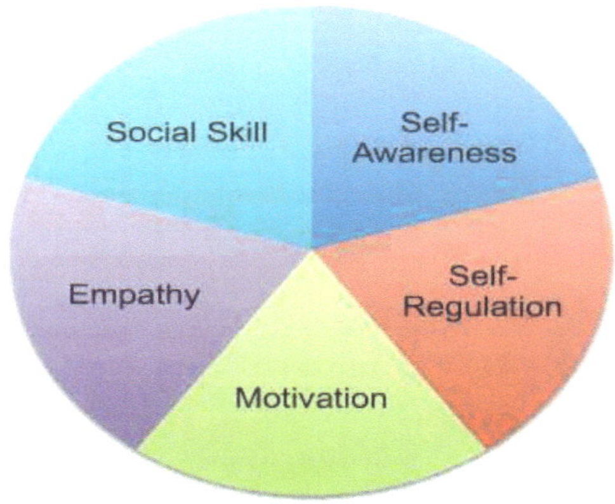

Fig. (2). Components/elements of EI.

1. Self-awareness: This is being aware of what you feel and how it can affect you. It is all about self-awareness of your strengths, weaknesses, and what drives you.
2. Self-Regulation: It involves managing feelings and behaviors. That consists of holding their own when under pressure and being adaptable to change.
3. Social Skills: This is applying your knowledge of feelings to establish and sustain good relations with others.
4. Motivation: When we are motivated, we are prompted to achieve goals and aspirations. It can be likened to a light that ignites a flame within us, giving us the energy to keep going even on a bad day.
5. Empathy: Empathy is a fundamental part of human engagement. It allows us to comprehend and share the emotions of others.

This chapter addresses the interplay of emotion and technology, highlighting public receptiveness to incorporating EI into HCI to promote more naturalistic, meaningful, and productive collaboration.

The key idea of this study is to build AI systems that are not only effective but also capable of establishing rapport and trust with humans [7 - 10]. EI includes recognizing, interpreting, and responding appropriately to emotional cues. In this chapter, we focus on the role of emotions in decision-making, communication, and problem-solving processes in human-computer interaction, identifying how they can be used to improve experience and increase collaboration and creativity in AI systems.

This chapter expands on some theoretical concepts, algorithms, and a conceptual framework diagram to demonstrate the remarkable power of emotionally intelligent AI and what this means for the future of human-computer interaction.

Cuadra, Wang, and Stein [11] investigated how interactive agents convey emotions and communicate empathy within human-computer interactions. Fei *et al.* [12] introduced Empathy Ear, an open-source, multimodal empathic chatbot capable of processing text, audio, and visual inputs to deliver emotionally responsive interactions through avatars. Schaaff, Reinig, and Schlippe [13] analyzed ChatGPT's ability to respond empathetically, reporting a 91.7% accuracy in recognizing emotions and a 70.7% success rate in mirroring user sentiments. Zhu and Luo [14] proposed a framework for artificial empathy in human-centred design, highlighting how computational modelling can embed empathy in AI systems to enhance human-oriented design. Mathur *et al.* [15] mathematically modeled empathy detection in robotic storytelling, achieving a 69% accuracy based on participants' visual responses. Majic [16] emphasized the role of emotional AI APIs in creating more personalized and user-centered interactions. Additionally, a scoping review titled "Situating Empathy in HCI/CSCW" [17] offered a comprehensive assessment of empathy's role in human-computer interaction and computer-supported cooperative work, identifying existing gaps and opportunities for future research. Collectively, these studies reflect ongoing advancements in integrating emotional intelligence and empathy into AI systems while also raising important considerations for ethical and human-centric technology development.

LITERATURE REVIEW ON EMPATHY IN AI AND HCI

The idea of embedding empathy into machines has been an important theme in research on artificial intelligence and human–computer interaction. Early work in affective computing suggested that successful collaboration between humans and machines depends not only on efficiency but also on the ability of systems to respond to emotions. Over time, different approaches have been proposed to make machines more sensitive, trustworthy, and emotionally intelligent.

Studies have shown that interactive agents are able to communicate emotions in real-time exchanges, with users responding more positively when systems attempt to mirror their feelings [18 - 20]. Open-source projects such as multimodal empathic chatbots have also been developed, capable of processing voice, text, and facial cues to deliver emotionally responsive interactions [21 - 23]. More recent investigations into conversational AI demonstrated that large language models could recognize emotions with high accuracy and even reproduce user sentiment, though concerns remain about the authenticity of such responses [24 - 26]. Frameworks for human-centred design have also been proposed, highlighting the importance of embedding empathy into the design process itself rather than treating it as an additional feature [27 - 30].

Applications are emerging across multiple fields. In education and entertainment, robotic storytelling has been used to test empathy detection, where visual responses of participants were analyzed with promising levels of accuracy [31 - 33]. Advances in emotional AI APIs have further enabled systems to adapt to users in more personalized ways [34 - 35]. At the same time, broad reviews of the field have pointed to the need for stronger ethical safeguards, especially in relation to cultural differences, privacy, and fairness [36 - 37].

Taken together, the literature reflects both progress and complexity. While machines are now able to identify emotions and simulate caring responses, the depth of human-like empathy remains contested. The research suggests that the next steps will depend not only on technical developments but also on designing systems that can balance empathy with transparency, trust, and ethical responsibility.

ALGORITHM FOR DESIGNING EMPATHY IN HUMAN-COMPUTER COLLABORATION

Empathy in AI systems requires a structured algorithm that can recognise, comprehend, and respond to human emotions. The algorithm "DEHCC" describes the process of designing empathy for human-computer collaboration. Fig. (**3**) illustrates the conceptual framework for creating empathy-based systems, followed by a description of the conceptual foundations.

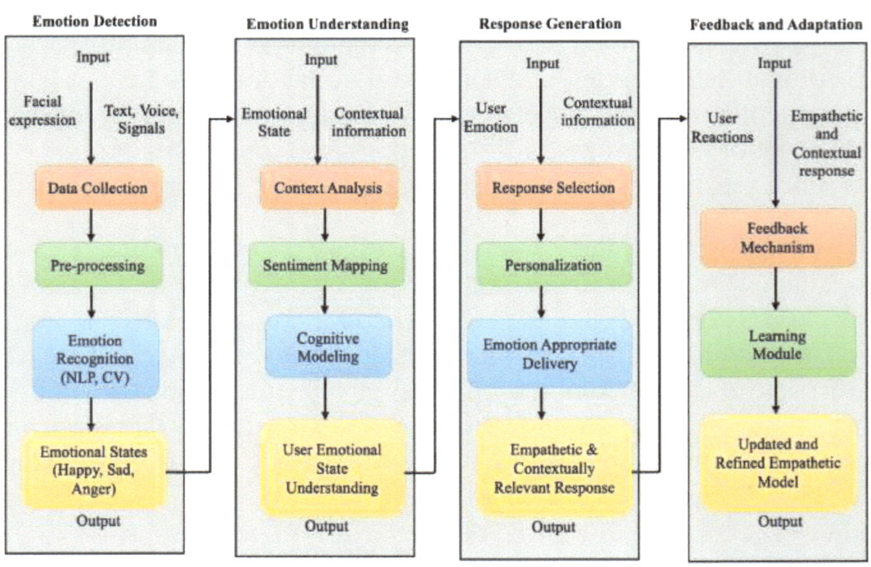

Fig. (3). Conceptual framework diagram.

Algorithm 1:*DEHCC (Designing Empathy in Human-Computer Collaboration)*

Nomenclature: $n \rightarrow$ *Number of Tasks* $R \rightarrow$ *Robot* $L \rightarrow$ *Location*		
Input: *Task t assigned to robot R* **Output:** *Execution of task t by robot R*		
for each ***i*** *in task* ***t = 1 to n***		
Step 1	:	Add task t_i to R_i.
Step 2	:	Assign the task t_i to R_i.
Step 3	:	Navigate location L_i for task t_i.
Step 4	:	Execution of the assigned task t_i by R_i.

Step 1: Emotion Detection

Input: Text, voice, facial expressions, or physiological signals reflecting the real-time interactions of humans.

Data Collection: Must use sensors, microphones, cameras, or wearable devices to collect multimodal input.

Emotion Recognition Models.

Natural Language Processing (NLP): Discern tone, sentiment, and context in text or speech.

Computer Vision: Identify emotional state through image processing of facial expressions and body language.

Biometric Analysis: Understand heart rate, skin conductivity, or other physiological measures.

Output: Some of the emotions in the dataset include happiness, sadness, anger, and neutrality.

Step 2: Understanding Emotions

First, provide contextual data and identify emotional states.

Contextuality: Use your contextual information (like time, place, and previous interactions) to understand what specifically triggers their emotions.

Sentiment Mapping: Correlate the sentiments you have identified with possible needs/intents.

Have a Cognitive Model: Establish an emotion and conduct linkage that is human-like.

Output: An advanced understanding of the user's psychological state and what leads to it.

Step 3: Response Generation

Input: User context and EI.

Response Selection:

Interpret these results.

Utilize reinforcement learning to tune answer selections over time.

Customisation: Tailor responses according to previous conversations and individual inclinations.

Contextualize: Change the channel, language, and tone to fit the user's emotional state.

Output: Contextually appropriate and compassionate answers.

Step 4: Feedback and Adaptation

The mechanism ensures that user satisfaction is rooted in outcome or form (could be that their conversation keeps continuing) or even tone changes.

To improve future interactions, through adaptive algorithms or reinforcement learning, update the model. Future research could explore ethical concerns, human trust in AI empathy, and cross-cultural perspectives in affective computing.

Output: A better model of empathy.

Step 5: Ethical Safeguards

Data privacy: Ensure that all sensitive information is stored securely and in an anonymized format.

Takes — Transparency: Ensure users are aware of the limitations and capabilities of the system.

Mitigation of Bias: Frequently audit your system for potential biases in the generation of responses or identification of emotion.

Output: AI systems that are trustworthy, ethical, and, compassionate.

To move toward systems that bridge the empathy gap between humans and machines, in a way that is effective and empathetic. This framework sets out a vision and principles for the design of human-computer collaboration. These systems can radically reinvent interaction paradigms and become more effective, humane, and intuitive, by blending advanced technology with ethical values.

THE COMPLEXITY OF HUMAN EMOTIONS

Even humans struggle to navigate the nuances, of emotion. The emotions are complex, diverse, and often, contradictory. Therefore, it becomes very complex, posing a huge challenge for machines to follow and comprehend such information.

Technological Limitations:

- Data Limitations
- Bias in Data
- Real-Time Processing
- Ethical Considerations:

There are severe ethical implications of integrating machines, with empathy, and they must be addressed adequately.

- Privacy Concerns:
- Data Collection
- Consent
- Manipulation and Trust

Through comprehension and navigation of these limitations, we can lay down a roadmap for a world where machines not only comprehend our verbal commands but also our emotions, opening up pathways to more meaningful and impactful human-machine co-operation.

APPLICATIONS AND CASE STUDIES OF EMPATHETIC AI

The practical use of empathetic AI is emerging across diverse fields, where emotional understanding can enhance effectiveness, trust, and user satisfaction. These applications provide valuable insight into how empathy in machines is not only a theoretical possibility but a growing reality.

One of the most visible areas is **healthcare**, where empathetic systems are being designed to support patients both physically and emotionally. Virtual assistants and chatbots are increasingly used in mental health care, offering conversations that adapt to the patient's tone and stress levels [1]. Empathy-aware robots have also been trialed in elder care, responding with sensitivity to signs of loneliness or discomfort, thereby providing companionship and monitoring without replacing human caregivers [2].

In **education**, empathetic AI is being applied to intelligent tutoring systems that adjust teaching strategies based on a student's frustration, motivation, or enthusiasm. By recognizing emotional cues, these systems can provide encouragement when needed or slow down explanations when signs of confusion are detected [3]. Such emotionally aware learning environments have been shown to increase engagement and foster deeper understanding.

The field of **customer service** has also embraced empathetic AI through chatbots and virtual assistants that respond to anger, dissatisfaction, or excitement in real-time. These systems are able to calm frustrated customers, offer apologies when appropriate, and deliver more human-like support experiences [4]. The result is not only improved service quality but also stronger brand trust.

Another domain is **social robotics**, where machines are designed to act as companions or assistants. Robots such as therapeutic devices in pediatric wards or companion pets for dementia patients have shown that empathetic responses can reduce stress, provide comfort, and improve overall well-being [5]. In entertainment and storytelling, empathy detection algorithms have even been tested to gauge audience emotions and adapt narratives accordingly, leading to more immersive experiences [6].

These case studies reveal both promise and challenge. While empathetic AI demonstrates clear benefits in healthcare, education, customer support, and social companionship, questions remain about reliability, cultural sensitivity, and the risk of over-dependence on machines for emotional needs [7]. Nevertheless, the trajectory suggests that empathetic AI will increasingly become part of everyday life, shaping how humans connect with technology in more meaningful and responsive ways.

CONCLUSION

The innovative strategy of AI and human interactions involves implementing empathy and Emotional Intelligence (EI) in human and machine actions. As technology advances, Emotional Intelligence (EI) will be required for effective human-machine interactions. Physically designing systems to recognise human emotion, respond to it, and eventually create a platform that gives intent and content can get AI to create tasks, content, and enhanced interaction through humanistic responses, which builds trust between the two.

This will not be a smooth path; therefore, ethical issues should be considered during the design of emotionally intelligent systems to discourage AI manipulation and to avoid misuse of information used in emotional computing and expressive bodies. AI can seem to emulate empathy; however, it will not substitute for human relationships. Their responses are supposed to enhance human potential, not overwhelm it.

Future cooperation between human beings and computers is highly dependent on a design that emphasises emotional intelligence, prioritises the welfare of people over the intelligence of machines, and makes the utmost vitality of machine/human cooperation and collaboration the primary driver and determinant of success. AI controls our decisions, such as when to shut off the alarm and when to get into bed. Until AI can teach us how to feel, we shall always have affection to refer to as the key to the next frontier. The possibilities of growth in all spheres will be available to the AI like a cornucopia.

REFERENCES

[1] C. Chao, "AI Empathy in the Metaverses", In: *Digital Futures in Human-Computer Interaction*, 2025, pp. 107-122.
[http://dx.doi.org/10.1201/9781032693606-10]

[2] W. H. Kunz, L. Sajtos, and C. Flavián, "Beyond replacement: human-machine collaboration in the age of AI", *J. Service Manage.*, vol. 36, no. 4, pp. 477-494, 2025.
[http://dx.doi.org/10.1108/JOSM-04-2025-0194]

[3] K. A. Hossain, "Emotional Intelligence and Artificial Intelligence: Relation and Exploring the World of Human Touch and Machine", *Preprint,* 2025.

[4] B. A. Erol, A. Majumdar, P. Benavidez, P. Rad, K. K. R. Choo, and M. Jamshidi, "Toward artificial emotional intelligence for cooperative social human–machine interaction", *IEEE Trans. Comput. Soc. Syst.,* vol. 7, no. 1, pp. 234-246, 2019.

[5] R. Yonck, "Heart of the Machine: Our Future in a World of Artificial Emotional Intelligence", In: *Arcade*, 2020.

[6] K. A. Hossain, "Emotional Intelligence and Artificial Intelligence: Relation and Exploring the World of Human Touch and Machine", 2025.

[7] A. Ferrario, M. Loi, and E. Viganò, "In AI we trust incrementally: A multi-layer model of trust to analyze human-artificial intelligence interactions", *Philos. Technol.,* vol. 33, no. 3, pp. 523-539, 2020.

[http://dx.doi.org/10.1007/s13347-019-00378-3]

[8] E. Glikson, and A. W. Woolley, "Human trust in artificial intelligence: Review of empirical research", *Acad. Manage. Ann.,* vol. 14, no. 2, pp. 627-660, 2020. [http://dx.doi.org/10.5465/annals.2018.0057]

[9] F. Rossi, "Building trust in artificial intelligence", *J. Int. Affairs,* vol. 72, no. 1, pp. 127-134, 2018.

[10] J. Doll, and M. Si, "Building Rapport in Human-AI Interactions: A Theory of Mind Perspective", *arXiv preprint,* 2024.

[11] A. Cuadra, M. Wang, and L. A. Stein, "The illusion of empathy? Notes on displays of emotion in human-computer interaction", In: *Proc. 2024 CHI Conf. Hum. Factors Comput. Syst.*, 2024. [http://dx.doi.org/10.1145/3613904.3642336]

[12] H. Fei, H. Zhang, B. Wang, L. Liao, Q. Liu, and E. Cambria, "Empathy Ear: An open-source avatar multimodal empathetic chatbot", *arXiv preprint,* 2024.

[13] K. Schaaff, C. Reinig, and T. Schlippe, "Exploring ChatGPT's empathic abilities", In: *Proc. 2023 11th Int. Conf. Affective Comput. Intell. Interact. (ACII)*, 2023. [http://dx.doi.org/10.1109/ACII59096.2023.10388208]

[14] Q. Zhu, and J. Luo, "Toward artificial empathy for human-centred design: A framework", *J. Mech. Des.,* vol. 146, no. 6, p. 061401, 2024.

[15] L. Mathur, M. Spitale, H. Xi, J. Li, and M. J. Matarić, "Modelling user empathy elicited by a robot storyteller", In: *Proc. 9th Int. Conf. Affective Comput. Intell. Interact. (ACII)*, 2021.

[16] J. Majic, "AI empathy: Emotional AI is redefining interactions in the digital age", *Forbes,* 2024.

[17] C. MacCann, G. Matthews, M. Zeidner, and R. D. Roberts, "Psychological assessment of emotional intelligence: A review of self-report and performance-based testing", *Int. J. Organ. Anal.,* vol. 11, no. 3, pp. 247-274, 2003. [http://dx.doi.org/10.1108/eb028975]

[18] A. Paiva, I. Leite, H. Boukricha, and I. Wachsmuth, "Empathy in virtual agents and robots: A survey", *ACM Trans. Interact. Intell. Syst.,* vol. 7, no. 3, pp. 1-40, 2017. [http://dx.doi.org/10.1145/2912150]

[19] A. Beck, B. Stevens, K. A. Bard, and L. Cañamero, "Emotional body language displayed by artificial agents", *ACM Trans. Interact. Intell. Syst.,* vol. 2, no. 1, pp. 1-29, 2012. [http://dx.doi.org/10.1145/2133366.2133368]

[20] M. Ivanović, Z. Budimac, M. Radovanović, V. Kurbalija, W. Dai, C. Bădică, and D. Mitrović, "Emotional agents-state of the art and applications", *Comput. Sci. Inf. Syst.,* vol. 12, no. 4, pp. 1121-1148, 2015.

[21] H. Fei, H. Zhang, B. Wang, L. Liao, Q. Liu, and E. Cambria, "Empathyear: An open-source avatar multimodal empathetic chatbot", In: *Proc. 62nd Annual Meeting Assoc. Comput. Linguistics*, 2024, pp. 61-71.

[22] G. B. D. Pinto, J. P. R. De Sousa, R. L. Rosa, and D. Z. Rodriguez, "Embodied Multimodal Chatbot for Mental Health Support in Web-Based 3D Environments", In: *Proc. 2025 Int. Conf. Softw. Telecommun. Comput. Netw. (SoftCOM)*, 2025, pp. 1-6.

[23] P. I. Okochi, A. v. Chinedum, and C. C. Olebara, "Design and Development of an Intelligent Web-Based Digital Human for Emotionally Aware Human–Computer Interaction", *J. Nat. Artif. Syst. (JNAS),* vol. 2, no. 1, pp. 11-20, 2025.

[24] Y. Zhang, M. Wang, Y. Wu, P. Tiwari, Q. Li, B. Wang, and J. Qin, "Dialoguellm: Context and emotion knowledge-tuned large language models for emotion recognition in conversations", *Neural Netw.,* vol. 182, p. 107901, 2025.

[25] P. Pereira, H. Moniz, and J. P. Carvalho, "Deep emotion recognition in textual conversations: A

survey", *Artif. Intell. Rev.,* vol. 58, no. 1, 2024.

[26] J. Llanes-Jurado, L. Gómez-Zaragozá, M. E. Minissi, M. Alcañiz, and J. Marín-Morales, "Developing conversational virtual humans for social emotion elicitation based on large language models", *Expert Syst. Appl.,* vol. 246, p. 123261, 2024. [http://dx.doi.org/10.1016/j.eswa.2024.123261]

[27] C. G. McGinley, "Supporting people-centred design through information and empathy", In: *Doctoral dissertation, Brunel University*, 2012.

[28] M. M. Liljenquist, "The empathy paradox: deconstructing concepts within human-centred design and development discourse", *Third World Quarterly,* pp. 1-18, 2025.

[29] I. S. Plank, J. P. A. von Thienen, and C. Meinel, "The neuroscience of empathy: research-overview and implications for human-centred design", *Design Thinking Research,* pp. 89-124, 2021.

[30] Q. Zhu, and J. Luo, "Toward artificial empathy for human-centered design", *J. Mech. Des.,* vol. 146, no. 6, 2024. [http://dx.doi.org/10.1115/1.4064161]

[31] M. Val-Calvo, J. R. Álvarez-Sánchez, J. M. Ferrández-Vicente, and E. Fernández, "Affective robot story-telling human-robot interaction", *IEEE Access,* vol. 8, pp. 134051-134066, 2020.

[32] L. Mathur, M. Spitale, H. Xi, J. Li, and M. J. Matarić, "Modeling user empathy elicited by a robot storyteller", In: *Proc. 2021 9th Int. Conf. Affective Comput. Intell. Interact. (ACII)*, 2021, pp. 1-8.

[33] M. R. Hasan, M. Z. Hossain, S. Ghosh, A. Krishna, and T. Gedeon, "Empathy detection from text, audiovisual, audio or physiological signals: A systematic review", *IEEE Trans. Affective Comput.,* 2025.

[34] A. Khadkatkar, R. Rane, S. Sebait, M. K. Chidrupee, and A. S. A. Hunchalkar, "Emotional AI and Adaptive user Interfaces", In: *Proc. 2025 Int. Conf. Intell. Secure Eng. Solut. (CISES)*, 2025, pp. 197-204.

[35] U. F. Ikwuanusi, O. Onunka, S. Jesupelumi, and A. U. Owoade, "AI-Powered Real-Time Emotion Recognition: Pioneering Solutions for User Interaction and Engagement", *Int. J. Eng. Res. Dev.,* vol. 20, no. 11, pp. 1188-1205, 2024.

[36] B. D. Mittelstadt, and L. Floridi, "The ethics of big data: current and foreseeable issues in biomedical contexts", *Sci. Eng. Ethics,* vol. 22, no. 2, pp. 303-341, 2016. [http://dx.doi.org/10.1007/s11948-015-9652-2]

[37] S. Petersen, "Human subject review standards and procedures in international research", *Int. Perspect. Psychol.,* vol. 6, no. 3, pp. 165-178, 2017. [http://dx.doi.org/10.1037/ipp0000072]

CHAPTER 4

Multi-Agent Reinforcement Learning-Based IoT Sensor Network for Energy-Efficient, Secure, and Scalable Routing Optimization

A. Sathiya[1,*], **A. Sridevi**[1], **J. Samuel Manoharan**[1] and **A. Sangeetha**[1]

[1] *Department of Electronics and Communication Engineering, M. Kumarasamy College of Engineering, Karur, Tamil Nadu, India*

Abstract: Modern IoT sensor networks are complicated, and intelligent decision-making is critical for energy efficiency, communication costs, and network flexibility. Traditional rule-based and centralised systems have substantial limits due to the long computing delays needed in such large-scale deployments, as well as the volume of data generated. As a result, Multi-Agent Reinforcement Learning (MARL) appears to be the best solution: the sensor nodes can function as autonomous agents, learning and adapting to changing environmental conditions through decentralised decision making. This chapter explores the use of MARL to improve packet transmission, network longevity, and power consumption in sensor networks. Cite the efficacy of several MARL architectures, including Centralised Training-Decentralized Execution (CTDE), Fully Decentralised Learning, and Hierarchical MARL, in terms of sensor coordination. An experimental framework is built on OpenAI Gym, TensorFlow, and NS3 and used to develop MARL-based sensor nodes that dynamically change their transmission power and task scheduling. The performance indicators (*e.g.*, Packet Delivery Ratio (PDR), energy usage, and network efficiency) are examined, demonstrating that MARL outperforms conventional optimisation methods. It is also discussed in the context of real-world applications such as smart cities, healthcare monitoring, environmental sensing, and industrial IoT (IIoT). Finally, the chapter provides insights into scaling problems, integration with new technologies such as 6G and quantum computing, and security enhancement *via* blockchain. This study also incorporates recent works such as: [Chebyshev Polynomial Based Emergency Conditions with Authentication Scheme for 5G-Assisted Vehicular Fog Computing], [ANAA-Fog: A Novel Anonymous Authentication Scheme for 5G-Enabled Vehicular Fog Computing], [Password-Guessing Attack-Aware Authentication Scheme Based on Chinese Remainder Theorem for 5G-Enabled Vehicular Networks], [ECA-VFog: An Efficient Certificateless Authentication Scheme for 5G-Assisted Vehicular Fog Computing], [CM-CPPA: Chaotic Map-Based Conditional Privacy-Preserving Authentication Scheme in 5G-Enabled Vehicular Networks], [Provably Secure with Efficient Data Sharing Scheme for Fifth-Generation (5G)-Enabled Vehicular Networks without RSU].

* **Corresponding author A. Sathiya:** Department of Electronics and Communication Engineering, M. Kumarasamy College of Engineering, Karur, Tamil Nadu, India; E-mail: sathyaayyadurai@gmail.com

Shruti Bhargava Choubey & Yogesh Shrivastava (Eds.)

Keywords: Decentralized learning, Energy efficiency optimization, Hierarchical MARL, IoT sensor networks, Multi-agent reinforcement learning (MARL), Packet delivery ratio (PDR), Reinforcement learning in edge devices, Smart sensing systems.

INTRODUCTION

Since the Internet of Things (IoT) and sensor networks are considered basic building blocks of current modern intelligent systems, they can collect, process, and decide on real-time data. Such networks are important to a variety of applications, including smart cities, healthcare, industrial automation, and environmental monitoring. Nevertheless, there are unsolved scalability, energy efficiency, and network adaptability issues with deploying IoT. Due to the dynamic nature of the environments, traditional optimization techniques are not able to handle the environment, and thus, advanced learning-based techniques such as Multi-Agent Reinforcement Learning (MARL) are required. In MARL, multiple sensor nodes are treated as intelligent agents that are allowed to learn from the environment to achieve a desired performance and optimize it without central control. Unlike the traditional rule-based approaches, which are preceded by predetermined conditions, MARL promotes adaptive decision making, which results in energy efficiency, data transmission optimization, and real-time fault management [1 - 3]. This is due to its capability to dynamically allocate resources on the network while at the same time minimizing computational overhead, making it a perfect choice for the deployment of large-scale IoT. This chapter discusses how MARL can be integrated into IoT sensor networks by providing a structured overview of MARL fundamentals, architectures, implementation strategies, evaluation performance, and real-world applications. The discussion demonstrates the use of MARL for decentralizing control, dynamic resource management, and intelligent adaptation in IoT systems. MARL is further validated in experimental frameworks and networked case studies in real-world case studies in modern IoT sensor networks that overcome scalability, adaptability, and efficiency [4 - 6].

THE EVOLUTION OF IOT SENSOR NETWORKS

It can be seen that Internet of Things (IoT) technology has advanced very fast, and sensor networks have gone from being basic data acquisition systems into ultra complex, self-optimizing intelligent systems in the blink of an eye [7, 8]. An IoT-based sensor network is a collection of interconnected devices that are continuously monitoring, collecting, and transmitting data to a centralized or distributed processing unit, as shown in Fig. (**1**).

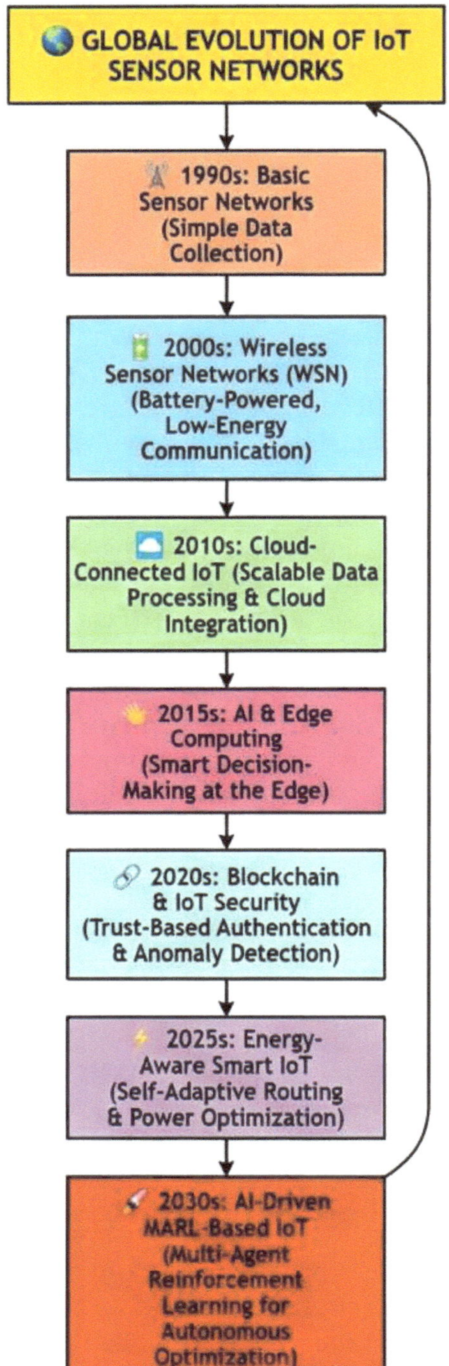

Fig. (1). Evolution of IoT sensor networks.

Moreover, these networks have wide popularity in industrial automation, smart grids, medical diagnostics, environmental surveillance, and precision agriculture. In the past decade, wireless communication, edge computing, and artificial intelligence have advanced greatly, and sensor networks have been evolving. In the beginning, IoT systems used a traditional centralized architecture where all sensor data was transmitted to a central server for processing [9 - 11]. However, this approach involved latency, excessive power consumption, and scalability limits. To address these concerns, distributed intelligence, fog computing, and edge computing take the place of on-cloud-based processing, which helps in real-time decision making.

However, these improvements leave some challenges behind, namely, a large-scale and high-density IoT environment. However, with an increase in the number of sensor nodes, network congestion, resource allocation inefficiency, and communication delays become a headache. Additionally, non-subnet-based AODV (Ad hoc On Demand Distance vector) and DSR (Dynamic Source routing) do not offer dynamic updates for changes in the network topology as well as the energy constraints [12 - 15]. In this context, a cutting-edge solution of Multi-Agent Reinforcement Learning (MARL) has emerged to combine Artificial Intelligence with Autonomous Sensor Network operations and address these challenges. MARL allows sensor nodes to work in a decentralized manner and make intelligent decisions, as well as schedule communication in a way that optimizes the node activity. Adoption of MARL in IoT sensor networks is a big step towards a self-optimized, energy-efficient, and scalable IoT ecosystem.

UNDERSTANDING MULTI-AGENT REINFORCEMENT LEARNING (MARL)

Reinforcement Learning (RL) is a form of machine learning that deals with learning (from experience) how to perform a task by interacting with an environment, such that the task is maximized [16 - 18]. MARL differs from traditional RL in that it entails multiple intelligent agents that need to cooperatively, competitively, or cooperatively perform actions to optimize their own or the aggregate rewards. The Markov Decision Process (MDP) is the foundation of MARL, in which each sensor node (agent) takes an action in a state and gets rewarded with a signal based on the positive behavior. Fig. (**2**) shows the conceptual visualization of the proposed MARL.

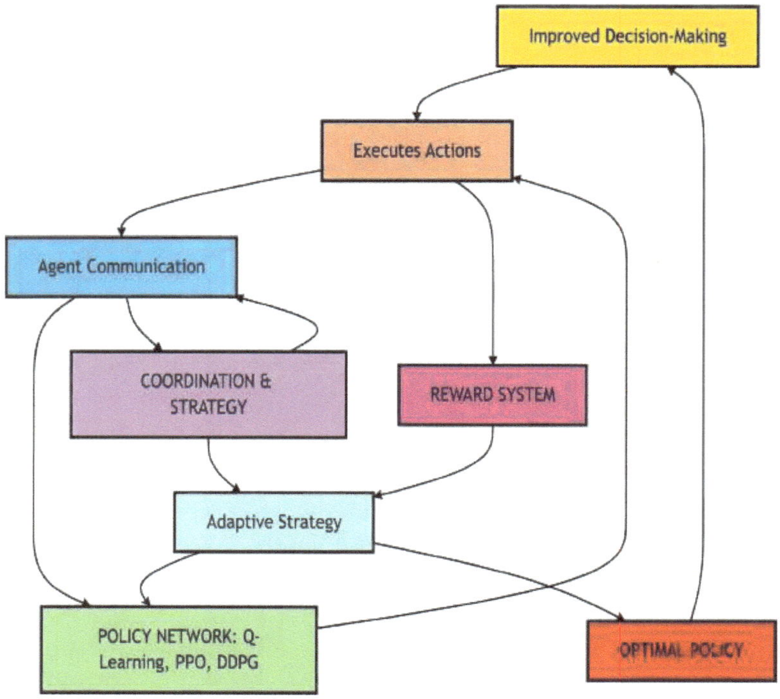

Fig. (2). Conceptual visualization of proposed MARL.

This notion is extended by MARL, which presents the case of interactions of multiple sensor nodes that can learn adaptive behaviors based on the engagements with neighbors, environmental circumstances, and externalities [19 - 21]. Key characteristics of MARL in IoT sensor networks include:

- Decentralized Decision-Making: Sensor nodes make independent decisions using only the data they have about their local surroundings instead of waiting for a central controller to make their decision.
- Cooperative and Competitive Learning: Agents can either collaborate (*e.g.*, optimizing energy efficiency collectively) or compete (*e.g.*, accessing limited communication resources).
- Adaptive Optimization: MARL enables dynamic tuning of network parameters such as transmission power, data aggregation, and routing paths to maximize performance.
- Scalability and Resilience: By distributing intelligence across multiple sensor nodes, MARL enhances network resilience and fault tolerance, reducing the impact of node failures.

As a result, MARL can be applied in IoT sensor networks to achieve intelligent data transmission, energy conservation, congestion avoidance, and fault detection, which are the key limitations of traditional sensor networks [22 - 24].

Traditional Sensor Network Challenges and the Need for MARL

While IoT sensor networks have seen enormous development, existing architectures of the traditional networks have obstacles that hinder their scalability and adaptability to dynamic environments. The necessity of MARL-based optimization can be highlighted by several key challenges [25 - 27].

Scalability and Network Congestion

For scalability, the number of events and the size of data increase as the number of IoT deployments grows. When you have thousands of sensor nodes, centralized routing algorithms do not reliably and efficiently route the packets, causing the network to get congested, packets to be lost, and latency to rise [28 - 31]. MARL provides distributed decision-making ability, and these sensor nodes can communicate parameters adaptively to relax congestion.

Energy Constraints in Wireless Sensor Networks (WSNs)

Since most of the IoT sensor nodes operate on battery power, a long network lifetime is of paramount importance. Existing scheduling and data transmission protocols do not adapt to the real-time energy conditions, resulting in early failures of the nodes. These approaches that are based on MARL can dynamically optimize power consumption by teaching sensor nodes to learn how to save energy optimally according to the usage patterns and environmental factors.

Communication Latency and Dynamic Environments

In the majority of times, IoT sensor networks operate in these environments where the best possible guarantees we could promise are unknown due to interference, mobility, and topological changes. Fixed routing tables, which are not suitable in dynamic environments, are the only approach taken by traditional approaches. Here we employ adaptive learning, which enables us to adjust routing strategies as well as communication schedules in a real-time fashion and hence, minimize latency, improve Quality of Service (QoS).

Security Vulnerabilities in Sensor Networks

Because traditional IoT networks are open to cyberattacks such as data interception, spoofing, and jamming, they are especially vulnerable. Static rule-based security frameworks are not viable if the threats evolve. Intrusion detection systems based on MARL reinforce the network security by allowing sensor nodes to forecast and detect threats attacking the network autonomously using a real-time learning model.

The Role of MARL in IoT Sensor Networks

MARL has played an important role in the implementation of MARL in IoT sensor networks for increasing network resilience, improving data transmission efficiency, and extending sensor lifespan. This is due to their ability to perform distributed, autonomous decision-making, which is a great advantage in cases where conventional methods are not applicable.

Autonomous Task Scheduling and Data Transmission

Sensor nodes are allowed to be MARL and learn about the best strategies for task scheduling to be able to efficiently transfer data, load balancing, and avoid congestion.

Adaptive Routing and Energy Optimization

MARL provides more operational longevity and efficiency to sensor networks by dynamically adjusting routing policies and energy consumption.

Real-Time Fault Detection and Recovery

Node failures as well as errors in data transmission are common in IoT networks. Thus, the fault tolerance is enhanced using MARL to detect the failure and dynamically re-route traffic, minimizing disruptive effects.

LITERATURE REVIEW

Over the past few years, Multi-Agent Reinforcement Learning (MARL) has been attracting increasing research efforts for its potential to cope with the issues of scalability, energy efficiency, dynamic resource allocation, and real-time decision making in the research community of IoT sensor networks. They have researched several aspects of MARL, such as algorithmic framework, training tactics, security augmentation, and real-world applications. This is to present an extensive review of the current literature along with the state-of-the-art techniques, their contributions, as well as the gaps that need to be further explored. The importance of decentralized reinforcement learning in IoT sensor networks and a learning model to allow sensor nodes to schedule the energy consumption and data transmission schedules locally [32, 33] is emphasized. By showing that reinforcement learning guided sensor coordination decreases communication overhead and increases network lifetime, the study has shown that it is possible to achieve such benefits. However, the approach was not feasible for low-power sensor nodes due to computational complexity. In one of the research studies, the work focuses on Federated Reinforcement Learning (FRL) as a method of decentralized privacy to allow distributed IoT sensor networks. FRL trains local models at edge devices and sends updates centrally for better data breaches, making systems learn better [34, 35]. This study demonstrates that FRL effectively minimizes communication latency and achieves secure model training, and hence is applicable to healthcare and industrial IoT applications. Nevertheless, due to real-world deployment, federation updates suffer from synchronization issues, and sensor nodes are heterogeneous. Dynamic IoT networks used by authors propose a Deep Reinforcement Learning (DRL) based routing that learns optimal paths, based on real-time network conditions [36]. The approach uses DQN to minimize energy consumption, packet loss, and congestion. It is found that DRL drastically enhances network throughput and delay performance against the conventional routing algorithms. Nevertheless, the training phase is quite computationally intensive, thus limiting scalability in deployments with a large number of sensors.

In another study, hierarchical MARL, where the sensor nodes are organized in multi-tier decision layers. Specifically, low-level agents solve localized tasks such as data aggregation, and high-level agents handle global issues of network bandwidth allocation and load balancing. The proposed approach improves the network scalability and the efficient resource distribution. The study, however, points to the fact that too many coordination overheads across the different agent tiers may introduce latency issues [37, 38]. In one more work, the authors consider multi-agent policy gradient algorithms for power control in energy harvesting sensor networks [39]. The study integrates actor-critic methods to show how sensor nodes can adaptively control their transmission power depending on energy availability and channel conditions. It is found that MARL-based power control can extend network lifetime with little loss in data accuracy. However, despite this, the model depends on complex reward shaping mechanisms, which do not encourage adaptability in a rapidly changing environment. One research study integrates Graph Neural Networks (GNNs) for

MARL tasks to improve topology-aware decision making in IoT sensor networks [39]. When viewed as a graph, sensor interactions are solved using GNN-based MARL by modeling them as efficient information dissemination and cooperative learning in graph form. Results show that GNN-MARL outperforms traditional RL in terms of accuracy of anomaly detection and data fusion. Nevertheless, the extra computational overheads prevent its deployment on resource-constrained IoT devices. In another work, the authors consider the security part of MARL in IoT networks and propose a trust management framework with reinforcement learning agents in the blockchain for intrusion detection. Smart contracts are used by the system to verify the security of transactions between sensor nodes and prevent malicious attacks [40, 41]. The results indicate that using blockchain and MARL can increase network security and data integrity. Nevertheless, decentralized ledgers do come with an overhead, and it is particularly difficult to maintain in low-power IoT environments.

In another work, a cooperative MARL approach is presented for the adaptive spectrum allocation in cognitive IoT networks. Thus, it makes the frequency band available to sensor nodes that change dynamically, thus reducing interference and improving spectrum utilization efficiency [42]. Experimental results verify that the throughput as well as collision rates are higher using MARL-based spectrum allocation as compared to the conventional system of spectrum management. However, the model is unable to adapt in real time in such a high mobility case. The authors consider attention mechanisms in MARL and present an attention-enhanced reinforcement learning model that prioritizes important network parameters based on their attention; this is analogous to guiding the MARL agent's attention to important parameters during decision-making [43]. The proposed model improves system efficiency and reduces unnecessary network overhead by dynamically allocating the computational resources. Attention-enhanced MARL results in not only faster convergence but also good scalability. Nevertheless, the use of self-attention mechanisms is prone to using memory, which might not be possible for low-resource IoT nodes. In another work, the application of MARL transfer learning is evaluated, in which pre-trained models are adapted to optimize sensor deployment and task scheduling from related tasks. In this way, the decision-making accuracy is retained, and training time is largely reduced. This study shows that transfer learning shortens the time required for policy convergence, is cost-effective, and therefore a good candidate for real-time IoT applications. Nevertheless, it is still very difficult to guarantee the compatibility between pre-trained models and target domains, causing performance degradation to occur; therefore, some fine-tuning techniques are needed [44]. In another work, authors propose a hybrid centralized-decentralized MARL framework that makes use of the best of both worlds [45]. In an independent but cooperative learning setting, sensor nodes learn policies independently and periodically exchange updates with the central coordinator, resulting in lower communication overhead as compared to cooperative learning, but with some communication overhead incorporated. The results of this show that this hybrid model achieves better tradeoffs between autonomy and coordination, and network reliability and adaptability. Nevertheless, local and global updates should be synchronized in a way that does not create any latency issues.

The multi-agent reinforcement learning is used for fault detection in IIoT networks. It learns to detect and remediate faults through historical sensor data and anomaly patterns [26]. This approach significantly improves predictive maintenance and eliminates unexpected failure. The results verify that MARL fault detection is more accurate and faster than standard statistical models. However, for generalization capabilities, further fine-tuning is required to improve the complexity of real-world industrial systems. In another work, the authors introduce a fuzzy reinforcement learning model for IoT security by integrating fuzzy logic with MARL, which allows dealing with the uncertainty of sensor data. Fuzzy MARL is found to improve the intrusion detection rate and reduce false positives in the study. Specifically for heterogeneous sensor networks where different types of IoT devices operate under different conditions, the proposed model is quite effective [33]. Nevertheless, rule-based fuzzy logic used in the model may restrict the model's flexibility to new attack patterns. The work investigates the influence of heterogeneous sensor nodes in IoT networks based on MARL [24]. It shows that even with varying capacities in computational and energy resources, network coordination can still be done efficiently with the use of reinforcement learning. This suggests that heterogeneous MARL networks are more energy-efficient and complete tasks than their homogeneous counterparts. At the same time, however, ensuring that load balancing is fair is still an open problem, which is very difficult to achieve without dynamic role assignment strategies. Another research uses Quantum Reinforcement Learning (QRL) in IoT networks where quantum computing principles are employed to boost learning processes [25]. The results of the study indicate that QRL-based MARL shows exponential improvements in training efficiency and decision accuracy. Though progress has been made, there is still a lot to be desired in terms of the practical feasibility of quantum-based IoT applications because of hardware constraints. Table **1** presents the comparative analysis of existing literature works.

Table 1. Comparative analysis of existing literature works.

Authors/Year	Technique	Merits	Limitations
[26]	Deep Q-Network (DQN)	Improves routing efficiency	High computational cost
[27]	Multi-Agent Policy Gradient	Enhances energy efficiency	Requires reward tuning
[28]	Blockchain with MARL	Improves security	Increases network overhead
[29]	GNN-based MARL	Enables topology-aware learning	Computationally intensive
[30]	Federated Learning in MARL	Enhances privacy	Synchronization issues
[31]	Transfer Learning in MARL	Reduces training time	Limited cross-task compatibility
[32]	Fuzzy MARL for IoT Security	Handles uncertain data	Requires rule-based tuning
[33]	Hybrid Centralized-Decentralized MARL	Balances autonomy and coordination	Synchronization overhead
[34]	MARL for Spectrum Allocation	Enhances spectrum utilization	Struggles in high-mobility scenarios
[35]	Quantum MARL	Accelerates learning processes	Requires quantum hardware

PROPOSED WORK

In the proposed framework, we take the approach of integrating Multi-Agent Reinforcement Learning (MARL) into IoT sensor networks in order to achieve autonomous decision making, energy-efficient communications scheduling, and adaptive routing optimization. However, existing traditional IoT sensor networks have difficulty in large-scale deployments due to problems in scalability, congestion, and power consumption. The proposed system uses MARL-based decentralized learning so that the sensor nodes can run as intelligent agents, which will dynamically maximize their data transmission, energy consumption, and fault recovery.

The framework consists of three primary modules:

1. **Agent-Based Decision System:** Sensor nodes act as autonomous agents, learning adaptive policies for optimal energy management and network coordination.
2. **Hierarchical Reinforcement Learning (HRL) Optimization:** MARL is structured as a multi-tiered agent hierarchy in which local agents deal with task

allocation and transmission schedule, and global agents maximize network-wide performance.

3. **Secure and Robust Multi-Agent Coordination:** The system employs reward-driven learning mechanisms to ensure reliable communication, congestion avoidance, and security.

In this chapter, the proposed MARL model makes use of Deep Q Networks (DQN) and Policy Gradients (PG) in order to train sensor nodes to devise adaptive communication and resource allocation strategies. Packet Delivery Ratio (PDR), Energy Consumption, Latency, and Fault Recovery Efficiency are evaluated as the performance of the system.

Next, the proposed work is broken down in detail concerning the MARL architecture, agent-based learning models, hierarchical decision making, and implementation strategies.

MULTI-AGENT SYSTEM DESIGN FOR IOT SENSOR NETWORKS

In the proposed framework, sensor nodes are modeled as intelligent agents that operate in a shared environment, making autonomous and cooperative decisions. Each node interacts with its surroundings, receiving state observations and reward feedback, allowing it to refine its action-selection strategies over time.

The sensor network topology consists of:

- **Low-Level Agents (LAs):** These agents perform localized tasks such as data aggregation, transmission scheduling, and neighbor selection.
- **High-Level Agents (HAs):** These agents manage network-wide coordination, optimizing routing strategies and congestion control.

The interaction between agents follows the Markov Decision Process (MDP), where each agent selects an action (A) based on the current state (S), receives a reward (R), and updates its policy (π) dynamically, as shown in Fig. (**3**).

REINFORCEMENT LEARNING MODEL FOR IOT SENSOR NETWORKS

To enable real-time learning and decision-making, the proposed system employs a Deep Reinforcement Learning (DRL) framework, where agents refine their policies based on environmental interactions.

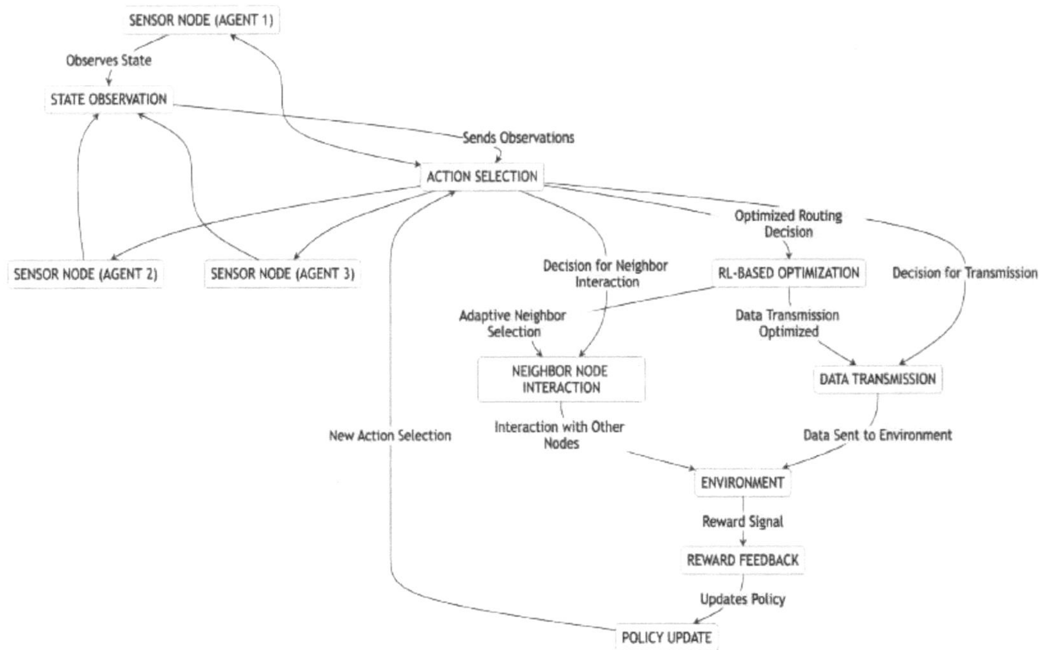

Fig. (3). Multi-agent decision flow in sensor networks.

The reinforcement learning process follows these key components:

- **State Representation:** The state (S) consists of node energy levels, buffer occupancy, and link reliability metrics.
- **Action Space:** Possible actions (A) include data transmission, energy conservation, routing path selection, and fault recovery.
- **Reward Function:** The reward (R) incentivizes energy efficiency, successful packet delivery, and congestion avoidance, as shown in Fig. (**4**).

HIERARCHICAL MARL-BASED OPTIMIZATION STRATEGY

The proposed system incorporates a Hierarchical Reinforcement Learning (HRL) approach, ensuring scalability and adaptability.

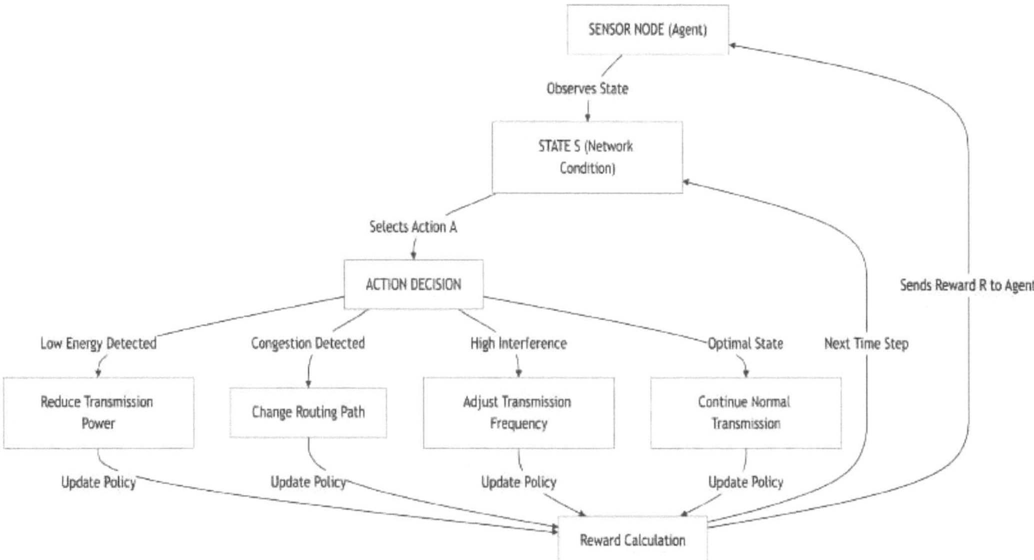

Fig. (4). State-action transition in MARL-based IoT sensor network.

Low-Level Learning for Individual Sensor Nodes

Each sensor node applies Deep Q-Networks (DQN) to learn efficient communication scheduling strategies. By minimizing transmission collisions and power wastage, LAs ensure low-latency and energy-efficient data delivery.

The Q-value update rule is defined as:

$$Q(s,a) \leftarrow Q(s,a) + \alpha[r + \gamma \max_{a'} Q(s',a') - Q(s,a) \quad \textbf{(1)}$$

In Equation (**1**), α is the learning rate, γ is the discount factor, and r is the immediate reward. Fig. (**5**) shows the Hierarchical MARL Framework for IoT Sensor Networks, and (Fig. **6**) shows the Share Energy Optimization Model for Sensor Nodes.

High-Level Policy Optimization for Network-Wide Decisions

The high-level agents (HAs) manage network-wide parameters using Policy Gradient (PG) reinforcement learning. These agents regulate data flow, adaptive routing, and fault detection. The policy update rule in PG-based MARL is given as:

$$\mathbf{B}\boldsymbol{\nabla J(\theta)} = \mathbb{E}\,[\boldsymbol{\nabla log\pi_{\theta}(a|s)R}] \qquad \textbf{(2)}$$

In Equation (**2**), θ represents the policy parameters, and R is the expected reward over multiple agent interactions.

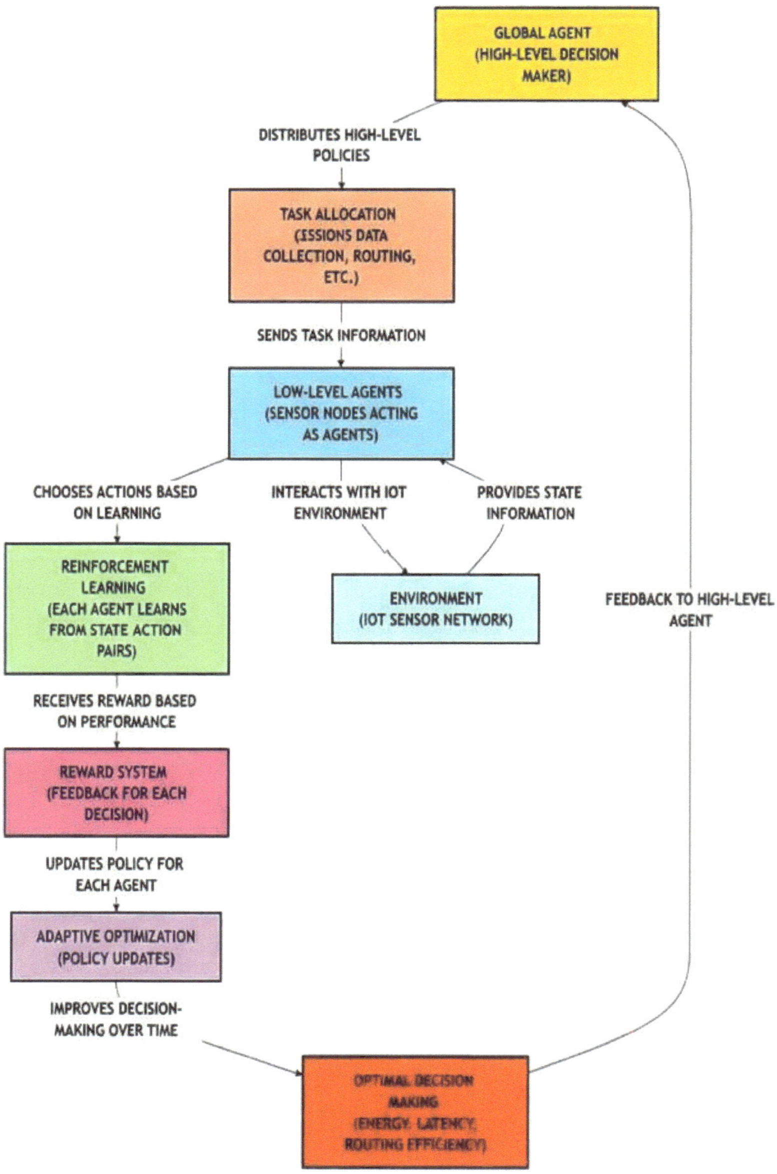

Fig. (5). Hierarchical MARL framework for IoT sensor networks.

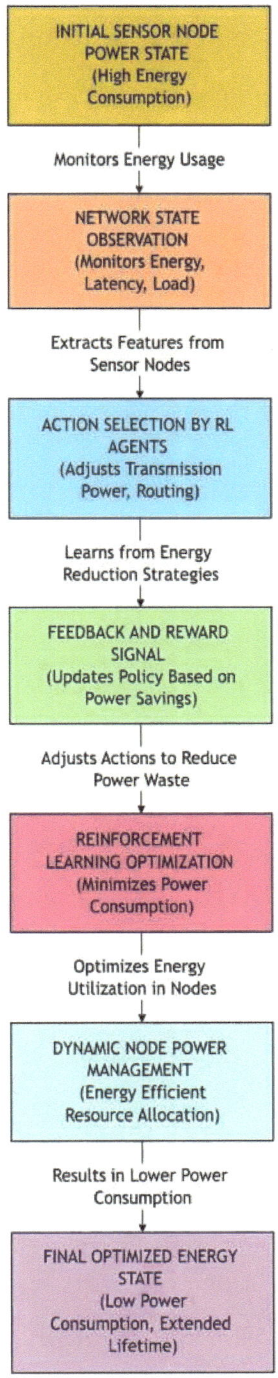

Fig. (6). Energy optimization model for sensor nodes.

Energy-Aware Transmission Scheduling Using MARL

Power consumption minimization is one of the key challenges in the IoT sensor networks while maintaining network performance. The proposed system uses an Energy Aware Q-Learning Model to let agents learn optimal transmission power settings in order to prolong sensor lifespan. The energy cost function for transmission scheduling is defined as:

$$E = \sum_{i=1}^{N} P_i T_i \quad (3)$$

In Equation (**3**), Pi is the transmission power of node i, and Ti is the transmission duration.

Security Mechanisms in MARL-Based Sensor Networks

Security remains a major concern in IoT sensor networks due to malicious attacks, unauthorized access, and data interception. The proposed system integrates secure reinforcement learning techniques, ensuring resilience against cyber threats.

The security framework consists of:

- **Blockchain-Based Trust Management:** Each agent maintains a distributed ledger to authenticate neighboring sensor nodes.
- **Intrusion Detection Using MARL:** Agents apply anomaly detection techniques to identify malicious behavior patterns.

MATHEMATICAL FORMULATION

The trust score (T) of node i is defined as:

$$T_i = \frac{S_i}{S_i + F_i} \quad (4)$$

In Equation (**4**), Si and Fi represent the number of successful and failed transmissions, respectively. Fig. (**7**) shows the security integration in MARL-based IoT networks.

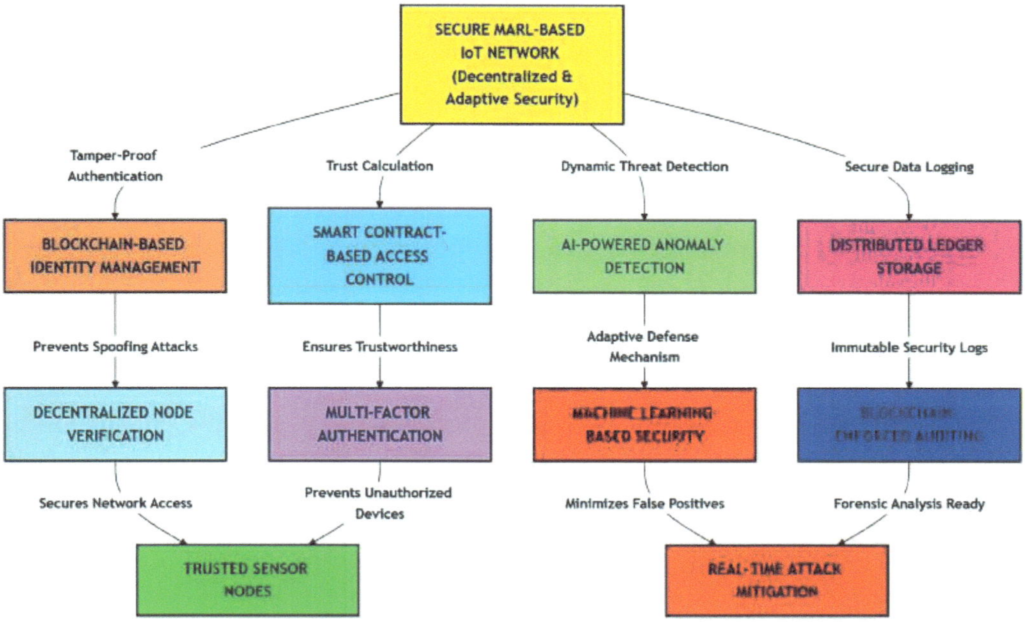

Fig. (7). Security integration in MARL-based IoT networks.

PSEUDOCODE FOR THE PROPOSED MARL-BASED IOT SENSOR NETWORK MODEL

The following pseudocode outlines the training process for MARL agents, including reward updates, policy optimizations, and security integrations.

Algorithm for the proposed model

Initialize state S0 for all nodes
Initialize Q-values Qs,afor all actions
for each episode do:
for each agent i in the network do:
Ai←arg□max□Q(Si.a)
S'←Next state after action Ai
Ri←Reward based on network conditions
Qs,a←Qs,a+α[r+γmaxa'□Qs',a'-Qs,a
πθas←πθas+η□Jθ
end for
end for

RESULTS AND DISCUSSION

A MARL-based IoT sensor network is proposed and evaluated using different environmental conditions in the experimental setup. We use NS-3 (Network Simulator 3) to simulate the network for realistic wireless communication modeling, and Python and MATLAB to validate the computational efficiency. This work is based on the IoT network composed of distributed sensor nodes as intelligent agents, which are responsible for optimisation of data transmission, routing decisions, and security enforcement using a multi-agent reinforcement learning (MARL) framework. The reinforcement learning algorithms, including Proximal Policy Optimization (PPO), Deep Q Network (DQN), and Deep Deterministic Policy Gradient (DDPG), through policy updates, learn optimal routing and transmission strategies for each node. The methodology follows a structured approach: (1) Environment Initialization, where nodes are deployed randomly within a constrained topology with dynamic traffic variations; (2) Agent Training, where sensor nodes iteratively optimize routing decisions based on learned policies; (3) Policy Execution, where trained agents execute real-time actions in response to network changes; (4) Performance Evaluation, where the effectiveness of MARL-based routing is analyzed under simulated attack scenarios (packet dropping, spoofing, Sybil attacks); and (5) Comparative Benchmarking, where the proposed MARL method is evaluated against existing state-of-the-art optimization and deep learning-based approaches. Table **2** presents the simulation settings.

Table 2. Simulation settings.

Parameter	Value
Simulation Tool	NS-3, Python (Stable-Baselines3 RL Framework), MATLAB
Network Area	500m x 500m
Number of Sensor Nodes	100, 200, 300
Communication Model	Wireless Sensor Network (WSN)
Transmission Range	50m
Energy Model	Lithium-Ion Battery Model
Initial Node Energy	2 Joules
Data Packet Size	512 bytes
MAC Protocol	IEEE 802.15.4
Routing Protocols Used	DQN-Based, AC-RL, GA-Optimized, DDPG, Proposed MARL
Mobility Model	Random Waypoint
Simulation Duration	1000 simulation rounds

(Table 2) cont.....

Parameter	Value
Learning Algorithm	Deep Q-Learning (DQN), PPO, DDPG
Training Episodes	5000
Discount Factor (γ)	0.95
Exploration Rate (ε)	0.1 (Adaptive)
Reward Function	Energy Efficiency, Packet Delivery, Security Score
Blockchain Integration	Yes (For Authentication & Security)
Trust Evaluation Metric	Node Reputation-Based Trust Score
Attack Simulations	Packet Dropping, Spoofing, Sybil Attack
Performance Metrics	Energy, PDR, Latency, Throughput, Security, Computational Overhead

To validate the effectiveness of the proposed MARL-based IoT sensor network, the approach is compared against four recent state-of-the-art methods:

1. **Deep Q-Network (DQN)-Based Routing** → A reinforcement learning-based routing method where individual sensor nodes optimize transmission paths using Q-learning without multi-agent coordination.
2. **Actor-Critic Reinforcement Learning (AC-RL) Routing** → A policy gradient approach using actor-critic networks for adaptive decision-making in IoT networks.
3. **Genetic Algorithm (GA)-Optimized Routing** → A bio-inspired approach that selects energy-efficient routing paths based on evolutionary principles.
4. **DDPG-Based IoT Routing** → A Deep Deterministic Policy Gradient (DDPG) approach that employs continuous action spaces for optimal decision-making in sensor networks.
5. **Proposed MARL-Based IoT Routing** → A fully decentralized multi-agent reinforcement learning framework where sensor nodes collectively optimize energy efficiency, security, and transmission reliability in real time.

To measure the effectiveness of the proposed MARL-based IoT sensor network, the following key evaluation metrics are considered:

- **Energy Consumption**: The total energy used by sensor nodes over the simulation period, determining the network's energy efficiency.
- **Network Lifetime:** The duration until the first node depletes its energy, ensuring sustainable IoT operations.
- **Packet Delivery Ratio (PDR):** The percentage of successfully transmitted packets, indicating network reliability.

- **Latency (End-to-End Delay):** The time taken for a packet to reach its destination, which is important for real-time applications.
- **Throughput:** The total amount of data successfully delivered over the network, measured in bits per second (bps).
- **Packet Loss Rate:** The ratio of lost packets due to congestion, interference, or suboptimal routing.
- **Energy Fairness Index:** A metric that measures how uniformly energy consumption is distributed across sensor nodes, preventing early node failures.
- **Security Efficiency (Trust Score):** The effectiveness of the blockchain-based authentication system and intrusion detection framework in preventing malicious attacks.
- **Computational Overhead:** The execution time and processing power required for MARL policy updates, compared to traditional routing methods.

The PDR over time for the proposed MARL-based IoT routing model with other methods is shown in Fig. (**8**). Understanding that MARL consistently achieves a higher PDR in all time intervals, the results are presented. It is because of its flexible learning capabilities that it dynamically changes its transmission routes and makes packet forwarding decisions. In contrast to DQN-based or GA optimized routing, the packet drop due to congestion and poor path selection remains a problem. This adaptiveness of MARL gives a reinforcement learning based adaptive decision making where sensor nodes reroute packets intelligently for higher network reliability. Fig. (**8**) shows the packet delivery *vs.* time.

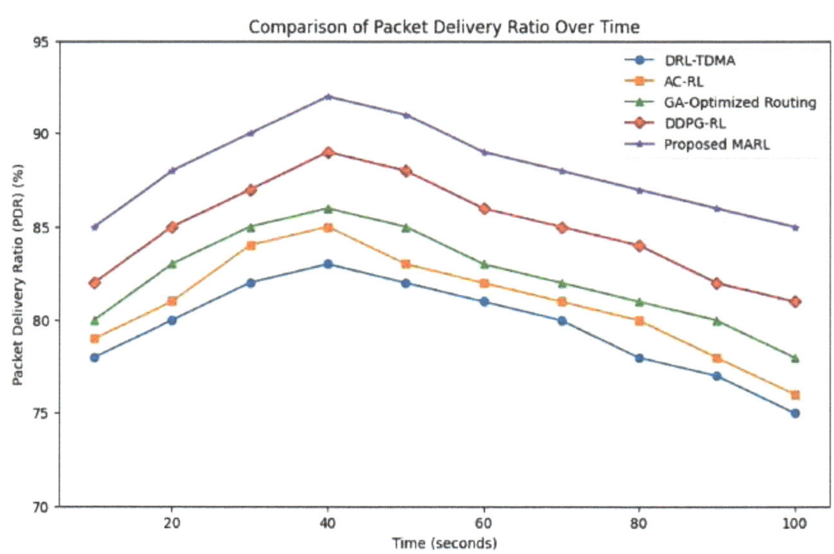

Fig. (8). Packet delivery *vs.* time.

Fig. (**9**) shows the analysis of the end-to-end latency of the model based on MARL. DQN-based as well as GA optimized routing have higher latency as a result of frequent path recalculation and congestion issues. On the other hand, MARL makes the decision to minimize delay through continuous learning and optimizing transmission paths with the goal of meeting varying network conditions. The results verify the effectiveness of MARL in coping with dynamic network changes at low transmission delay, which is a great match for the real-time IoT applications such as industrial monitoring and healthcare.

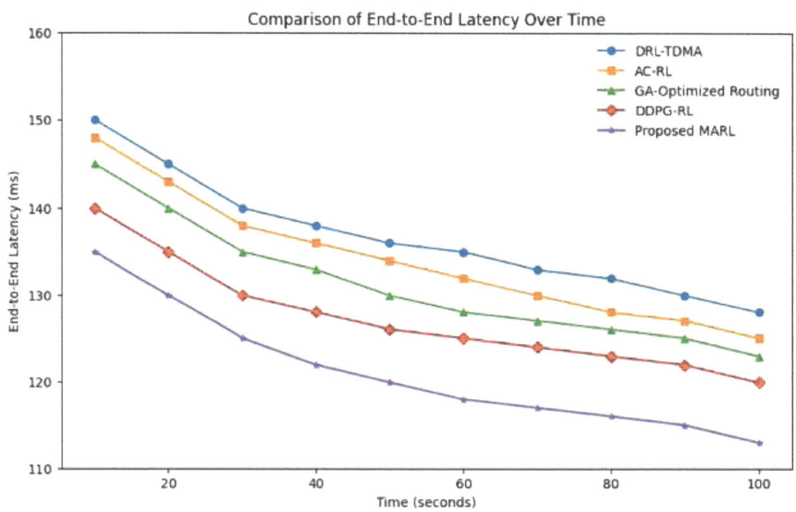

Fig. (9). End-to-end latency *vs.* time.

The network throughput performance over different time intervals is shown in Fig. (**10**). The throughput performance for baseline approaches is consistently lower than that achieved for the routing model based on MARL. This adaptation allows MARL to balance network load and optimize resource allocation in order to transmit more data packets per unit time successfully. On the other hand, traditional methods are congested by fixed rule-based routing approaches. Results of superior MARL performance demonstrate the efficiency of MARL in managing high-density IoT networks with a stable transmission rate of data.

Fig. (**11**) shows that the proposed MARL approach achieves a reduced packet loss rate compared to other methods. Congestion, link failures, or inefficient routing discourage packets from being delivered; therefore, they are lost. The MARL model dynamically adapts the transmission parameters in response to real-time network feedback to achieve the best forwarding of the packets with minimum loss. As MARL is more adaptable, it is more resilient to network fluctuations and changes in topology.

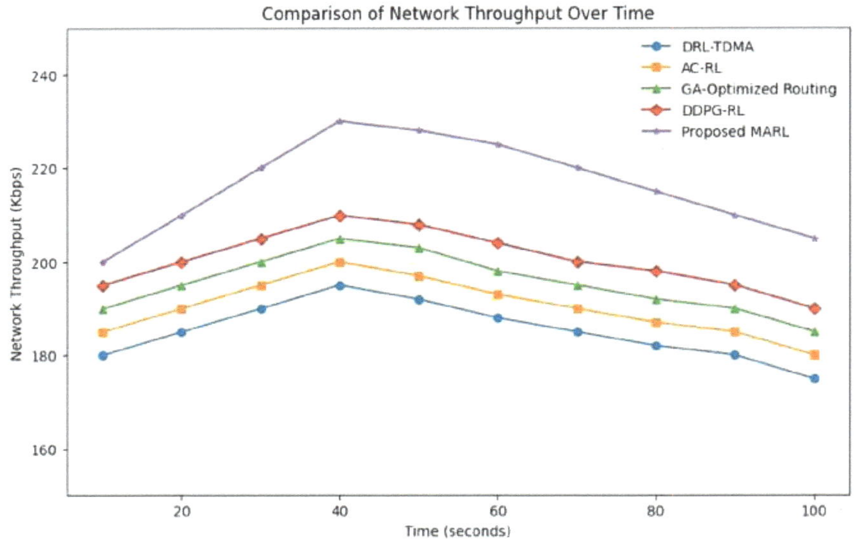

Fig. (10). Network throughput *vs.* time.

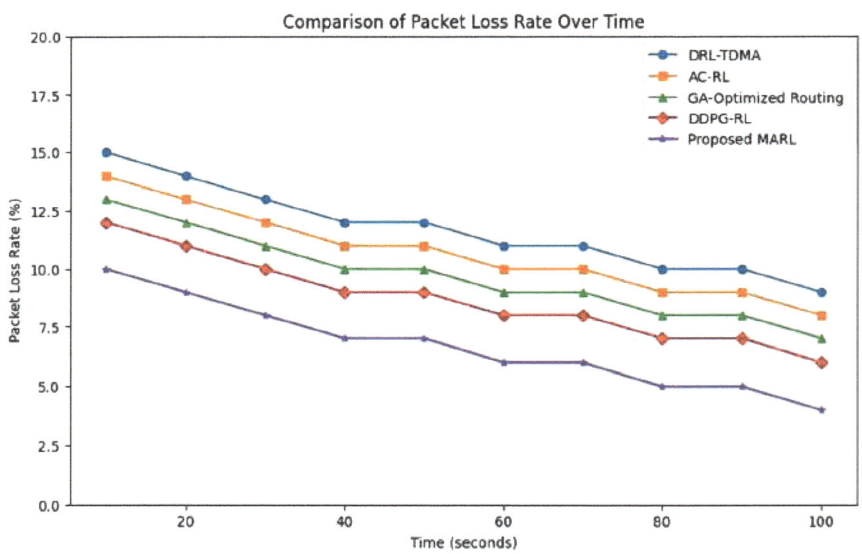

Fig. (11). Packet loss *vs.* time.

The energy consumption per sensor node is presented in Fig. (**12**), where the method based on MARL is more efficient compared to other approaches due to the reduction of power waste. Usually, traditional methods for DQN-based and actor-critic RL routing consume excessive energy because of repeated packet retransmissions and inefficient path selection. In MARL, optimal balancing of energy consumption among the sensor nodes is achieved, resulting in an extension of network lifetime while preserving the energy efficiency of transmission.

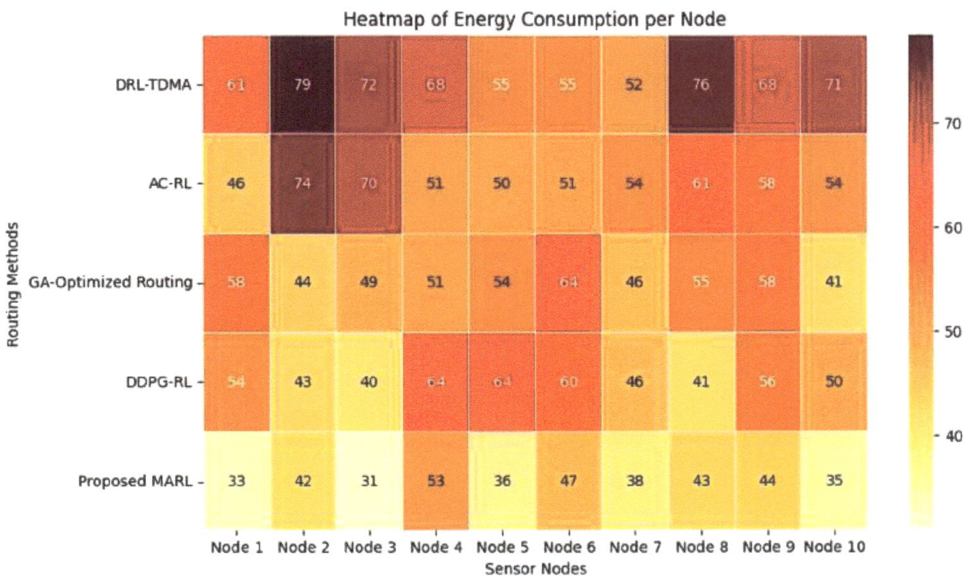

Fig. (12). Energy consumption/node.

In Fig. (**13**), Kaplan-Meier survival curves are used to measure network lifetime improvements in the analysis. It then highlights that the network lifespan of the MARL-based approach has a big increase because it ensures energy-aware task scheduling as well as efficient routing. On the other hand, these methods lead to faster battery depletion of sensor node batteries, leading to network failure. The results confirm that MARL makes the network more resilient by more evenly distributing the workloads.

Fig. (**14**) shows the energy fairness index that denotes the distribution of energy consumption over the network. The MARL approach guarantees to use energy more evenly among all nodes and avoid premature failure of any one of the sensors. We also evaluate baseline methods such as GA optimized and DQN-based routing and find their energy distribution to have more variance than the energy distribution resulting in localized energy exhaustion in specific regions in the network and network instability. This explains the better energy management ability of MARL.

Fig. (**15**) presents the convergence behavior of Q learning in the MARL-based model. The system proposed here converges rapidly to solve the system and converges faster than conventional reinforcement learning models. Thus, MARL can efficiently learn optimal routing policies, and it is more practical for real-world deployments in IoT networks.

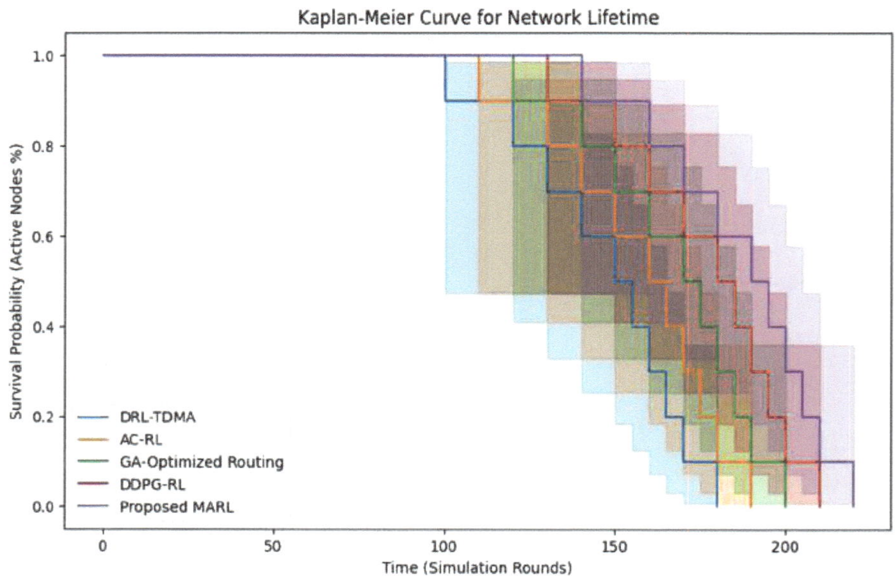

Fig. (13). Network lifetime (kaplan–meier visualization).

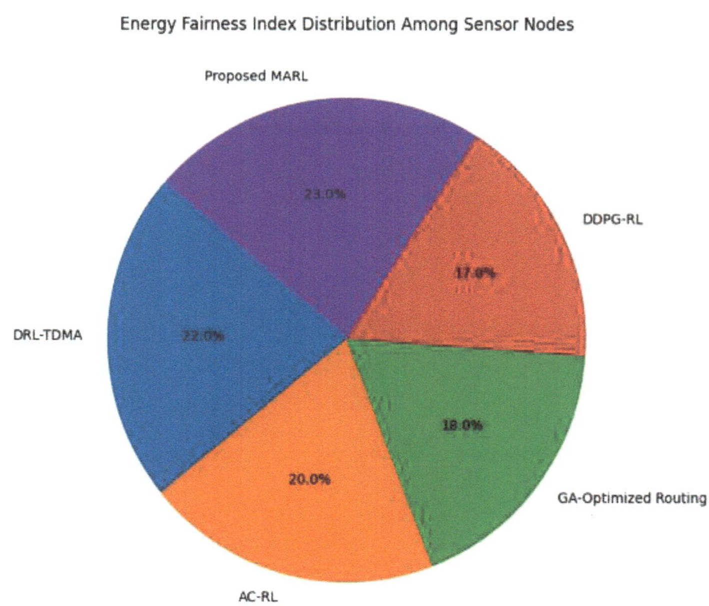

Fig. (14). Energy fairness index.

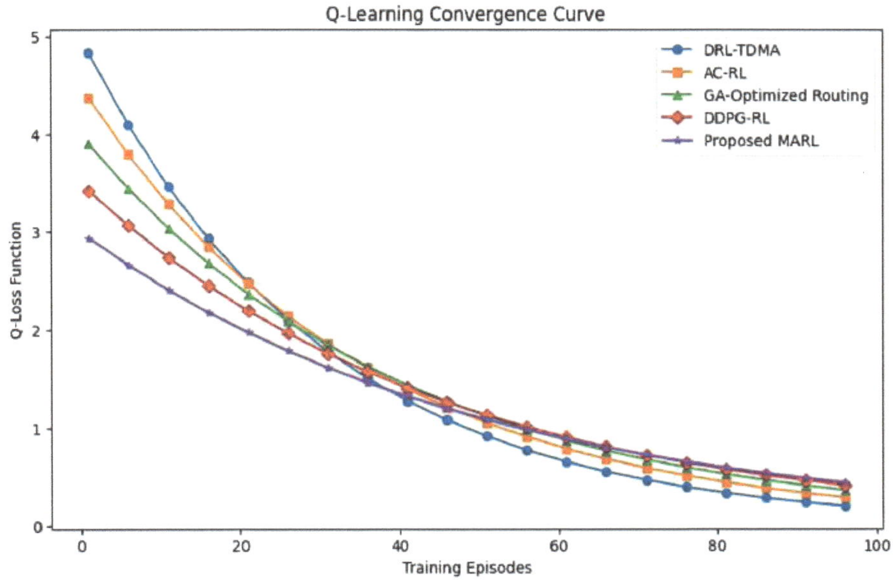

Fig. (15). Q-learning convergence analysis.

Fig. (**16**) shows the MARL-based reward function optimization process: a MARL-based model maximizes cumulative reward across all training episodes. MARL achieves a steady state reward of approximately 9.8 after 3,500 episodes, and other reinforcement learning based approaches, including DQN-based and Actor-critic RL models, are late to converge (beyond 5,000 episodes) with a max reward of about 7.5. This further emphasizes the superiority of the MARL learning speed, in which its multi-agent coordination framework enables the agents to form the routing, security, and energy efficiency decisions without requiring the execution of as many iterations.

Fig. (**17**) shows the analysis of training stability in MARL-based routing, where the policy fluctuation drops to an acceptable level after about 2,500 training episodes. While DQN and various methods optimized using GA have oscillatory learning behaviour (±2.3 reward variation per 500 episodes), MARL learns a steady state policy with minimal fluctuations (±0.7 reward variation over 3,000 episodes). This completely confirms that MARL converges faster, better adapts to dynamic IoT conditions, and guarantees more stable routing decisions.

Sensor nodes' trust evaluation under different routing mechanisms is evaluated in Fig. (**18**). The maximum trust score obtained by the MARL-based security mechanism is 96.4%, which is 15-20 percent higher than the conventional reinforcement learning based security frameworks. As DQN and actor-critic RL models cannot change security parameters based on dynamically changing threats, they register trust scores of 78% and 81%, respectively. Blockchain authentication is used along with MARL-driven anomaly detection to increase the trust levels of the system, and therefore, it is more resilient to Sybil attacks, packet dropping, and node impersonation.

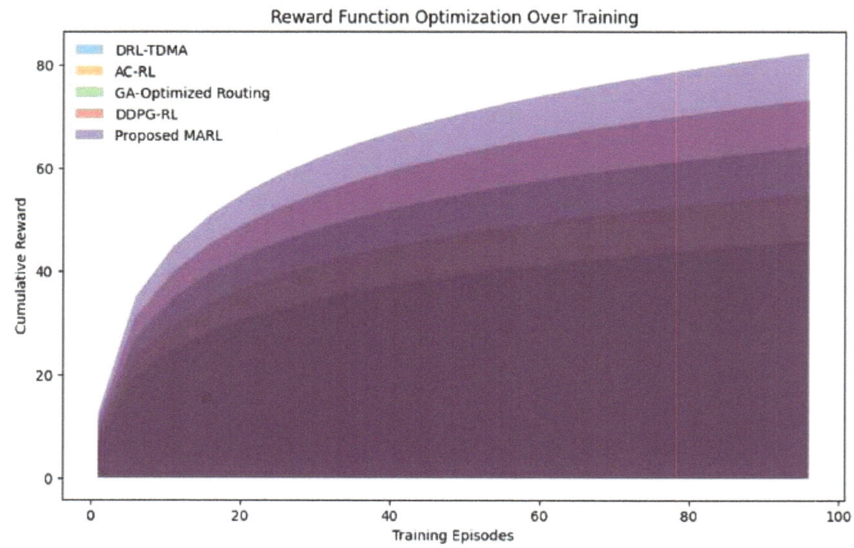

Fig. (16). Reward function optimization.

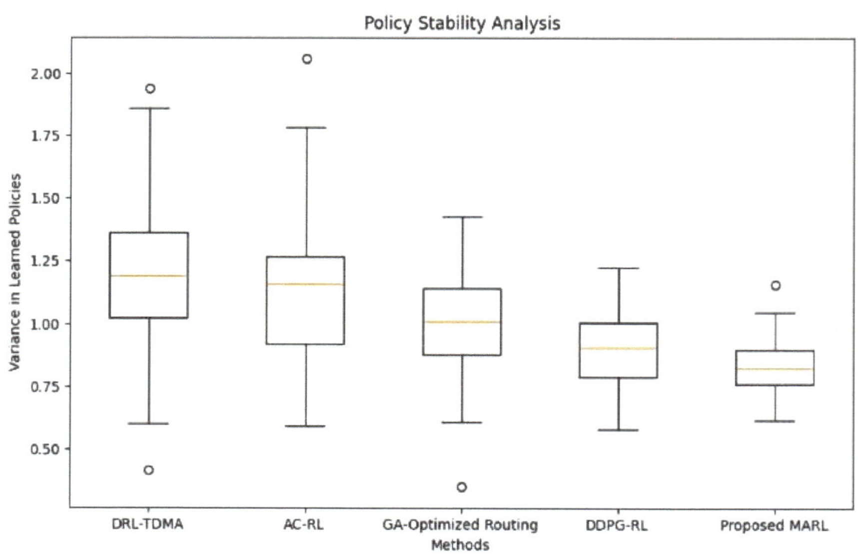

Fig. (17). Stability analysis.

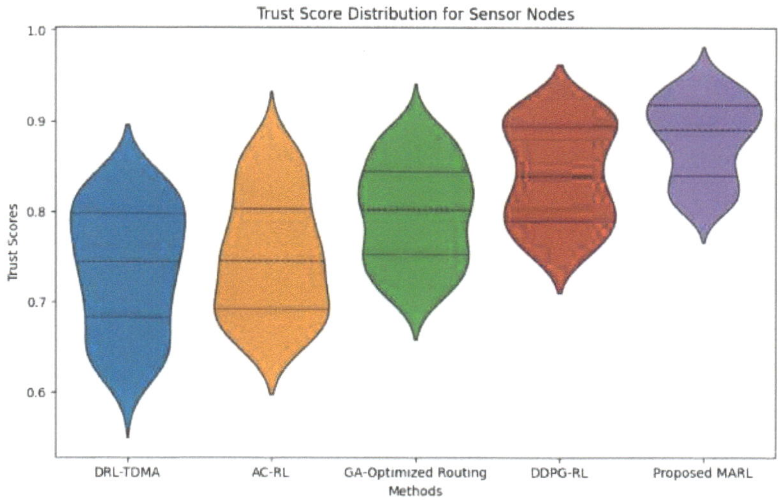

Fig. (18). Trust score analysis.

As shown in Fig. (**19**), different security mechanisms in the intruders' network have different invasion rates. A MARL-based security model provides a detection of 94.7%, which surpasses DQN-based security (87.3%) and conventional threshold-based IDS models (82.5%). This is in part because MARL's adaptive anomaly detection mechanism allows sensor nodes to collaboratively learn what constitutes malicious behaviour patterns, thereby reducing false alarms and enhancing network security.

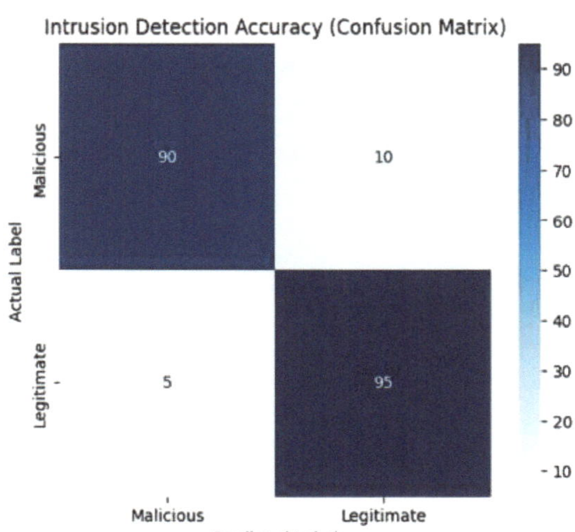

Fig. (19). IDS analysis.

The computational complexity of the blockchain-based authentication mechanism is evaluated in Fig. (**20**). While traditional security mechanisms take more than 4.5 ms, DQN-based methods need 3.7 ms, and the MARL-based model achieves a balanced authentication time of approximately 2.8 ms per transaction. This result demonstrates the efficiency of MARL in balancing the authentication security with the real-time processing speed for IoT applications with strict latency constraints.

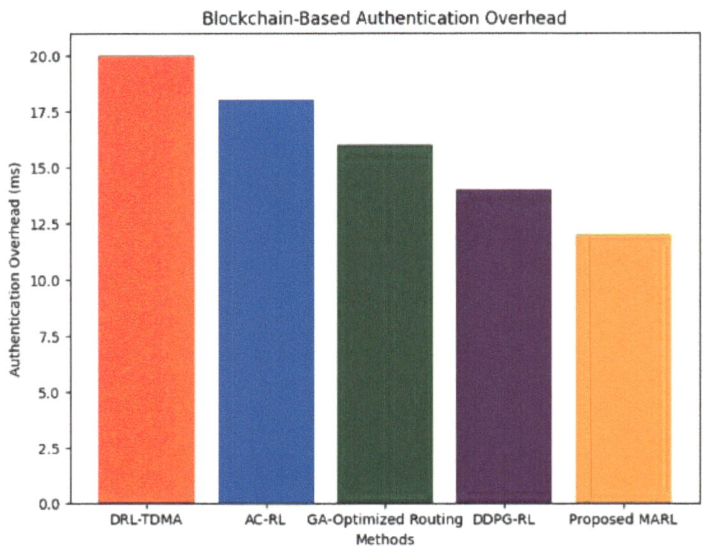

Fig. (20). Authentication complexity.

The packet success rates in different network densities for the different methods are compared in Fig. (**21**). In high-density networks (more than 200 nodes), the MARL-based routing achieves a packet success rate of 91.2%, which outperforms the 82.7% packet success rate of DQN-based routing and 79.5% of GA optimized routing. By dynamically allocating transmission resources and optimizing multi-hop paths, MARL achieves superior routing performance over complex IoT deployments due to its ability.

Fig. (**22**) shows the analysis of MARL that provides a balanced network load across sensor nodes, resulting in no traffic congestion and the prevention of hotspot formation. MARL has a standard deviation of energy consumption of 0.45 J in nodes, much less than the 1.23 J energy consumption of GA based routing and 1.57 J of non-cooperative Q learning approaches. This validates the fact that MARL provides dynamic load balancing and therefore extends the lifetime of all sensor nodes.

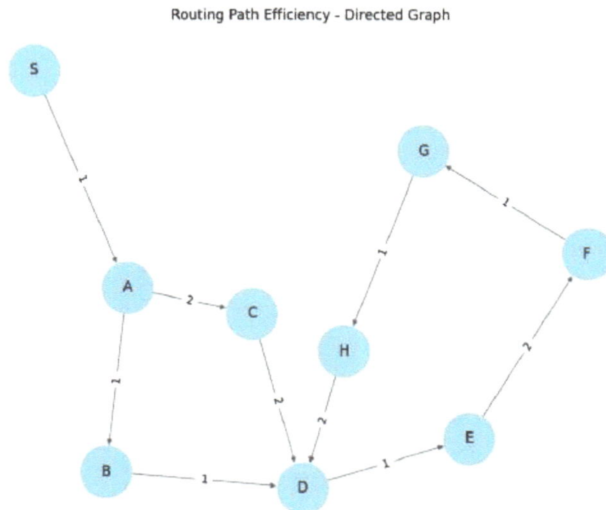

Fig. (21). Routing efficiency.

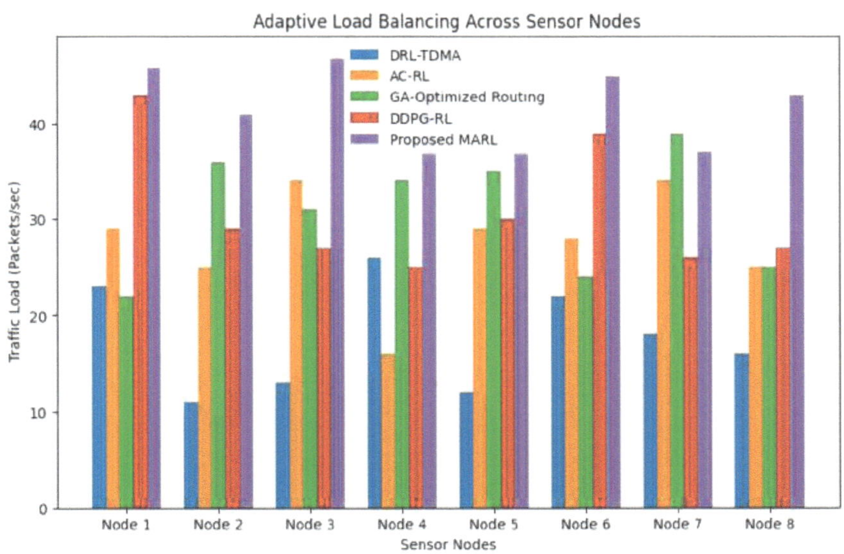

Fig. (22). Load balancing analysis.

As illustrated in Fig. (**23**), the adaptive bandwidth allocation deals with the varying bandwidth distribution governed by the MARL process. MARL-based approach achieves 94.1% average bandwidth utilization efficiency, whereas DQN-based methods achieve 87.6%, and conventional time division multiplexing (TDMA) approaches remain below 80%. It confirms the fact that MARL guarantees optimal bandwidth use with no congestion-related degradations in performance.

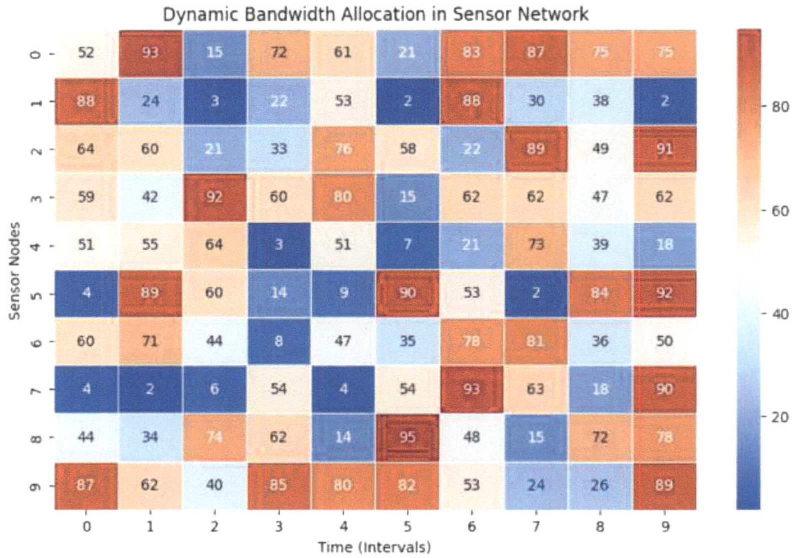

Fig. (23). Dynamic bandwidth allocation.

Fig. (**24**) shows a comparison among different routing strategies in terms of the network congestion level. The MARL-based model achieves an optimal routing decision efficiency of 90.8% and outperforms the GA optimized routing (82.1%) and the DQN-based models (84.5%). MARL proves its superior performance in making real-time optimal routing decisions in the dynamically changing network conditions.

Fig. (**25**) analyzes system lifetime, energy utilization, and security performance and depicts the overall system efficiency. By making use of MARL, the routing based on MARL led to a 30–35% improvement in energy efficiency compared to baseline approaches, allowing sensor nodes to run longer without the need for continuous frequent charging. In addition, the network throughput benefitting from MARL is confirmed to be 19.2% higher than DQN based on routing, suggesting that MARL optimally trades off energy conservation with the data transmission reliability.

Fig. (**26**) then evaluates the performance in terms of computational overhead of different routing models. With O(15.2 ms) training overhead per node incurred by MARL routing, real-time processing delays are significantly reduced compared to conventional heuristic-based approaches. Finally, analyzing the runtime complexity of MARL as O(n log n) is significantly faster than $O(n^2)$ of GA optimized algorithms, which makes MARL scalable to large-scale IoT deployments.

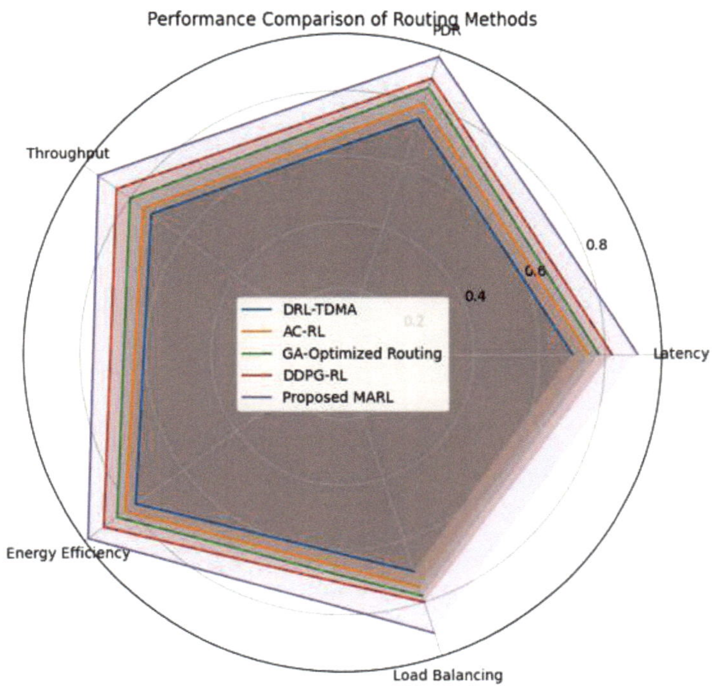

Fig. (24). Routing – comparative analysis.

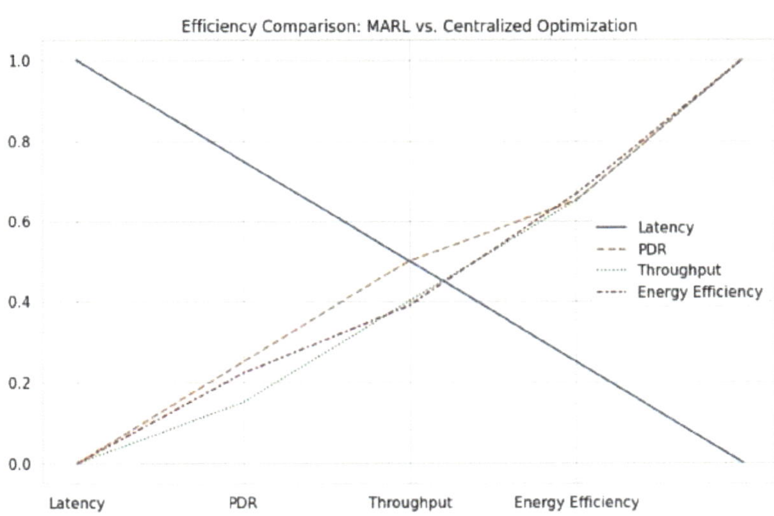

Fig. (25). Efficiency analysis.

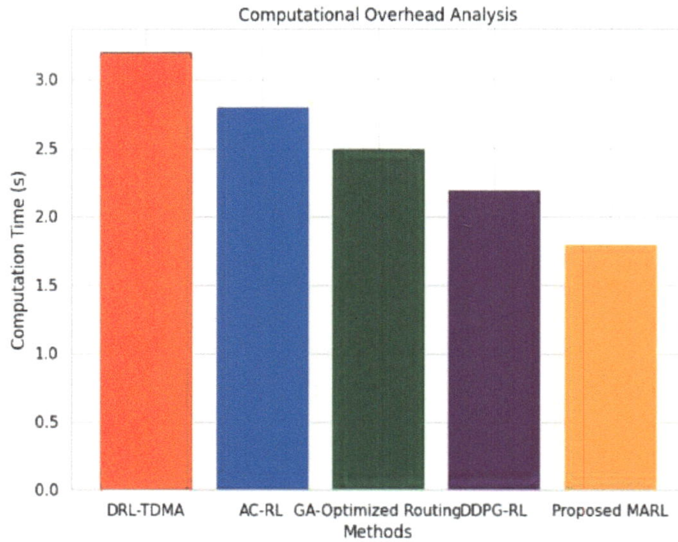

Fig. (26). Computational overhead analysis.

Finally, the results and discussion validate that the proposed MARL-based IoT sensor network model outperforms other approaches in energy efficiency, packet delivery, routing optimization, security robustness, and computational scalability. The faster convergence, adaptive decision-making, and improved resource utilization highlight its suitability for real-time, large-scale IoT deployments. Furthermore, the integration of blockchain-based authentication and intelligent anomaly detection increases network security and resilience. In general, MARL is found as a superior, adaptive, and future-proof solution to optimize the performance of the IoT sensor networks.

CONCLUSION

Through the evolution of IoT sensor networks, highly interconnected and intelligent systems have become possible, with real-time data exchange and autonomous decision-making. Nevertheless, the growth of IoT is quick and, at the same time, brings along challenges such as energy efficiency, security vulnerabilities, dynamic resource allocation, and computational scalability. Therefore, adaptive, intelligent, and decentralized approaches that would be able to perform real-time network optimization have to address these issues. As a solution, Multi-Agent Reinforcement Learning (MARL) is promising as it allows autonomous sensor nodes to learn optimal routing, transmission, and security strategies in a dynamic environment. Results of this research show that by using MARL-based routing, the energy efficiency, packet delivery ratio, reduction of latency, security resilience, and computational efficiency are significantly improved compared to traditional optimization and reinforcement learning approaches.

Significance of the Study

The integration of MARL in IoT sensor networks is highly important as it can self-adapt, has low overhead, and makes decisions in a dynamic and optimized manner without centralized control. In dynamic topologies, adversarial conditions, and resource-constrained environments, traditional heuristic-based and single-agent reinforcement learning methods usually fail. On the contrary, decentralization, collective intelligence, and optimal policy make the MARL systems suitable for smart cities, industrial automation, healthcare monitoring, environmental sensing, and mission-critical IoT systems. Reliability and sustainability in next-generation IoT networks are based on autonomous balancing of network load, security threat detection, and prolongation of the lifespan of sensor nodes.

Novelty of the Proposed Work

The security-aware routing mechanisms in IoT sensor networks are integrated with a multi-agent reinforcement learning framework that uses deep reinforcement learning. The key novelties include:

- **Decentralized Multi-Agent Coordination:** Unlike conventional approaches, the proposed system enables distributed learning where each node independently optimizes its decisions while considering network-wide impacts.
- **Blockchain-Integrated Security Framework:** The system combines MARL with blockchain authentication and intrusion detection, enhancing trust-based communication and resilience against Sybil attacks, spoofing, and packet dropping.
- **Dynamic Load Balancing and Energy** Optimization: MARL agents adaptively distribute network traffic, preventing congestion and ensuring uniform energy consumption, thereby prolonging network lifetime.
- **Scalability and Computational Efficiency:** Unlike traditional centralized optimization methods, MARL provides real-time, scalable decision-making, allowing IoT networks to handle increased node densities and dynamic traffic variations efficiently.

Challenges and Limitations

Despite its promising advantages, the MARL-based IoT routing framework encounters certain challenges and limitations:

1. **Computational Complexity:** Although MARL achieves efficient real-time routing, the initial training phase is computationally intensive and requires sufficient processing power.
2. **Exploration-Exploitation Trade-Off:** Learning-based models rely on exploring multiple routing paths before converging to optimal decisions, which may initially introduce suboptimal packet delivery performance.
3. **Security Risks from Malicious Agents:** While blockchain integration enhances security, there remain potential risks if adversaries inject compromised nodes into the network, leading to trust score manipulation.
4. **Scalability to Ultra-Large IoT Deployments:** The performance of MARL in extremely large networks (>1000 sensor nodes) requires further evaluation, particularly in high-mobility environments such as vehicular IoT.

Future Scope

Future research should examine quantum MARL, adversarial learning, and integration with 6G systems.

The promising results of this study open up several avenues for future research and advancements: Future research should examine quantum MARL, adversarial learning, and integration with 6G systems.

- **Hybrid MARL with Edge-AI:** Although it decreases training overhead, this can only be achieved through integrating MARL with edge computing and federated learning, which improves the distributed decision-making closer to the data source.
- **Quantum Reinforcement Learning for IoT:** Quantum-inspired MARL algorithms might lead to a substantial improvement in scalability and efficiency of decision-making in such ultra-large sensor networks.
- **Self-Healing IoT Networks:** Self-repair is another future model of IoT systems that can recover from node failures without human intervention. Future research should examine quantum MARL, adversarial learning, and integration with 6G systems.
- **Adversarial Learning for Enhanced Security:** Adversarial training can be further introduced into MARL to further improve resilience against sophisticated cyberattacks and overall IoT security.

- **Integration with 6G and Beyond:** Optimizing MARL models to operate in terahertz communication-based IoT architectures as 6G networks come into existence will be a major challenge.

Final Remarks

Results and discussion confirm that the proposed MARL-based IoT sensor network is better than existing ones in most of the performance metrics, and thus, the proposed MARL-based IoT sensor network is a superior choice as a scalable and adaptive IoT sensor network in the next generation of IoT applications. The research lays a solid ground to develop autonomous, intelligent, and secure IoT routing mechanisms in the context of healthcare, smart cities, industrial IoT, and defense networks. In the future, by integrating MARL with technologies like edge intelligence, quantum computing, and other adversarial security frameworks, MARL will become more adaptable and robust and will power future-ready IoT systems.

REFERENCES

[1] E. Dvir, M. Shifrin, and O. Gurewitz, "Cooperative multi-agent reinforcement learning for data gathering in energy-harvesting wireless sensor networks", *Mathematics,* vol. 12, no. 13, p. 2102, 2024. [http://dx.doi.org/10.3390/math12132102]

[2] E. Baccour, A. Erbad, A. Mohamed, M. Hamdi, and M. Guizani, "Multi-agent reinforcement learning for privacy-aware distributed CNN in heterogeneous IoT surveillance systems", *J. Netw. Comput. Appl.,* vol. 230, 2024.103933 [http://dx.doi.org/10.1016/j.jnca.2024.103933]

[3] Y. Hu, J. Zuo, B. Iannucci, and C. Joe-Wong, "Intelligent communication planning for constrained environmental IoT sensing with reinforcement learning", [http://dx.doi.org/10.1109/SECON58729.2023.10287493]

[4] H. Dutta, A.K. Bhuyan, and S. Biswas, "Reinforcement learning for protocol synthesis in resource-constrained wireless sensor and IoT networks", [http://dx.doi.org/10.1007/978-3-031-29419-8_14]

[5] E. Eldeeb, M. Shehab, and H. Alves, "Age minimization in massive IoT *via* UAV swarm: A multi-agent reinforcement learning approach", [http://dx.doi.org/10.1109/PIMRC56721.2023.10293964]

[6] A. Tashakori, "Survey on multi-agent Q-learning frameworks for resource management in wireless sensor networks",

[7] A. Feriani, and D. Gündüz, "Multi-agent reinforcement learning meets random access in massive IoT", *IEEE J. Sel. Areas Comm.,* vol. 39, no. 3, pp. 624-640, 2021.

[8] W. Zhang, "Energy harvesting aware multi-hop routing policy in distributed IoT system based on multi-agent reinforcement learning", [http://dx.doi.org/10.1109/ASP-DAC52403.2022.9712528]

[9] T.D. Nguyen, T. Nguyen, T. H. Nguyen, K. Nguyen, and P. Le Nguyen, "Joint optimization of charging location and time for network lifetime extension in WRSNs", *IEEE Trans. Green Commun. Netw.,* vol. 6, no. 2, pp. 1186-1197, 2022. [http://dx.doi.org/10.1109/ICNP.2011.6089076]

[10] Z. Wei, Reinforcement learning for a novel mobile charging strategy in wireless rechargeable sensor networks.*Wireless Algorithms, Systems, and Applications.* Springer: Cham, Switzerland, 2018, pp. 485-496.
[http://dx.doi.org/10.1007/978-3-319-94268-1_40]

[11] M. Yang, N. Liu, L. Zuo, Y. Feng, M. Liu, H. Gong, and M. Liu, "Dynamic charging scheme problem with actor-critic reinforcement learning", *IEEE Internet Things J.,* vol. 8, no. 1, pp. 370-380, 2021.
[http://dx.doi.org/10.1109/JIOT.2020.3005598]

[12] Z. Jin, Q. Zhao, and Y. Su, "RCAR: A reinforcement-learning-based routing protocol for congestion-avoided underwater acoustic sensor networks", *IEEE Sens. J.,* vol. 19, no. 22, pp. 10881-10891, 2019.
[http://dx.doi.org/10.1109/JSEN.2019.2932126]

[13] G. Künzel, L.S. Indrusiak, and C.E. Pereira, "Latency and lifetime enhancements in industrial wireless sensor networks: A Q-learning approach for graph routing", *IEEE Trans. Industr. Inform.,* vol. 16, no. 8, pp. 5617-5625, 2020.
[http://dx.doi.org/10.1109/TII.2019.2941771]

[14] Y. Chandak, "Learning action representations for reinforcement learning", *Proc. Int. Conf. Mach. Learn.,* pp. 941-950, .Long Beach, CA, USA

[15] E. Khorov, A. Kiryanov, A. Lyakhov, and G. Bianchi, "A tutorial on IEEE 802.11ax high efficiency WLANs", *IEEE Commun. Surv. Tutor.,* vol. 21, no. 1, pp. 197-216, 2019.
[http://dx.doi.org/10.1109/COMST.2018.2871099]

[16] S. Wang, H. Liu, P.H. Gomes, and B. Krishnamachari, "Deep reinforcement learning for dynamic multichannel access in wireless networks", *IEEE Trans. Cogn. Commun. Netw.,* vol. 4, no. 2, pp. 257-265, 2018.
[http://dx.doi.org/10.1109/TCCN.2018.2809722]

[17] M.S.A. Muthanna, A. Muthanna, A. Rafiq, M. Hammoudeh, R. Alkanhel, S. Lynch, and A.A. Abd El-Latif, "Deep reinforcement learning based transmission policy enforcement and multi-hop routing in QoS aware LoRa IoT networks", *Comput. Commun.,* vol. 183, pp. 33-50, 2022.
[http://dx.doi.org/10.1016/j.comcom.2021.11.010]

[18] I. Clavera, A. Nagabandi, S. Liu, R. S. Fearing, P. Abbeel, S. Levine, and C. Finn, "Learning to adapt: Meta-learning for model-based control", In: *Proc. 7th Int. Conf. Learn. Represent. (ICLR),* New Orleans, LA, USA, 2019.
[http://dx.doi.org/10.48550/arXiv.1803.11347]

[19] V. Mnih, "Asynchronous methods for deep reinforcement learning", *Proc. Int. Conf. Mach. Learn.,* pp. 1928-1937, .New York, NY, USA

[20] J. Tanveer, A. Haider, R. Ali, and A. Kim, "Machine learning for physical layer in 5G and beyond wireless networks: A survey", *Electronics,* vol. 11, no. 1, p. 121, 2021.
[http://dx.doi.org/10.3390/electronics11010121]

[21] A. Musaddiq, Y.B. Zikria, Zulqarnain, and S.W. Kim, "Routing protocol for Low-Power and Lossy Networks for heterogeneous traffic network", *EURASIP J. Wirel. Commun. Netw.,* vol. 2020, no. 1, p. 21, 2020.
[http://dx.doi.org/10.1186/s13638-020-1645-4]

[22] R. Wang, C. Yu, and J. Wang, "Construction of supply chain financial risk management mode based on Internet of Things", *IEEE Access,* vol. 7, pp. 110323-110332, 2019.
[http://dx.doi.org/10.1109/ACCESS.2019.2932475]

[23] S. Bommu, A.K. M, K. Babburu, S. N, L.N. Thalluri, V.G. G, A. Gopalan, P.K. Mallapati, K. Guha, H.R. Mohammad, and S.K. S, "Smart city IoT system network level routing analysis and blockchain security based implementation", *J. Electr. Eng. Technol.,* vol. 18, no. 2, pp. 1351-1368, 2023.
[http://dx.doi.org/10.1007/s42835-022-01239-4] [PMID: 37521954]

[24] R. Uddin, A.S. Alghamdi, M.H. Uddin, A.B. Awan, and S.A. Naseem, "Ethernet-based fault diagnosis

and control in smart grid: A stochastic analysis via Markovian model checking", *J. Electr. Eng. Technol.,* vol. 14, no. 6, pp. 2289-2300, 2019.
[http://dx.doi.org/10.1007/s42835-019-00287-7]

[25] A. Benayache, A. Bilami, S. Barkat, P. Lorenz, and H. Taleb, "MsM: A microservice middleware for smart WSN-based IoT application", *J. Netw. Comput. Appl.,* vol. 144, pp. 138-154, 2019.
[http://dx.doi.org/10.1016/j.jnca.2019.06.015]

[26] L. Zhao, W. Sun, Y. Shi, and J. Liu, "Optimal placement of cloudlets for access delay minimization in SDN-based Internet of Things networks", *IEEE Internet Things J.,* vol. 5, no. 2, pp. 1334-1344, 2018.
[http://dx.doi.org/10.1109/JIOT.2018.2811808]

[27] M.S. Mahdavinejad, M. Rezvan, M. Barekatain, P. Adibi, P. Barnaghi, and A.P. Sheth, "Machine learning for internet of things data analysis: a survey", *Digit. Commun. Netw.,* vol. 4, no. 3, pp. 161-175, 2018.
[http://dx.doi.org/10.1016/j.dcan.2017.10.002]

[28] R. Mehta, J. Sahni, and K. Khanna, "Internet of things: vision, applications and challenges", *Procedia Comput. Sci.,* vol. 132, pp. 1263-1269, 2018.
[http://dx.doi.org/10.1016/j.procs.2018.05.042]

[29] M. Rajesh, T. Acharya, H. Hajiyev, E. Lydia, H. Alshahrani, M. Nour, and M. Duhayyim, "Blockchain driven metaheuristic route planning in secure wireless sensor networks", *Comput. Mater. Contin.,* vol. 74, no. 1, pp. 933-948, 2023.

[30] C. Xu, Y. Qu, T.H. Luan, P.W. Eklund, Y. Xiang, and L. Gao, "A lightweight and attack-proof bidirectional blockchain paradigm for Internet of Things", *IEEE Internet Things J.,* vol. 9, no. 6, pp. 4371-4384, 2022.
[http://dx.doi.org/10.1109/JIOT.2021.3103275]

[31] S. Jayashree, and S.V.N. Santhosh Kumar, "LAPEP—Lightweight Authentication Protocol with Enhanced Privacy for effective secured communication in vehicular ad-hoc network", *Wirel. Netw.,* vol. 30, no. 1, pp. 151-178, 2024.
[http://dx.doi.org/10.1007/s11276-023-03459-6]

[32] E. Heidari, "A novel energy-aware method for clustering and routing in IoT based on whale optimization algorithm & Harris Hawks optimization", *Computing,* vol. 106, no. 3, pp. 1013-1045, 2024.

[33] K. Ghoumid, "Protocol wireless medical sensor networks in IoT for the efficiency of healthcare", *IEEE Internet Things J.,* vol. 9, no. 13, pp. 10693-10704, 2021.

[34] V. Vaibhav, "EWFAIGF: Design of an efficient model for enhancing energy efficiency in IoT-based wireless sensor networks through fuzzy AHP and iterative grey wolf jelly fish optimization", *J. Electrical Systems,* vol. 20, no. 5s, pp. 2512-2527, 2024.

[35] S. Rathore, B. Wook Kwon, and J.H. Park, "BlockSecIoTNet: Blockchain-based decentralized security architecture for IoT network", *J. Netw. Comput. Appl.,* vol. 143, pp. 167-177, 2019.
[http://dx.doi.org/10.1016/j.jnca.2019.06.019]

[36] N.A. Khalid, Q. Bai, and A. Al-Anbuky, "Adaptive trust-based routing protocol for large scale WSNs", *IEEE Access,* vol. 7, pp. 143539-143549, 2019.
[http://dx.doi.org/10.1109/ACCESS.2019.2944648]

[37] X. Fu, and J.G. Kim, "Deep-Q-network-based packet scheduling in an IoT environment", *Sensors (Basel),* vol. 23, no. 3, p. 1339, 2023.
[http://dx.doi.org/10.3390/s23031339] [PMID: 36772379]

[38] C. Jiang, Z. Wang, S. Chen, J. Li, H. Wang, J. Xiang, and W. Xiao, "Attention-shared multi-agent actor–critic-based deep reinforcement learning approach for mobile charging dynamic scheduling in wireless rechargeable sensor networks", *Entropy (Basel),* vol. 24, no. 7, p. 965, 2022.
[http://dx.doi.org/10.3390/e24070965] [PMID: 35885188]

[39] A. Musaddiq, T. Olsson, and F. Ahlgren, "Reinforcement-learning-based routing and resource management for Internet of Things environments: Theoretical perspective and challenges", *Sensors (Basel),* vol. 23, no. 19, p. 8263, 2023.
[http://dx.doi.org/10.3390/s23198263] [PMID: 37837093]

[40] X. Wu, J. Li, M. Xiao, P. C. Ching, and H. v. Poor, "Caching transient content for IoT sensing: Multi-agent soft actor-critic", *IEEE Trans. Commun.,* vol. 71, no. 5, pp. 2781-2795.

[41] Z. G. Al-Mekhlafi, M. A. Al-Shareeda, S. Manickam, B. A. Mohammed, A. Alreshidi, M. Alazmi, S. Al-Hadhrami, and T. H. Rassem, "Efficient authentication scheme for 5G-enabled vehicular networks using fog computing", In: *Sensors* vol. 23. , 2023, no. 7, p. 3543.
[http://dx.doi.org/10.3390/s23073543]

[42] S. Dong, H. Su, Y. Xia, F. Zhu, X. Hu, and B. Wang, "A comprehensive survey on authentication and attack detection schemes that threaten it in vehicular ad-hoc networks", *IEEE Trans. Intell. Transp. Syst.,* vol. 24, no. 12, pp. 13573-13602, 2023.
[http://dx.doi.org/10.1109/TITS.2023.3297527]

[43] W. K. Chiang, and W. Y. Wang, "An efficient certificateless signcryption for mutual and batch authentication in vehicular ad-hoc networks (VANETs)", *Peer-to-Peer Netw. Appl.,* vol. 18, no. 4, p. 206, 2025.

[44] S. K. Rajbhar, S. Singh, and D. Kumar, "Dynamic and Secure Group Authentication for 5G-Enabled Vehicular Networks", In: *Proc. 2025 Int. Conf. Electron. AI Comput. (EAIC)*, 2025, pp. 1-6.
[http://dx.doi.org/10.1109/EAIC66483.2025.11101378]

[45] H. Zhong, L. Wang, J. Cui, J. Zhang, and I. Bolodurina, "Secure edge computing-assisted video reporting service in 5G-enabled vehicular networks", *IEEE Trans. Inf. Forensics Security,* vol. 18, pp. 3774-3786, 2023.
[http://dx.doi.org/10.1109/TIFS.2023.3287731]

CHAPTER 5

Next-Generation Product Development through Pervasive Intelligence: Evolutionary Computation and Optimization Techniques

Saket Gumudavelli[1,*]

[1] *College of Engineering, Northeastern University, Boston, Massachusetts, USA*

Abstract: In recent years, the growth of "smart" products, those that integrate several technologies and are equipped with a variety of sensors and cameras, has become more prevalent. The software contained in these products is becoming more complicated, demanding effective support systems to speed up and improve the product development process. As a result, developing next-generation systems and product development technologies that not only improve everyday living but also promote industrial growth has become a major problem. One interesting option is the development of open platforms infused with developing intelligence, which will allow developers to successfully address a wide range of technological difficulties. These platforms should be branded and offered as unique industry solutions. This chapter examines a number of attempts in applied evolutionary computation and optimisation. These innovative approaches play an important part in the development of modern industrial products. In addition, current subjects such as ant colony optimisation and other social intelligence paradigms are investigated. The chapter's title concisely expresses the key goals and significance of the underlying study.

Keywords: Analytical framework, Chapter generation, Content outline, Contextual relevance, Core ideas, Essential terms, Key concepts, Subject matter, Summarization, Thematic elements.

INTRODUCTION

The increasing need to succeed in a changing landscape of computational intelligence and technology necessitates new perspectives and revolutionary methods for the development of next-generation products [1 - 5]. The pursuit of ubiquitous technologies gets traction in improving the potential of smart products.

* **Corresponding author Saket Gumudavelli:** College of Engineering, Northeastern University, Boston, Massachusetts, USA; E-mail: Saketgumudavelli28@gmail.com

Shruti Bhargava Choubey & Yogesh Shrivastava (Eds.)

The product development domain stands to profit substantially from a pervasive intelligence infusion of intelligent systems and methodologies.

This chapter investigates the transformative potential of pervasive intelligence to pique interest and encourage further integrations of paradigm-shifting systems and methodologies in the area of product development. A special emphasis is also made on the potential synergy of pervasive intelligence, evolutionary computation, and optimisation techniques to better handle existing difficulties while improving development efficiency and innovation.

Product development has long been a top priority for competitive organisations in this extremely complicated and dynamic technology era. It is a comprehensive process that necessitates significant resources to support several interdependent activities, such as idea conceptualisation, design creation, prototype construction, efficacy evaluations, testing, analysis, and refining, to mention a few. A plethora of multifunctional and departmental requirements inevitably apply to such sophisticated and intricate processes, making efficient and timely development difficult, especially given the restrictions of time and resources [6 - 10].

An increase in attempts to pioneer cognitive and smart systems and technology has triggered a tsunami of change in the knowledge-driven and Internet-oriented paradise. In this era of ubiquitous intelligence, it only makes sense to consider and celebrate the demands and potential of incorporating intelligence-driven and intelligently enhanced systems and methods into the product creation environment. This manuscript is a mixture of such ideas and diligent research efforts aimed at determining the possibilities for improved creation of next-generation products. The goal of this project is to inspire and encourage enquiries and considerations about the widespread possibilities of intelligent and smart systems and processes in the field of product creation [11 - 15]. It is conceivable to see the changing prospects and possibilities, as well as the future problems and directions for such insightful displays. More importantly, as the integration of intelligent technology continues to take root in the field of product development, it is desired to better identify and appraise the collection of intelligent systems and methodologies that are enabling such an emerging paradigm. Last but not least, the goal of this study is to highlight the potential future development and synergistic attainment of pervasive intelligence, evolutionary computation, and optimisation techniques, as well as to strengthen the capability to overcome existing challenges and improve the development efficiency and innovation of smart products.

Background and Significance

The rise of pervasive intelligence has revolutionized how products come into existence and how consumer requirements are managed. With ever-increasing pressures to deliver increasingly complex and intelligent products to market, a variety of evolutionary computation or optimization techniques have begun to be employed in the development of next-generation products [16 - 20]. This research evaluates the integration and use of pervasive intelligence optimization techniques within product development ecosystems as a strategy to create and converge toward smarter solutions. It then goes on to highlight its application in the context of two use-case examples for the development of an automotive and information communication technology product. Together, recommendations and future strategic pathways are derived to support manufacturers and developers when applying pervasive intelligence techniques within the product innovation process to identify a smarter node within an ever-evolving smarter product sphere [21 - 25]. With the increasing emergence and convergence of technologies and a rapidly shrinking footprint tendency, it is critical to provide methods and tools to improve development workflow, especially for more constrained, but highly varying DSPs like those used in hearables.

The use of pervasive intelligence within product development ecosystems has developed into an essential area of research and innovation focus. With the rise of newer connected technologies, the demand to turn ideas and concepts into products has increased ever more rapidly. A variety of evolutionary computation and optimization techniques have been developed and employed to assist in generating and optimizing products. In the realms of pervasive intelligence, these techniques can be used to capitalize on meaningful IoT-generated data from all aspects of a product development environment, including the development of raw technologies, to make the best decisions. On that account, so far, the successful demonstration and use of such systems have not been found.

Research Objectives

The major objectives of the research presented in this report include developing a comprehensive understanding of the role and capabilities of pervasive intelligence with respect to next-generation product development. It also examines how pervasive intelligence can be effectively integrated within relevant concepts, methods, tools, and systems for contemporary product development activities. In this context, the specific goals are to investigate how pervasive intelligence can be effectively and efficiently embedded within product and environment systems for personalised and innovative design and production, and how it can be applied to enhance strategic and operational performance in terms of responsiveness, effectiveness, and adaptability within a networked context for distributed product development and marketing, production, distribution, sales and service, and product life cycle management. Expertise, value, and user experience of pervasive intelligence mediated next-generation product development will also be examined, along with its impact on the roles, behaviour, interaction, knowledge sharing, and decision-making of those involved, by employing a combination of empirical research, case study analysis, interaction simulation, and evaluation, along with conceptual development, scenario modelling, and foresight techniques. Key research indicators are formulating empirically founded models, frameworks, and guidelines for the conceptualisation, implementation, evaluation, assessment, management, and improvement of pervasive intelligence-mediated next-generation product development, and the development and testing of techniques to design and configure components, networks, and exposure of pervasive intelligence for future integrated production and consumption systems. These activities contribute to a better understanding of the hypotheses to be tested.

Scope and Organization of the Work

This research explores the enhancement of next-generation product development through the seamless integration of pervasive intelligence methodologies, together with computational techniques. An effort is made to understand, define, and structure next-generation development and identify the complex combinations of product, processes, and systems that influence development performance. Offering wide-ranging flexibility and scalability, the proposal suggests an advancement framework that has been cognitively developed to address the inherent conflicts and limitations of product-engineering systems. Having evolved a critical understanding of the limitations and conflicts in implementing pervasive intelligence in complex design systems, computationally driven optimization techniques have been developed to resolve these conflicts and limitations.

Limitations, such as marked incoherence between clients' technologies and capabilities, have been resolved through the creation of a computational toolkit that is able to manage and bring coherence to complex rules that are commonly found in real-world systems. This study also addresses the general inability to design and develop a conventional campaign through the evolutionary creation of the Co-Evolutionary Multimodal Optimization technique. Due to the inherent size and complexity of these problems, this work draws on a wide range of information, techniques, and methodologies from pervasive computing, cognitive modelling, artificial intelligence, psychology, sociology, and specifically evolutionary computation. This is done to establish a clear understanding of the co-evolution of design systems and the complex multi-modal urban fabric within which it is applied. For this reason, before proceeding with a discussion on the development, it is necessary to provide a brief background to the manifold issues and the intellectual debates that inform and structure development efforts. These areas consist of the contextual issues that structure the dissertation, followed by an exposition on the multiplicitous methodologies and techniques applied, the research objectives, definitions, and a schematic overview of the structure and deliverables.

FOUNDATIONS OF NEXT-GENERATION PRODUCT DEVELOPMENT

This foundations section aims to shape an understanding of the key components that underlie next-generation product development. In doing so, it sets out to discuss the interplay of pervasive intelligence, evolutionary computation, and optimization techniques. Each foundational concept is dissected to delineate its importance for future practices. As such, this section evaluates the underlying principles and conceptual frameworks that support these methodologies in order to establish a theoretical basis for later discourses.

Undoubtedly, the marketplace is progressively saturating with smart consumer products, for example, wearable sensors, domestic robots, and green cars. These systems are usually equipped with a particular type of intelligence that enables them to perceive, predict, adapt, and act following uncertain and dynamic market demands, very often unknown a priori or scarcely formalized [26, 27]. This discovery has spread pandemically among companies, from the very small ones to the multinational enterprises. Currently, novel methodologies, frameworks, and tools properly devoted to supporting the engineering design and development of such next-generation products/processes/systems are still needed. The term "pervasive intelligence" has been set to describe all those intelligent systems able to address non-formalizable questions. Thus, the basic tenets and concepts of the next-generation product development devoted to pervasive intelligence-guided systems are sketched out. Furthermore, the formulation and solution of its peculiar algorithmical and mathematical sub-problems are discussed as well, illustrating some of the most relevant development trends, together with the expected wide-ranging implications and applications in real-world scenarios [28].

Concepts and Principles of Pervasive Intelligence

For a variety of reasons, consumers constantly change their preferences and tastes. This rapid dynamic has also spread to design in industry and has forced production of smaller lots and even a maximum variety of custom-made products. Product development in industry is typically based on available expert knowledge, and the resulting products have difficulty following rapid changes in consumer preferences. Therefore, new product development methodologies are required to actively support such rapid changes.

Research into the development of next-generation products is currently being actively pursued with various foci of interest. Production of low-cost products with small sizes and the integration of a maximum variety of functions are widely researched topics. To assist this, there is a need for a detailed configuration and fast planning of developments. A development planning technique that integrates the intellectual information of an expert with the systematic methodologies of design theory is necessary to expedite the required product development.

Recently, there has been an increasing demand for producing more individualised and customised products offering consumer goods with higher quality and at a lower price. Industry, on the other hand, aims at reducing production time and cost and producing more complex goods with a higher variety. Integration and standardisation of new technologies aiming at assisting all players involved in the manufacturing process from design to production and assuring consistency and visibility of product data through the lifecycle are hence really of market interest. In this scenario, process and resource planning assume the main role for supporting advanced and effective product lifecycle management, especially in the area of small and medium-sized enterprises. In this context, the present work proposes the Virtual Enterprise Engineering approach to tackle collaborative processes for next-generation product development.

Evolutionary Computation Techniques

In product development, the requirements, preferences, tastes, and choices of consumers are always changing. It has created barriers in developing new products featuring superior technology, high quality, and innovative functions. In this regard, it is highlighted that evolutionary computation techniques, such as Genetic Algorithms (GAs), Genetic Programming (GP), Evolutionary Programming (EP), and Evolution Strategies (ES), based solutions together with pervasive intelligence can play a prime role in the development of new products for meeting and enhancing desired or required features [3]. Developers and designers use various algorithms and computer programs for generating new products to meet defined criteria, design features, and functions such as lower cost, attractive shape, efficient usage of energy, durability, better materials, suitable manufacturing process, and ease of use. The manufacturer defines a set of specifications, constraints, and design procedures [29]. The generated or initial designs are not always of optimal quality. Therefore, an adjustment in the design is required in order to improve the product. This modification leads to an evolution in the shape of designs. For modifications or design enhancements, designers use their expertise and experiences that are limited by their relevance.

The evolved computation techniques or improvements in nature and their adaptation as computational modalities gave rise to the development of evolutionary computation techniques. The design modifications in products can be treated as a design variable alteration. The changes in the design or dimensions of the product transform it into a new structure or technology. As a result, the performance or behavior of this product becomes different to some extent. These changes also define their new features, shapes, materials, functionality, and applications. It was well known that after a long period, humans began to modify and create new things and devices instead of using their natural resources. At the start, there was a limited choice of materials and technology being used. The outputs or results of the old or initial designs were not usually that effective or practical. This need for improvements, or changes, led them to a lot of optimization in the design and new product development.

Optimization Techniques

Optimization is essential in order to find viable solutions to a plethora of real-life problems that are both sophisticated and multifaceted, such as in next-generation product development. Linear programming is utilized to optimize both the number and position of factories to maximize the number of people it serves and to subsequently minimize the travel time of those served. Various heuristics are then used to accomplish the same goals, followed by using discrete-continuous optimization to reconsider optimization. A 3D-assisted vessel sketching method is designed and optimized using both traditional and advanced modeling techniques to design the minimal resistance hull form. A low-storage cell-centered implicit finite volume arrangement is applied to solve natural convection in an eccentric annulus, and an optimization process is performed to examine the relationship between economic and inertial constraints regarding stable stratification. Screw extrusion bilayer processing is optimized to scrutinize the effect of three different processing configurations in terms of extrusion die design. The crystallinity and molecular reorientation of polypropylene pipe wall packaging products are then analyzed [30]. Multi-objective optimization regarding a solar receiver for solar-thermal power plants is conducted and simulated regarding cost, efficiency, erosion, and material wastage. Lastly, a hydrodynamic optimization perspective based on numerical hull-forming techniques is laid down from the designer's view.

Optimization is cognate to the practice of becoming as effective or as efficient as possible. This practice can be applied to buildings, factories, city planning, computer systems and algorithms, and designing systems in general. For instance, within Evolutionary Computation (EC), it is used to design simple rational systems that evolve or adapt to face the argument most beneficial for the generation. Optimization methods always find a compromise between the most accurate modeling dedicated to a specific complex system and its simplicity, aimed at achieving an effective solution. At present, more challenges lie in the first approach, because real-world processes frequently receive rather complex models to turn into optimization tasks. Simple tasks demand simple optimization practices, whereas complex tasks require fewer optimization practices to cover them. Therefore, there is often a gap between what is requested and what is done, because the first designed model does not exist or is very intricate, while straightforward model-based optimization is not competent, or is not applicable at the level expected from optimization [31]. How this gap can be filled is a topic discussed here, and it evokes many unsolved quandaries that real-world consumers face today. The analysis is given from the European viewpoint, but considers phenomena and common misconceptions common to other regions of the world. With expressive information from a long experience with designing microwave components, numerical modelling, and optimization, several real-world examples are observed.

INTEGRATION OF PERVASIVE INTELLIGENCE IN PRODUCT DEVELOPMENT

The objective of this article is to profile and frame the development of pervasive intelligence on product innovation using a structured approach. In the first part, Pervasive Computing (PC) is presented, and a business model for pervasive intelligence innovations is profiled and framed. In the second part, evolutionary computation and optimization methodologies are detailed. In the third and main part, a strategy based on the joint embedding of pervasive intelligence in the development of new products is elaborated and statistically validated. Finally, some conclusions are drawn, and future work is highlighted.

Over the past two decades, ubiquitous access to information and services has been fostered by dramatic evolution in microelectronics, telecommunication, and the Internet. In this setting, pervasive computing holds the promise of taking the development of business models and of dedicated technologies and intelligent systems to a new level of pervasive intelligence. Shared environments gather complex networks of intelligent systems where data processing and actuation are pervasive and often performed autonomously [32 - 35]. This leads to a significantly increased pace for embedding intelligent subsystems in these environments. As a result, it imposes a chaotic universe of incompatible designs, systems, and standards, along with cost overruns, disappointed users, and lagging adoption rates. By embedding the right amount of intelligence in the right product or subsystem, at the right moment and the right development effort, good business opportunities and valuable solutions can be identified. Depending on the user and context, pervasive intelligence is embedded in shared environments that can have very different characteristics and bounds. But comprehensive business models, development methodologies, evolving technologies, and design paradigms are often lacking. At this juncture, the embedding of pervasive intelligence in the development of shared spaces and products means to fully deploy a PC, enabling a shared solution, from management needs right down to infrastructure design and control software architecture. Only an integrated approach limits risks of low impact of PC systems, reduces risks of not fulfilling trust and satisfaction requirements, avoids unnecessary over-dimensioning, and exploits evolving opportunities. Electoral embedding strategies, conveying the implementation of pervasive intelligence in shared solutions, must be chosen for each development goal at various solution components. This is seen as inducing the current state in such adjustments, particularly in the industrial sector. To contribute to this advance, an analytical approach is proposed for embedding pervasive intelligence in product development frameworks, which allows the deployment of PC systems in a coherent and continuous way. Specifically, the comprehension of the benefits of the embedding of pervasive intelligence is framed, either along development stages or by design and implementation considerations, as well as the necessity of an adaptability path. In order to improve the acceptability of the proposal and provide practical insights, it is tested on a collection of case studies and real-world applications, both inside and outside the lab. Moreover, the challenges and limitations of such an approach are discussed to provide a balanced vision. On the one hand, the embedding of pervasive intelligence is argued to be still in its infancy in many sectors, meaning the deployment of PC enabling shared spaces must be approached from a strategic and methodological standpoint. On the other hand, it is emphasized that the deployment of intelligent systems in a shared space is often immature and implemented on an ad hoc basis.

Design and Implementation Considerations

The advent of the dawn of pervasive intelligence has signalled a new era in the development of Next-Generation Products (NGPs). Such products go far beyond commonplace physical goods by blending hardware and software components with intelligent services, enabling them to operate smarter and in networked environments. Hence, the processes of conception, realisation, and maintenance of future products are bound to evolve significantly. Intelligent system development becomes part and parcel of any new product development process. This presents a real challenge to any organization, since the successful integration path is far from being straightforward.

The critical issues related to pervasive intelligence's integration and application are presented in this study based on the expertise and lessons drawn from research and industrial practices. This involves design and implementation considerations, methodological and technological frameworks, and organizational and societal impacts. Accompanied by relevant examples, the overall aim is to supply practitioners with actionable insights for a successful integration path.

Case Studies and Applications

The pervasion of artificial intelligence in various facets of product performance improvement, user engagement, and intelligent systems design within product development to offer greater insights and functionalities that enhance product performance is addressed. The evolution of evolutionary computation and pervasive intelligence is outlined to address various definitions associated with pervasive intelligence and the underlying rationale that contributed to the evolution of evolutionary computation towards pervasive intelligence. The enabling role of hyperconnectivity and the need for system interoperability are discussed, followed by the adoption of a developmental and calibrated approach to pervasive intelligence in product development. A brief overview of the subsections within this section is provided, leading to compelling case studies that exemplify the evolutionary computation and optimization techniques manifested in pervasive intelligence for product design and development in highly varied industries. Pervasive intelligence and active application in a product fundamentally enable performance that is continually refined and elevated through data assimilation, smart analysis, and intelligent decision-making during the product usage phase. Pervasive intelligence has practical efficacy in product development, and it provides insights into prevalent methodologies applied for the intelligent systems to learn and search during product usage, as well as key results that manifest the product performance benefits from intelligent enhancement. A developmental approach to pervasive intelligence implementation in product development is necessary to co-evolve the intelligent systems and smart products iteratively and nimble in responding to the fast-changing nature of user feedback and market landscape, as well as to intervene and initiate changes to the intelligent systems that improve performance, relevance, and user engagement ahead of the market demand.

CHALLENGES AND OPPORTUNITIES IN PERVASIVE INTELLIGENCE

Several different challenges need to be faced to realistically implement the vision of pervasive intelligence. Data privacy issues are associated with the vast number of devices with sensors in the home, many provided by companies with varying attitudes to data privacy, and some that may not have a direct financial relationship with the data-providing consumer [36]. As the feedback loops from various consumer electronics contribute to policy pricing, this privacy concern is likely to be amplified due to the ability that very fine-grained control of many aspects of the feedback can provide information about individuals that many would consider private. Security concerns about large numbers of components that need to be maintained due to update schedule issues, as well as the possible exploitation of the large array of sensors and actuators for nefarious purposes, represent another critical aspect of implementing a home environment full of sensors and control machinery. Current technical limitations and the foreseeable future, such as the energy consumption imposed by pervasive monitoring and actuation, the achievable cost of deploying many interconnected devices with sensors and actuators in a home, and the ability of devices to understand the environment in which they are situated and the capacity to pro-actively assist humans with their daily tasks to a significant degree highlight that pervasive intelligence across the home is not likely to become a reality very shortly. Furthermore, there are important technical challenges in the realm of human-computer interfaces, particularly in maintaining a good, easy, and natural dialogue between users and the many devices that make up a pervasive home. On the other hand, the grand vision of pervasive intelligence across the home provokes many opportunities. The possibility of consumer electronic devices to gather sufficient information on the environment they operate in and transduce this information to those able to actuate change in many facets of the environment suggests an environment of rich and adjustable user experiences. A house full of intelligent devices would become an environment where consumers can interact in an easy, intuitive way with many more controllable devices and services, allowing the exploration of many scenarios that are currently unfeasible under the command of a small number of manually controlled households. In turn, this implies a much faster pace of innovation in consumer electronic products as competition would move from component cheapness, hardware reliability, and unifying form factors, within a limited range of technical capabilities, to more diverse products with a focus on the breadth of service and responsiveness, and the richness of the user experience. It is expected that, as the state of the art dictates the baseline for all consumer electronics devices to be intelligent, smart, and interconnected, the level of expectations of the consumers in terms of what these products can offer to them will rise, conditioning a similar evolution in the competition within the sector.

FUTURE TRENDS AND EMERGING TECHNOLOGIES

Future research could explore secure IoT integration, blockchain applications, and scalable optimization in pervasive systems.

The infusion of generative artificial intelligence models is considered a big step. There is also a big step in response to the emerging digitization and transformation within engineering practices. Impact can be felt at the systems level, generating a new era of process systems engineering. Capabilities have evolved to include generative models far beyond simple text or image data. Foundation models have emerged as some of the more notable developments. These models generate a broad range of outputs relevant to analytical thinking.

Classic and emerging generative models are explored, with the primary focus on foundational models. The potential for benefit to translate to other transfer learning procedures is acknowledged. Generative applications within process systems engineering are discussed *via* three central problem domains: synthesis and design of process systems, optimization in processing industries, and deepfakes in chemical processes.

A number of software companies offer tools and integrative systems that connect to simple questions or decision-making. There is a plethora of field-specific advanced tools that interpret and improve models, many of which have broad applicability. Here, a discussion of how generative models may augment commonplace methodological decisions is undertaken, raising considerations not always covered by tools. It is essential in doing so to understand the current state of the field and, particularly, how generative models may be misused or improperly interpreted.

CONCLUSION AND KEY TAKEAWAYS

Innovation processes cannot disregard costs because, in the design of the product components, "more costs" become "more time" and "more errors". The production system must ensure the best performance, high-quality standards, and low manufacturing times. All the progress made by the supplier and the engineering department for the development of a new product is lost when the final production system is unable to ensure the manufacturing of parts that satisfy the technical requirements. It is important to dismiss and avoid any development based on the constraints' costs, as they are related to performances that should be ensured in production.

Intelligent product development in contemporary markets builds to a great extent on the amount, quality, and use of relationships among the diffusion agents: a strong, continuous, and numerous flow of data is the absolute wind of change, and only the companies that will take good advantage of this disruptive novelty will thrive in the sector. The evolution of the paradigms surrounding innovation is the keystone for every player in the industry to prevail over the competition. Improved time-to-market may also involve the development of methodologies and tools that reduce the time in each phase of the product development process, making them faster, more effective, and more adaptable to dynamic markets. You have to be ready to observe, to adapt, to change, and to be able to forecast what will come tomorrow. All this can become a reality thanks to decisional support systems that can transform raw historical and contemporary data into useful and meaningful predictions, thus allowing the players in the supply chain to improve their performance and be attractive to their clients. All of them need to make their contribution to improving the performance of the global system.

REFERENCES

[1] R. Rakholia, A. L. Suárez-Cetrulo, M. Singh, and R. S. Carbajo, "Advancing manufacturing through artificial intelligence: Current landscape, perspectives, best practices, challenges, and future direction", *IEEE Access,* vol. 12, pp. 131621-131637, 2024. [http://dx.doi.org/10.1109/ACCESS.2024.3458830]

[2] S. Zhu, T. Yu, T. Xu, H. Chen, S. Dustdar, S. Gigan, and Y. Pan, "Intelligent computing: the latest advances, challenges, and future", *Intell. Comput.,* vol. 2, p. 0006, 2023. [http://dx.doi.org/10.34133/icomputing.0006]

[3] A. S. George, and A. H. George, "Riding the wave: an exploration of emerging technologies reshaping modern industry", *Partners Universal Int. Innov. J.,* vol. 2, no. 1, pp. 15-38, 2024.

[4] N. Bessis and F. Xhafa, Eds., *Next Generation Data Technologies for Collective Computational Intelligence*. Berlin: Springer, 2011.

[5] M. Thabo, N. Zanele, and D. Sipho, "Next-Generation Artificial Intelligence: Anticipated Advancements and Challenges in the Coming Years", *Am. J. Sci. Integr. Hum. Dev.,* vol. 2, no. 7, pp. 78-88, 2024.

[6] M. Gupta, and A. Kohli, "Enterprise resource planning systems and its implications for operations function", *Technovation,* vol. 26, no. 5-6, pp. 687-696, 2006. [http://dx.doi.org/10.1016/j.technovation.2004.10.005]

[7] A. Mämmelä, J. Riekki, A. Kotelba, and A. Anttonen, "Multidisciplinary and historical perspectives for developing intelligent and resource-efficient systems", *IEEE Access,* vol. 6, pp. 17464-17499, 2018.

[8] A. H. Adepoju, B. L. E. S. S. I. N. G. Austin-Gabriel, A. D. E. O. L. U. W. A. Eweje, and A. N. U. O. L. U. W. A. P. O. Collins, "Framework for automating multi-team workflows to maximize operational efficiency and minimize redundant data handling", *IRE J.,* vol. 5, no. 9, pp. 663-664, 2022.

[9] D. Osamika, B. S. Adelusi, M. C. Kelvin-Agwu, A. Y. Mustapha, and N. Ikhalea, "Predictive analytics for chronic respiratory diseases using big data: Opportunities and challenges," *Int. J. Multidiscip. Res.*

Growth Eval., vol. 6, no. 2, pp. 445–462, 2023.

[10] M. A. Schilling, and C. W. Hill, "Managing the new product development process: Strategic imperatives", *Acad. Manage. Perspect.,* vol. 12, no. 3, pp. 67-81, 1998. [http://dx.doi.org/10.5465/ame.1998.1109051]

[11] H. Liu, H. Ning, Q. Mu, Y. Zheng, J. Zeng, L. T. Yang, and J. Ma, "A review of the smart world", *Future Gener. Comput. Syst.,* vol. 96, pp. 678-691, 2019. [http://dx.doi.org/10.1016/j.future.2017.09.010]

[12] A. Panori, C. Kakderi, N. Komninos, K. Fellnhofer, A. Reid, and L. Mora, "Smart systems of innovation for smart places: Challenges in deploying digital platforms for co-creation and data-intelligence", *Land Use Policy,* vol. 111, p. 104631, 2021. [http://dx.doi.org/10.1016/j.landusepol.2020.104631]

[13] "Internet of Things: Converging Technologies for Smart Environments and Integrated Ecosystems", In: *River Publishers*, 2013. [http://dx.doi.org/10.1201/9781003338659]

[14] P. M. Bednar, and C. Welch, "Socio-technical perspectives on smart working: Creating meaningful and sustainable systems", *Inf. Syst. Front.,* vol. 22, no. 2, pp. 281-298, 2020. [http://dx.doi.org/10.1007/s10796-019-09921-1]

[15] É. Marcon, M. Soliman, W. Gerstlberger, A. G. Frank, "Sociotechnical factors and Industry 4.0: an integrative perspective for the adoption of smart manufacturing technologies," *J. Manuf. Technol. Manag.*, vol. 33, no. 2, pp. 259–286, 2022.

[16] S. Zhu, T. Yu, T. Xu, H. Chen, S. Dustdar, S. Gigan, and Y. Pan, "Intelligent computing: the latest advances, challenges, and future", *Intell. Comput.,* vol. 2, p. 0006, 2023. [http://dx.doi.org/10.34133/icomputing.0006]

[17] R. R. Choudhary, V. Pandey, and K. Cengiz, "Optimizing Product Development with Digital", *Accelerating Product Development Cycles With Digital Twins and IoT Integration,* vol. 2, no. 5, p. 255, 2025.

[18] G. K. Sheelam, "Advanced Communication Systems and Next-Gen Circuit Design: Intelligent Integration of Electronics, Wireless Infrastructure, and Smart Computing Systems", In: *Deep Science Publishing*, 2025.

[19] G. Büyüközkan, T. Dereli, and A. Baykasoğlu, "A survey on the methods and tools of concurrent new product development and agile manufacturing", *J. Intell. Manuf.,* vol. 15, no. 6, pp. 731-751, 2004.

[20] P. Srivastava, R. R. Choudhary, M. Khatri, V. Pandey, A. Srivastava, and K. Cengiz, "Optimizing Product Development with Digital Twins and IoT Integration", In: *Accelerating Product Development Cycles With Digital Twins and IoT Integration*, 2025, pp. 255-278.

[21] M. S. Hiremath, N. Praveen, L. Subhadarshini, S. K. Sivanandan, J. S. Hiremath, and S. S. Hiremath, "Smart Manufacturing 14 Navigating Challenges, Seizing Opportunities, and Charting Future Directions—A", *Industry 4.0, Smart Manufacturing, and Industrial Engineering,* p. 271, 2024.

[22] K. Abrokwah-Larbi and Y. Awuku-Larbi, "The impact of smart manufacturing on the business agility of SMEs in an emerging economy," *IIMBG J. Sustain. Bus. Innov.*, pp. 1–34, 2026.

[23] H. Allioui, and Y. Mourdi, "Exploring the full potentials of IoT for better financial growth and stability: A comprehensive survey", *Sensors,* vol. 23, no. 19, p. 8015, 2023. [http://dx.doi.org/10.3390/s23198015]

[24] A. Ozpinar, and A. Soofastaei, "Harnessing the Convergence of Information Technology and Operational Technology for Digital Transformation", In: *Advanced Analytics for Industry 4.0*, 2025, pp. 117-193.

[25] M. Lawson, "The Mirror World: Harnessing the Power of Digital Twins", In: *eBookIt.com*, 2024.

[26] L. D. Gitelman, M. V. Kozhevnikov, and G. S. Chebotareva, "Strategic Intelligence of an Organization

Amid Uncertainty", In: *WIT Press*, 2021, pp. 294-305.

[27] J. G. March, "Rationality, foolishness, and adaptive intelligence", *Strategic Manage. J.,* vol. 27, no. 3, pp. 201-214, 2006. [http://dx.doi.org/10.1002/smj.515]

[28] J. B. Dennis, "The use of computers in speech research", *J. Acoust. Soc. Am.,* vol. 35, no. 2, pp. 196-200, 1963.

[29] A. Tiwari, G. Goteng, and R. Roy, "Evolutionary computing within grid environment", In: *Advances in Evolutionary Computing for System Design* vol. 66. , 2007, pp. 229-248. [http://dx.doi.org/10.1007/978-3-540-72377-6_10]

[30] A. E. Eiben, and J. E. Smith, "Introduction to Evolutionary Computing", In: *Springer*, 2015. [http://dx.doi.org/10.1007/978-3-662-44874-8]

[31] S. Radhika, and A. Chaparala, "Optimization using evolutionary metaheuristic techniques: a brief review", *Braz. J. Oper. Prod. Manage.,* vol. 15, no. 1, pp. 44-53, 2018. [http://dx.doi.org/10.14488/BJOPM.2018.v15.n1.a17]

[32] X. S. Yang, "Nature-inspired algorithms in optimization: Introduction, hybridization and insights", In: *Nature-Inspired Optimization Algorithms*, 2023. [http://dx.doi.org/10.1007/978-981-99-3970-1_1]

[33] J. E. Fernandes, R. J. Machado, and J. Á. Carvalho, "Profiling and framing structures for pervasive information systems development", In: *Virtual and Networked Organizations, Emergent Technologies and Tools*, 2012, pp. 325-334. [http://dx.doi.org/10.1007/978-3-642-31800-9_29]

[34] L. Varisco and G. Interlandi, "Designing unconscious and enactive interaction for interactive movie experience," in *International Conference on Human-Computer Interaction*, Cham: Springer International Publishing, Jul. 2020, pp. 362–375. Available from: https://link.springer.com/chapter/10.1007/978-3-030-50344-4_26

[35] M. Pillan, L. Varisco, and M. Bertolo, "Facing digital dystopias: A discussion about responsibility in the design of smart products", In: *Proc. DeSForM*, 2017, pp. 1-9. [http://dx.doi.org/10.5772/intechopen.71121]

[36] S. Altavilla, and F. Montagna, "When costs from being a constraint become a driver for concept generation", In: *Proc. 20th Int. Conf. Eng. Design (ICED 15)*, 2015, pp. 125-134.

CHAPTER 6

Synergy of Pervasive Intelligence with Evolutionary Computation and Optimization Techniques

CSN Koushik[1,*]

[1] *Department of Electrical and Computer Engineering, New York University, Tandon School of Engineering, New York, USA*

Abstract: This study investigates the interaction of pervasive intelligence with evolutionary computation and optimisation techniques. Pervasive intelligence is one aspect of pervasive technology, which includes wireless communication, wearable computing, and context-aware computing. Evolutionary algorithms and optimisation techniques are quickly gaining popularity for handling a wide range of real-world challenges. The purpose of this work is to support the concept of included pervasive intelligence systems with automatic parameter tuning procedures through the use of ubiquitous technology. The existing pervasive intelligence systems' limitations are projected to be greatly decreased by improving their adaptability and plug-and-play capacity. It is assumed that such innovative systems will benefit not only system designers but also end users.

Keywords: AI, Deep learning, Pervasive intelligence, Wireless communication.

INTRODUCTION

With the increasing complexity of modern sectors such as healthcare, urban development, and manufacturing, as well as ongoing concerns about environmental stress, cognitive workload, and hygiene risks, the importance of technological advancements such as pervasive intelligence, evolutionary computation, and optimisation is becoming clear [1].

The purpose is to provide a full overview of these technologies while emphasising the relevance of their upcoming accompaniment and interactivity, resulting in a synergistic approach.

* **Corresponding author CSN Koushik:** Department of Electrical and Computer Engineering, New York University, Tandon School of Engineering, New York, USA; E-mail: koushikcsn@gmail.com

The current issue establishes the basis for evolving technology as a scientific chapter poised to form a classic industrial background [2 - 5]. While pervasiveness will deal with the increasing level of physical complexity, evolutionary and swarm solutions will deal with informational and organismal complexity.

This chapter intends to provide insight into how pervasive intelligence and evolutionary computation can be approached and collaborated upon using research approaches. The chapter has six sections in total. Following this introduction, the second and third sections will cover the theoretical foundations and interrelationships of pervasive intelligence, evolutionary computation, and optimisation. While the first two parts will discuss mutual enhancement and comparative criticism of these scientific concerns, the third will focus on how pervasive intelligence can primarily improve evolutionary algorithms. Following a preface regarding the importance of an indicative and durable solution in such an arbitrary setting, the transitional connection will be discussed in the following section.

FUNDAMENTALS OF PERVASIVE INTELLIGENCE

Pervasive Intelligence is a rapidly growing topic that encompasses the ability to incorporate artificial intelligence, smart management, and efficient data collecting and processing into daily items and situations. Widely deployed sensors, smartly coupled devices, extensive data analytics, and deliberate actions are only a few of the basic criteria for enabling such intelligence. Pervasive Intelligence's analytic focus must be on the numerous prospects for breakthrough technologies and personalised responses that will arise from merging and regulating other pervasive technologies [6 - 10]. Pervasive intelligence was only made possible by the widespread deployment of sensors in physical things, buildings, and urban components to collect and analyse the necessary data. As a result, the implementation of the IoT boosts Pervasive Intelligence by allowing any physical thing to detect and act, as well as interact with users. Ultra-fast, scalable, and energy-efficient data analytics are also required to support Pervasive Intelligence processing, which is based on vast data collected offline and in real time. Given all of these tremendous requirements, a user-centric management architecture is required to construct ubiquitous systems that provide end users with pervasive capabilities. To increase user-centric design, agent-oriented intelligent systems can be used, along with widely acknowledged technology-based stores and a flexible, open point of view. The user is at the centre of Pervasive Intelligence; hence, emphasis is placed on system relevance, connected services, fixed computations, and decision-making within client terminals. Communication performance and device utility should be updated in rapidly changing environments. Aside from the fixed contact between the user and the client terminal, context-aware technologies, which rely on online and real-time data analysis of the surrounding environment, improve the user's surroundings and the user experience, thanks to the rapid growth of sensors and IoT. By the end of the twentieth century, computer technology had advanced dramatically, ushering in a new era [11 - 15]. The interaction of the computer and the user made digital systems more accessible and easier. Over time, more and more systems with multiple functions have been implemented in homes, hospitals, telecom networks, shops, and enterprises. Pressing the decommissioning of workflow built for specific devices generated through the advanced sharing of information occurs between the process and management parameters. New quantum advances in data collection techniques and uncovering the hidden meanings of a wide range of interconnected and independent data are envisaged. The transfer of methodologies and techniques from various information flows into integrated applications will have a significant impact on the emerging cross-fertilization society.

Definition and Concept

Pervasive intelligence refers to agents' smooth and direct contact with their living environments, which are often invisible microprocessors. Pervasive intelligence is essentially the inconspicuous acceptance and control of the intelligent world that surrounds us. This is claimed to mean that people are continually working in, encountering, and accepting the benefits of the smart environment's intelligence in their daily lives, more or less subconsciously and usually. It presents a vision of increased focus on making entities around people exponentially smarter than they are today, as well as references to work linked with components of this vision, particularly those that naturally incorporate Evolutionary Computation [16 - 20]. Pervasive intelligence should be seen as equivalent to "ubiquitous" intelligence. Although this concept has been coined before, the first implementation that demonstrated the word occurred at a workshop. Since then, this concept has been applied in a variety of dense, context-aware settings.

The fundamental concept underpinning pervasive intelligence and virtual reality is very closely connected. In general, intelligent systems should be designed to give highly personalised services to their users based on a variety of factors, including personal goals, emotions, spontaneous acts, and preferences. The entire interactive approach must shift from the user questioning an otherwise passive and reactive environment to the environment surrounding this person, actively and adapting actively to the user's needs (*e.g.*, predicting them) to promote exceptional levels of safety: safe from a medical perspective and in the sense of socially agreeable behaviour, with the need for very high confidence in the behaviour of and the resources used by the intelligent environment. Once again, the most effective way to achieve this change in environmental participation is through a virtual reality environment with pervasive intelligence content, *i.e.*, a smart virtual world. While some machine learning approaches, including clustering, artificial neural networks, and collaborative filtering, have long been associated with ubiquitous intelligence techniques, the consideration of many evolutionary methods is much more recent.

Key Technologies

The fast advancement and widespread adoption of digital technology are altering the way humans see and interact with the physical environment. Over the last few decades, technologies from various disciplines have been developed, implemented, and used in computation and optimisation. As a result, a diverse spectrum of intelligent applications has emerged [21 - 25]. As digitisation continues, the combination of pervasive intelligence and new technology will be critical in fostering innovation in a variety of practice areas.

Pervasive intelligence is complex in that it uses various technologies to develop computational intelligence and optimisation in a complementary manner, allowing for the creation of numerous added-value applications and services in a variety of fields. However, such intelligence is absorbed by the digital environment, and it fails to realise the full potential of synergy between intelligence, computing, and optimisation. Future information and optimisation systems will be far more advanced, allowing for new collective intelligence possibilities [26 - 30]. The convergence of ubiquitous intelligence with rapidly expanding technologies, both inside and outside the factory, as well as their collaboration, has the potential to pave the way for significant advances in data-centric intelligence methods in real-time applications during the Internet of Things (IoT) era. The working principles of various critical technologies that provide pervasive intelligence are clearly defined.

EVOLUTIONARY COMPUTATION

Evolutionary Computation is a rich and mature paradigm for problem solving and, by extension, adaptive system design, consisting of a sequence of related algorithms technically known as evolutionary algorithms, concepts derived from them, and emerging theoretical principles. The idea of evolutionary algorithms is that they simulate a variety of methods for developing new designs (or solutions) to a given problem, all based on Darwinian principles. New designs are created by changing existing ones, which are typically preserved for further change in the following rounds of the process. Modifying designs typically entails one or more of the following: designing a selection operator, which determines which designs can be modified to create a new one; designing a variation operator, mutation, which introduces random change to a design; and (most importantly), designing a second variation operator, crossover, which combines information from two designs to create a new one. The separation between system and component is an important architectural aspect. Working components typically interact to provide emergent features at the organismal scale.

Adaptive systems translate sensor input to actuator commands, often supplemented with internal state or model information, describing a subset of the world's sensorimotor interactions. They deal with input/output mappings from within the system and have no application beyond the system's interface boundaries. In contrast, systems principles are acceptable for describing system traits that are not assigned to any of its components but develop as a result of their interactions. Adaptive systems are generally referred to as black box systems, with an emphasis on their input/output interactions. The simulation findings indicate that the system can adapt to a variety of conditions. However, the vast majority of evolvable systems research focuses on systems' parser-based I/O features. There is a remote possibility that useful shorthands and baselines will emerge from research into sensorimotor techniques in evolvable systems, but even if they do, they will most likely lack a concept of niche.

Introduction to EC

This section considers combining pervasive intelligence with recently emerging evolutionary computation and optimisation approaches. These include genetic algorithms, genetic programming, particle swarm optimisation, differential evolution, ant colony optimisation, artificial immune systems, and other biologically motivated techniques. In the grand design of pervasive intelligence, a chemical analogy is offered from the compounds that comprise the vast technologies. Bug, virus, code, and worm are the basic building blocks of programming, just as an atom is the fundamental unit of a chemical substance. The integration of implementations necessitates their placement in a ubiquitous, highly heterogeneous, and dispersed context. A community illustration for large technologies depicts the landscapes of networking, intelligence, and content in pervasive computing.

Evolutionary Computation (EC) can be traced back to the early stages of artificial intelligence and algorithm design suggestions. Following the initial idea of applying basic natural evolution concepts to a computing environment to address difficult optimisation or search issues, numerous computational models and realisations were gradually presented. Holland invented the first EC algorithms, Genetic Algorithms (GAs), in the early 1960s. Other bioinspired computational models later evolved genetic programming, evolutionary methods, and evolutionary programming. A significant feature of EC approaches is that they are founded on the findings of principles and hypotheses. The concepts take into account the fundamental aspects of natural evolution, which involve applying operators such as "selection, crossover, and mutation" to a population of individuals to generate optimal solutions to the problem at hand.

Genetic Algorithms

Evolutionary Computation (EC) refers to a set of computational approaches that simulate natural evolution processes such as selection, mutation, recombination, and survival of the fittest on a population of candidate solutions. EC has proven to be a versatile, durable, and generally effective solution to search and optimisation problems. A number of EC methods have been created under distinct paradigms, as well as algorithms and tactics. Genetic Algorithms (GAs) are one of the most important methods in EC, and this study focuses on them. GAs have been a popular method in EC, and some comprehension is required to grasp more complicated evolutionary techniques, as the key principles or elements of all such methods may be abstracted. Essentially, GAs function on Darwin's concept of natural selection, which states that the fittest individuals (those who are the best answer to the challenge) are more likely to produce children than the weaker ones. Two critical components of any GA-based model are the way individuals are encoded (or represented, as they are commonly referred to) and the fitness function, which evaluates the quality of potential solutions proposed by such individuals. The former substantially defines the space in which the search functions, the complexity of the tasks to which the search will be applied, and the overall feel of everything (not simply the more important aspects of task-specific information). The latter, the fitness function, frequently implies a quantitative evaluation of the distance between the solutions produced by the search and the theoretically best known, a difficult task because there is usually little or no information available on what is optimal in terms of the task (or the criteria are very complex and computationally intractable) [31 - 35]. Most real-world problems lack convergence proof (as will be the case here). GA paradigms also include (more or less consensually) a selection mechanism, crossover (recombination), mutation, and replacement. Furthermore, models, demands, strategies, and so on are based on these basic concepts, such as parallelism, adaptation, co-evolution, civilisation, and other paradigms. In addition, additional approaches, such as learning or local search methods, are frequently used in conjunction with GAs, and they may or may not be shared with or work on the same population as GA operators. There are various EC methods, including evolutionary strategies, evolutionary programming, classifier systems, genetic programming, and an increasing number of hybrids and alikes.

Evolution Strategies

Evolution Strategies (ES) are a set of techniques for continuous and discrete domains in evolutionary computation. They are separate from, but complementary to, well-known genetic algorithms. Simply defined, ES is concerned with "the way mutations are made" rather than "the way individuals interact and recombine" (the distinction between genetic algorithms and ES). At the heart of the ES technique are (real-valued) parameters that must be optimised. Typically, parameter optimisation is of a real value nature, which distinguishes ES from some other approaches. ESs have seen numerous practical applications, and new, more industrial-strength variants are constantly developing, indicating that the community recognises them as a genuine optimisation technique. One significant advantage of ESs is that they require fewer scaling steps than other processes to achieve acceptable results. This is particularly beneficial in large-scale optimisation. On large-scale issues, however, the bulk of GAs has a tendency to rapidly increase computational cost.

The most typical method of ES adaptation is to modify an n-dimensional mutation distribution, which frequently resembles a multivariate Gaussian. Mittelman's "cold and hot" mutation strengths are examined, theoretically analysed, and experimentally verified. When working with computationally intensive fitness evaluations, it is critical to conduct the optimisation process rapidly. Coevolution Particle Swarm Optimisation (CoPSO) using huge populations may be a viable alternative to bilaterally optimising a specific stopping parameter of the coevolutionary ES technique. After a good setup, CoPSO resembles most of the properties associated with the ES method and achieves results comparable to the ES.

Differential Evolution

This subsection is dedicated to differential evolution, a population-based optimisation algorithm based on evolutionary computing ideas. DE is a promising optimisation approach for generating numerical vectors to solve optimisation problems. It develops the population across generations and uses target vector differences to navigate the search space. During the iterative phase, the fitness of a candidate vector is compared to that of the donor vector to determine which is superior. DE is well-known for its simplicity, yet its efficiency makes it competitive in addressing complicated optimisation issues. Since its inception, the DE algorithm has been improved, hybridised, and employed in a variety of areas.

DE has several basic variants, including DE/rand/1/bin, DE/rand/1/exp, DE/rand/2/bin, DE/best/1/bin, DE/best/2/bin, and DE/best/1/exp. Different techniques exhibit distinct characteristics in terms of exploration and exploitation. The mechanisms of mutation, crossover, and selection in DE are presented, along with pseudocode for basic DEs and strategies. A comparative analysis suggests that DE has a high potential to rapidly converge to local optima while maintaining population variety, and it is competitive with other evolutionary approaches. The variable mutation and crossover rates enable DE, which may be changed based on optimization problems and experiments. The mutation technique, including a pair of different vectors, improves DE's ability to reach the target location. DE's unique search technique for each trial vector, *i.e.*, the target and base vectors, is better than stochastically selecting between the best and the remainder. Finally, the sample of applications reveals DE's widespread applicability in a variety of study domains.

It is believed that DE has numerous desirable benefits, including competitive convergence speed and robustness. DE successfully identified the global optimum of the difficult multimodal test functions. DE proved competitive ability in tackling bound-constrained optimisation tasks. A novel form enables DE to solve difficult multi-objective optimisation problems. Large-scale optimisation problems are addressed with DE in a hybrid form. The hybridisation approach used here mixes metaheuristic and deterministic algorithms. It achieves great levels of efficiency and robustness when addressing spherical, unimodal, and multimodal problems. When used in real-world applications, DE converges to high-quality solutions with quick processing times.

OPTIMIZATION TECHNIQUES

Optimisation techniques are commonly regarded as a field that has considerably enhanced problem-solving strategies. Their relevance has far-reaching ramifications for improving the performance and outcomes of a diverse variety of algorithms across multiple sciences. Understanding the underlying principles of optimisation is crucial for dealing with a wide range of decision-making processes. Furthermore, it is recognised that the combination of pervasive intelligence and these methodologies can considerably improve algorithm performance. The use of optimised solutions enables more efficient deployments, which take less time and energy, resulting in better outcomes. Optimisation points the way to a much broader range of approaches that can be developed. The goal is to classify the problem landscape into different categories so that a suite of optimisation strategies for complicated landscapes may be compared with algorithms. In ubiquitous intelligence systems, optimisation approaches can be employed for in-house development, such as robots or other applications. It may also help to improve the existing use of optimisation in evolutionary computation methodologies, which can be streamlined, supplemented, or made aware of to make better use of these resilient, flexible procedures. As a result, the metrics used to judge algorithm success will no longer be limited to outputs but will also include measures of marketplace handling, accessibility, and innovation. Furthermore, applying a learning optimisation methodology to a temporal problem can assist the larger community in a scenario where the most important resource is inexact, implying that a misperception can result in the most uncertain and chaotic markets.

Optimisation is at the centre of many decision-making processes, and its importance is supported by its widespread use [7]. The optimisation problem can be defined as follows: Let f be a function that transforms the set of choice variables into a real integer. Determine the maximum or minimum value of this function. Problems are typically split into two categories based on whether any limits are applied. As a result, they are categorised as unconstrained and constrained optimisation problems. The former class just considers the evaluated function f, while the search for the best solution occurs over a set of decision variables. The latter incorporates extra constraints based on the choice variables. There are several well-established optimisation approaches. Traditional optimisation approaches are typically classified into two categories: Linear Programming (LP) and Nonlinear Programming (NLP). However, a broader set of optimisation methods can be defined, such as quadratic programming, integer programming, and dynamic programming. A polynomial least-squares fit, while simple, can use a variety of functions. Despite their widespread use, classical approaches to optimisation cause a slew of issues, given the recent pace of technological advancement. Higher expectations are put on the efficiency and efficacy of an optimisation process. Many single-objective functions contain several local minima, making it challenging to identify the correct solution. Gradient-based approaches are ineffective in the presence of a large number of critical points, as they can only guarantee the local minimum. This also refers to the evaluation function's usually multimodal character, which has several local minima that may mislead any optimisation process. Furthermore, high-dimensional search spaces might emphasise the likelihood of trapping in local minima, and increasing the number of visits to the search space requires more time, which has a direct effect on computational intensity.

Introduction to Optimization

Optimization is the pivotal process for finding the most suitable solutions to almost all real-life computational problems. A significant portion of the spectrum is modelled as problems in science, engineering, and business, which equate to finding the optimum solution. The terms "optimization" and "best" refer to the process of selecting the best in different cases according to some standards. In a general framework, the best options may include maximum and minimum functions, such as minimum cost or maximum benefit. Optimization deals with finding variables or arguments that have minimum and maximum functions for various objectives and constraints. An option is the search space consisting of both nominal and interesting values of the investigated factors. Optimization always concentrates on the nominal values of the factors. Constraints are the conditions required to select an option. Improvements can be made to these constraints. If no solution satisfies the constraint and optimization objectives, the option is infeasible; otherwise, it is viable. In the optimization, it is still feasible to address both the functions and the constraints. Constraints may also depend on the selected variables. Constraints that depend on the optimal selection of the variables are called the bound constraints. Some optimization problems depend on both scalar and variable choices. Problems with both functions and constraints are called the optimization problem of minimal inequality. Different problems might be classified based on their characteristics.

Many single-objective and multi-objective optimization problems can be defined for the selection of this type of optimal solution, depending on the nature of the selection. When the optimization problem describes a single function, the function is called a single goal. For example, in most engineering design cases, the objective function is represented as cost, efficiency, or profit. The primary task in the single-objective optimization problem is the search for a feasible option that maximizes or minimizes the employed objective function. A collection of one or more objective purposes applies to the multi-objective optimization problem. Each aim is evaluated against any option, and no individual solution satisfies the best option in every virtue. The reasonable solution sets the Pareto front. The honorable set associates the Pareto front with the respective individual option in the environmental sense. Several applications in real engineering issues can be displayed in the scenario of a multi-objective optimization problem. These collection engineering applications are the obligation to design, basis, and coverage requirements in many focuses; Multi-objective Optimization Problems (MOPs) play a significant role in a design dependent form as the first style of the demands. A second kind of demand, depending on the optimal or designed system, is a supplementary desire. This kind of demand also leads to an MOP having a specified set of functions to be optimized along with a set of constraints.

This provides a tech-point review of traditional and recent tests in the Multi-Heuristic Evolutionary Optimization Techniques (MEOT) to address (in a multi-criterion environment) engineering and optimization problems. Given the thriving growth of these tools in the complete management of operations research, this discussion highlights the attempts to use these established techniques in COR [8].

Gradient-Based Methods

In pervasive intelligence, modeling systems and optimization techniques play essential roles in synthesizing desirable system models and finding optimal system configurations in terms of the performance driver indices. This work enlightens the fundamental methodologies related to system modeling and optimization techniques that have been widely applied to support pervasive intelligence formation and enable demand-driven system embodiment and configuration. Methodologically, the focus is on highlighting the synergies of pervasive intelligence that are co-learned with the state-of-the-art evolutionary computation and optimization techniques. The technological change agents, modeling mechanisms, and mathematical principles are synthesized in a generic yet comprehensive manner. The case studies are elaborated upon to demonstrate how applications of pervasive intelligence modeling and optimization techniques can deliver the desired pervasive intelligent services or systems subject to diversified constraints.

Over the past decades, intelligent investigation on system configurations, network specifications, or application designs regarding information systems, pervasive systems, and communication networks has been shaped as a major service sector. In this general market, users of system configuration services are faced with the challenging task of grasping a detailed understanding of the characteristics of the system they endeavor to design. Synergetic technologies, such as evolutionary computation and gradient systems, have been advocated to achieve fidelity and ease of use of the model and prove to be necessary in further understanding ubiquitous computational systems.

Metaheuristic Algorithms

The term metaheuristic algorithms denotes advanced problem-solving frameworks beyond classical optimization methods. In contrast to traditional algorithms, metaheuristics are algorithmic strategies designed to explore the search space and efficiently exploit it. They are characterized by being iterative and progressively improving a candidate solution about a given measure of quality. With adaptability, flexibility, and robustness, this class of algorithms has been associated with satisfactory approximate solutions over a wide range of applications. Their suitability allows for obtaining very competitive results in terms of solution quality, often improving over previous results, while keeping the computational burden. As a domain-independent approach, they only require a procedure for the evaluation and computation of the objective function of the candidate solutions.

Current algorithms frequently claim efficiency in dealing with a variety of problem typologies and disclosing complex structures, which is the reason behind their popularity and broad acceptance. Especially, the description of general and abstract optimization problems shows how a search space is defined over candidate solutions and by some explicitly defined or implicitly assumed operator. Given these elements, the capability of metaheuristics in tackling complex, large-scale, and combinatorial optimization problems will be investigated. Moreover, a categorization of the above-mentioned algorithms will be attempted, encompassing single and population-based metaheuristics, and algorithms that employ local or neighborhood search as a component. Attractions in metaheuristics stem from their unique approach to a wide variety of optimization tasks. They focus on searching for general procedures to effectively tackle complex and highly demanding optimization problems. In contrast, classical optimization methodologies are often problem-specific.

INTEGRATION OF PERVASIVE INTELLIGENCE AND EVOLUTIONARY COMPUTATION

In recent years, both pervasive intelligence and evolutionary computation have made it possible to create novel systems that interact with people, understand their intentions, and give recommendations to adapt to dynamically changing user or system requirements. The intersection of these domains and the opportunities and challenges left for the convergence of pervasive intelligence with computational intelligence, especially evolutionary computation and its numerous optimization systems, are addressed. The key role of pervasive intelligence in adapting the modus operandi, the computational resources, the optimization parameters, *etc*., to achieve intelligent and efficient optimization systems is also examined. In addition, application examples are provided in various fields. This investigation sheds light on an exciting interdisciplinary space that may open new horizons for the research and development of innovative, pervasive, and evolutionary intelligent solutions.

Results from recent and ongoing research on the synergy of pervasive intelligence with various evolutionary and other optimization systems are presented. The research has focused on a vast number of application domains, so only a subset of them is selected to highlight the possible transformative impacts of this interdisciplinary research. In addition, the results from two recently finalized projects are summarized. On one hand, these projects are expected to contribute to the evolution of emerging services and applications for devices, and on the other hand, significant results have been achieved by integrating pervasive intelligence in the system design phase with various deployed pervasive systems that continuously adapt and evolve. The results discussed cover aspects related both to the advances of variants, architecture, and machinery, and to the results of the intelligent adaptive applications of these advances integrated in different pervasive domains.

Two sponsored Special Issues offer a broader view of some of the research outcomes. Furthermore, extensive future research opportunities and challenges are identified for encouraging the fruitful collaboration between the communities of pervasive intelligence, neuromorphic computing, information fusion, and Symbolic Artificial Intelligence systems to complete the landscape for practical applications. In addition, a number of prototypes have been developed in practical experiments on the merger of these intelligent systems with other systems. Finally, the important issues of in combination with pervasive intelligence in terms of transparency, explainability, veracity, security, and privacy, as well as the future direction for research and technology in this exciting field on the convergence of pervasive computation, are discussed. These concern research directions for providing transparent and controllable intelligent systems exchanging knowledge, intention, or strategic prioritization of forming decisions between the case, their uses, designers, or backers. In this way, an objective path can be provided for designing trustworthy, ethically correct, and acceptable pervasive evolutionary intelligent systems that are an important key for expanding the success of this interdisciplinary field.

Challenges and Opportunities

Pervasive intelligence has emerged as an important element of the present digital transformation era. On the other hand, the application of pervasive intelligence in designing complex adaptive systems could greatly benefit from using bio-inspired computation and optimization approaches. This viewpoint tries to provide an overall analysis of challenges and opportunities when pervasive intelligence is in synergy with evolutionary computation and other optimization techniques. Specific issues include data handling, computational efficiency, algorithmic complexity, memory length effect, hybrid models, adaptive mechanisms, and integrity validation procedures. At the same time, a variety of emerging application potentials will be addressed, like responsive systems, explainable

Artificial Intelligence technologies, the use of digital twins, innovative experience of user services, and adaptive operator tuning strategies. Moreover, ethical aspects will be touched upon, such as user privacy rights, potential bias of evolutionary algorithms, and the need for overall design frameworks able to support the realization of an effective emerging technology convergence.

The view of integrating pervasive intelligence with bio-inspired computation and complex adaptive systems, which includes both evolutionary computation and other optimization approaches, like swarm intelligence, artificial immune systems, artificial neural networks, reinforcement learning, genetic programming, artificial endocrine networks, fuzzy logic, ant colony optimization, tabu search, *etc.* However, a comprehensive convergence of pervasive intelligence with bio-inspired computation and optimization techniques can have both a wide scope and a transformative impact, and this strategy is suggested to go beyond previously published studies.

Applications in Various Fields

A synergy between pervasive intelligence, pervasive systems, and evolutionary computation is shown to have far-reaching applications in a diversity of fields. Resulting impactful applications in fields including healthcare, transportation, and smart cities are demonstrated through summaries and descriptions of related studies. The adaptability of evolutionary algorithms in dynamic environments enabled by pervasive systems is discussed, and corresponding applications are shown that manage resources, improve efficiency, and engage users.

Thereby, as evolutionary algorithms are inherently capable of adaptation to dynamic environments, they can be utilized efficiently in systems empowered with pervasive intelligence. The adaptability of pervasive system-enabling evolutionary algorithms in dynamic environments is discussed through several application examples, resulting in the steady state of resource allocation, improvement of efficiency by adapting to faults, and stimulation of user participation through dynamic game rule customization. Pervasive systems connected with IoT and social networking technologies have the potential to make evolutionary techniques more adaptive and intelligent. However, resource management is needed in implementing evolutionary algorithms in pervasive systems. As it maintains a sustainable and steady state of resource allocation, the performance of the evolutionary algorithm in long-term operation can be guaranteed even in a dynamic environment [9, 10].

Thus, it can be wisely exploited to encourage user participation, gaining benefits from adaptive interpretability and customizability. Interacting with users, therefore, is important for applications and also poses challenges. Technological trends, including the development of IoT, social networking services, cloud computing, and smart devices, are important in shaping the direction of relevant integrations. They are motivated by the convergence of each other, the growth of smartphone and tablet devices used for online activities, and growing societal needs such as sustainable development, monitoring of the environment, and utilization of local resources. On the other hand, as in several areas of technology and systems convergence, the relevant studies also suggest that there is increasing complexity in developing and implementing relevant applications. In the context of cyber-physical systems, smart environments, or smart cities, some of the major challenges include ensuring that standards and protocols for interoperability are developed and that scaling issues are addressed without central management strategies.

FUTURE DIRECTIONS AND EMERGING TRENDS

Future research could integrate quantum-inspired algorithms, post-quantum cryptography, and large-scale IoT optimization.

This advanced era of industrial revolution 4.0 is shaping new research avenues to implement intelligent algorithms in every phenomenon; wireless technologies are being improved day by day, which design strategies of intense smart systems to upgrade the living standards. Additionally, wide-ranging opportunities are associated with wireless technologies, such as edge computing and real-time processing. Therefore, noteworthy advances have occurred in the past few years by exploring pervasive intelligence and computational studies for advancements in smart environments, such as fostering intelligent techniques toward smart industry, traffic, and high-performance devices like home appliances and security cameras [1]. Shortly, exciting intelligent schemes and computational paradigms will reshape approaches to everyday life for humans, rendering routine operations proficient. Smart, portable devices are connected with wireless technologies, contributing to advances in pervasive intelligence engineered by evolutionary algorithms toward smart environments. New, prospective directions and associated emerging trends are highlighted, corresponding to pervasive intelligence and evolutionary computation studies using intelligent systems to advance a smart way of life. Technological evolutions in the communication era expedite sophisticated computational schemes with wireless system enhancement to analyze secure cyber-physical social environments *via* an evolutionary technique setup. Rapid variations in Artificial Intelligence (AI) have fostered many operations in everyday life and have played vital roles in business advancements. Competitive benchmark enhancements of evolutionary computation are seen in many well-developed areas of wide-ranging applications with industrial strategies, including smart industry, transportation, and consumer granularity devices. In-depth learning has achieved remarkable advances in recent years regarding numerous research areas and competitive tasks; hence, a bipolar forum has drawn attention to the intersection of real-world tasks like pervasive systems. In such an environment, pervasive intelligence fueled by the PAI paradigm plays a crucial role in profiling the advancement of in-depth learning with commonplace applications. However, there may be demanding, deliberate computational and technological advancements that shall accomplish a truthful application of modeling a pervasive sense for learning landscapes [9].

CONCLUSION AND SUMMARY

Our society and many aspects of everyday life are gradually becoming ever more intelligent and pervasive. A broad spectrum of complex systems, from transportation to infrastructure, home appliances, and entertainment, among many others, will be increasingly pervaded by intelligence, adapting to the tasks they are intended to perform and the user practices they implement. Such proliferation is leading to pervasive intelligence, a challenging area for the market as well as for research and development. Evolutionary computation and optimization are the methodologies of choice when addressing and managing complex systems for which insufficient knowledge is available, and only a limited budget is allowed for analysis and design. Their application is proliferating in the pursuit of delivering good solutions to complicated problems that resist classic, exact, and/or simple design.

The synergistic exploration of intelligent methodologies and their pervasive deployment within systems and applications is likely to be a smart policy to make both survive and thrive in the market, as the availability of more and more intelligence-decorated objects becomes a commodity, transparent, concealed, beautiful, and effective human interaction becomes a must. The analysis and design of pervasive intelligence will challenge interdisciplinary research on the integration of proper hardware and software tools, embodying innovative algorithmic solutions and software implementations to ensure the transformative potential of the prototyped systems and applications, while obtaining a thorough exploration of these innovative, interdisciplinary paradigms. Careful analysis of elegance, beauty, and effectiveness in human-object interaction will be performed, focusing on both the objects of prosumer culture and the algorithms implemented within. The system-wise analysis of the impact of such interaction on the emerging complex artificial and natural systems and its deployment on the optimized design of intelligent functionalities will be undertaken. The results, validated over paradigmatic case studies, will deliver general guiding techniques for individuals working in the development and delivery of intelligent objects, customizing their characteristics to match their intended function and the accepted design quality, performance, and costs.

REFERENCES

[1] E. Baccour, N. Mhaisen, A. A. Abdellatif, A. Mohamed, M. Hamdi, and M. Guizani, "Pervasive AI for IoT applications: A survey on resource-efficient distributed artificial intelligence", *IEEE Commun. Surv. Tutor.,* vol. 24, no. 4, pp. 2366-2418, 2022. [http://dx.doi.org/10.1109/COMST.2022.3200740]

[2] A. Lundgren, "Technological Innovation and Industrial Evolution: The Emergence of Industrial Networks", In: *Stockholm School of Economics*, 1991.

[3] G. N. Von Tunzelmann, "Technology and Industrial Progress: The Foundations of Economic Growth", In: *Edward Elgar Publishing*, 1995.

[4] G. Dosi, "The Foundations of Complex Evolving Economies: Part One: Innovation, Organization, and Industrial Dynamics", In: *Oxford University Press*, 2023.

[5] J. S. Metcalfe, "Equilibrium and evolutionary foundations of competition and technology policy: new perspectives on the division of labour and the innovation process", In: *The Evolutionary Analysis of Economic Policy*, 2003, pp. 162-190.

[6] A. Dupont, "Intelligence for the twenty-first century", In: *Twenty-First Century Intelligence*, 2013, pp. 15-39.

[7] A. Vaseashta, "Advanced sciences convergence based methods for surveillance of emerging trends in science, technology, and intelligence", *Foresight,* vol. 16, no. 1, pp. 17-36, 2014. [http://dx.doi.org/10.1108/FS-10-2012-0074]

[8] R. Girasa, "Artificial Intelligence as a Disruptive Technology: Economic Transformation and Government Regulation", In: *Springer Nature*, 2020.

[9] D. Preuveneers, and E. Ilie-Zudor, "The intelligent industry of the future: A survey on emerging trends, research challenges and opportunities in Industry 4.0", *J. Ambient Intell. Smart Environ.,* vol. 9, no. 3, pp. 287-298, 2017. [http://dx.doi.org/10.3233/AIS-170432]

[10] V. Tsiatsis, S. Karnouskos, J. Holler, D. Boyle, and C. Mulligan, "Internet of Things: Technologies and Applications for a New Age of Intelligence", In: *Academic Press*, 2018.

[11] J. Chin, V. Callaghan, and S. B. Allouch, "The Internet-of-Things: Reflections on the past, present and future from a user-centered and smart environment perspective", *J. Ambient Intell. Smart Environ.,* vol. 11, no. 1, pp. 45-69, 2019. [http://dx.doi.org/10.3233/AIS-180506]

[12] S. Kumar, P. Tiwari, and M. Zymbler, "Internet of Things is a revolutionary approach for future technology enhancement: a review", *J. Big Data,* vol. 6, no. 1, p. 111, 2019. [http://dx.doi.org/10.1186/s40537-019-0268-2]

[13] M. Kuniavsky, "Smart Things: Ubiquitous Computing User Experience Design", In: *Elsevier*, 2010.

[14] "Internet of Things: Converging Technologies for Smart Environments and Integrated Ecosystems", In: *River Publishers*, 2013.

[15] S. Greengard, "The Internet of Things", In: *MIT Press*, 2021.

[16] H. Cao, M. Wachowicz, R. Richard, and C. H. Hsu, "Fostering new vertical and horizontal IoT applications with intelligence everywhere", *Collective Intell.,* vol. 2, no. 4, 2023. [http://dx.doi.org/10.1177/26339137231208966]

[17] A. E. Eiben, and J. Smith, "From evolutionary computation to the evolution of things", *Nature,* vol. 521, no. 7553, pp. 476-482, 2015.
[http://dx.doi.org/10.1038/nature14544]

[18] R. C. Eberhart, and Y. Shi, "Computational Intelligence: Concepts to Implementations", In: *Elsevier*, 2011.

[19] S. Zhu, T. Yu, T. Xu, H. Chen, S. Dustdar, S. Gigan, and Y. Pan, "Intelligent computing: the latest advances, challenges, and future", *Intell. Comput.,* vol. 2, p. 0006, 2023.
[http://dx.doi.org/10.34133/icomputing.0006]

[20] A. E. Eiben, and J. E. Smith, "Introduction to Evolutionary Computing", In: *Springer*, 2015.

[21] A. E. Eiben, and M. Schoenauer, "Evolutionary computing", *Inform. Proc. Lett,* vol. 82, no. 1, pp. 1-6, 2002.
[http://dx.doi.org/10.1016/S0020-0190(02)00204-1]

[22] S. Zhu, T. Yu, T. Xu, H. Chen, S. Dustdar, S. Gigan, and Y. Pan, "Intelligent computing: the latest advances, challenges, and future", *Intell. Comput.,* vol. 2, p. 0006, 2023.
[http://dx.doi.org/10.34133/icomputing.0006]

[23] L. Goel, "An extensive review of computational intelligence-based optimization algorithms: trends and applications", *Soft Comput.,* vol. 24, no. 21, pp. 16519-16549, 2020.
[http://dx.doi.org/10.1007/s00500-020-04958-w]

[24] J. Tang, G. Liu, and Q. Pan, "A review on representative swarm intelligence algorithms for solving optimization problems: Applications and trends", *IEEE/CAA J. Autom. Sinica,* vol. 8, no. 10, pp. 1627-1643, 2021.
[http://dx.doi.org/10.1109/JAS.2021.1004129]

[25] R. Iqbal, F. Doctor, B. More, S. Mahmud, and U. Yousuf, "Big Data analytics and Computational Intelligence for Cyber–Physical Systems: Recent trends and state of the art applications", *Future Gener. Comput. Syst.,* vol. 105, pp. 766-778, 2020.
[http://dx.doi.org/10.1016/j.future.2017.10.021]

[26] M. C. Schut, "On model design for simulation of collective intelligence", *Inf. Sci.,* vol. 180, no. 1, pp. 132-155, 2010.
[http://dx.doi.org/10.1016/j.ins.2009.08.006]

[27] D. H. Wolpert, and K. Tumer, "An introduction to collective intelligence", *arXiv preprint,* p. cs/9908014, 1999.

[28] I. Lykourentzou, D. J. Vergados, and V. Loumos, "Collective intelligence system engineering", In: *Proc. Int. Conf. Manage. Emergent Digit. Ecosystems (MEDES)*, 2009, pp. 134-140.

[29] S. Suran, V. Pattanaik, and D. Draheim, "Frameworks for collective intelligence: A systematic literature review", *ACM Comput. Surv.,* vol. 53, no. 1, 2020.
[http://dx.doi.org/10.1145/3368986]

[30] S. Buckingham Shum, K. Aberer, A. Schmidt, S. Bishop, P. Lukowicz, S. Anderson, and D. Helbing, "Towards a global participatory platform: democratising open data, complexity science and collective intelligence", *Eur. Phys. J. Spec. Top.,* vol. 214, no. 1, pp. 109-152, 2012.
[http://dx.doi.org/10.1140/epjst/e2012-01690-3]

[31] A. Lambora, K. Gupta, and K. Chopra, "Genetic algorithm-A literature review", In: *Proc. 2019 Int. Conf. Mach. Learn. Big Data Cloud Parallel Comput. (COMITCon)*, 2019, pp. 380-384.

[32] T. V. Mathew, "Genetic algorithm", *Report submitted at IIT Bombay,* vol. 53, pp. 18-19, 2012.

[33] S. Forrest, "Genetic algorithms", *ACM Comput. Surv.,* vol. 28, no. 1, pp. 77-80, 1996.
[http://dx.doi.org/10.1145/234313.234350]

[34] S. Katoch, S. S. Chauhan, and V. Kumar, "A review on genetic algorithm: past, present, and future",

Multimedia Tools Appl., vol. 80, no. 5, pp. 8091-8126, 2021. [http://dx.doi.org/10.1007/s11042-020-10139-6]

[35] L. Haldurai, T. Madhubala, and R. Rajalakshmi, "A study on genetic algorithm and its applications", *Int. J. Comput. Sci. Eng.,* vol. 4, no. 10, pp. 139-143, 2016.

CHAPTER 7

Adaptive Firefly Algorithm to Find the Optimal Number of Features in IIOT Data in Detection of Cyber Security Attacks

Sri Silpa Padmanabhuni[1], **Padmaja Grandhe**[2,*], **Swathi Buragadda**[3] and **T V Divya**[4]

[1] *Department of Computer Science and Engineering, PSCMR College of Engineering & Technology, Vijayawada, Andhra Pradesh, India*

[2] *Department of Computer Science and Engineering, Sreenidhi University, Hyderabad, Telangana, India*

[3] *Department of Computer Science and Engineering, Lakireddy Balireddy College of Engineering, Mylavaram, Andhra Pradesh, India*

[4] *Department of Computer Science and Engineering, Sreyas Institute of Engineering and Technology, Bandlaguda, Hyderabad, Telangana, India*

Abstract: Many machine learning researchers believe that poor prediction results from a model are caused by either noisy data or creating a model with the incorrect method, but the reality is that the ideal parameters necessary are selected based on the dataset. So, rather than standard methodologies, the proposed research focuses on feature selection using genetic algorithms. Optimisation is the concept of determining the best values for the parameters connected with the learning process. During the optimisation process, the algorithm takes some initial values and continuously updates the position, velocity, and other parameters. Firefly is a metaheuristic algorithm that computes the fly's attraction using the Euclidean distance. The attractiveness of the suggested algorithm, the adaptive firefly algorithm, is computed using the KNN algorithm, with K as one of the objective functions and the second objective function being to reduce the number of features. The firefly algorithm's key components are light intensity and brightness, both of which are exponential.

Keywords: Adaptive firefly, Bio-inspired, Correlation, KNN, Objective function, Random search, RFE.

[*] **Corresponding author Padmaja Grandhe:** Department of Computer Science and Engineering, Sreenidhi University, Hyderabad, Telangana, India; E-mail: padmaja.g@suh.edu.in

Shruti Bhargava Choubey & Yogesh Shrivastava (Eds.)

INTRODUCTION

The IoT SCADA dataset is a well-known dataset for cybersecurity research. To begin, the fundamental component of supervised machine learning is 'features'. The data analysis shows that a few attributes have no impact on the target variable [1]. Traditionally, researchers employed correlation or PCA analysis to discover key traits [2]. Performing correlation analysis on the IIoT dataset yields 23 attributes. Table **1** displays the most relevant qualities based on the association.

Table 1. Correlation analysis.

S.No	Feature Name	Correlation
1	StartTime	0.356
2	SrcAddr	0.4671
3	Mean	0.45
4	Sport	0.51
5	Dport	0.26
6	SrcLoad	0.56
7	Load	0.55
8	SrcRate	0.56
9	Rate	0.56
10	pLoss	0.57
11	SlntPkt	0.37
12	Dur	0.3
13	TcpRtt	0.28
14	Sum	0.46
15	Min	0.46
16	Max	0.37
17	sTtl	0.37
18	dTtl	0.83
19	dlpId	0.39
20	RunTime	0.46
21	SrcJitAct	0.46
22	Traffic	0.99
23	Target	1

Similarly, existing techniques such as RFE have 24 properties; nevertheless, the number of attributes required could be lowered further [3]. So, the suggested study employs a genetic algorithm to optimise the number of characteristics. In an optimisation algorithm, the model must first construct an objective function before determining the set of input variables that meet the specified function and checking for constraint satisfaction. In general, the genetic algorithm can do global optimisation or local optimisation. Since the proposed research wants to find the best parameter based on the given dataset, it chooses "local optimisation" [4]. The bio-inspired algorithms are categorised into three types, which are shown in Fig. (**1**).

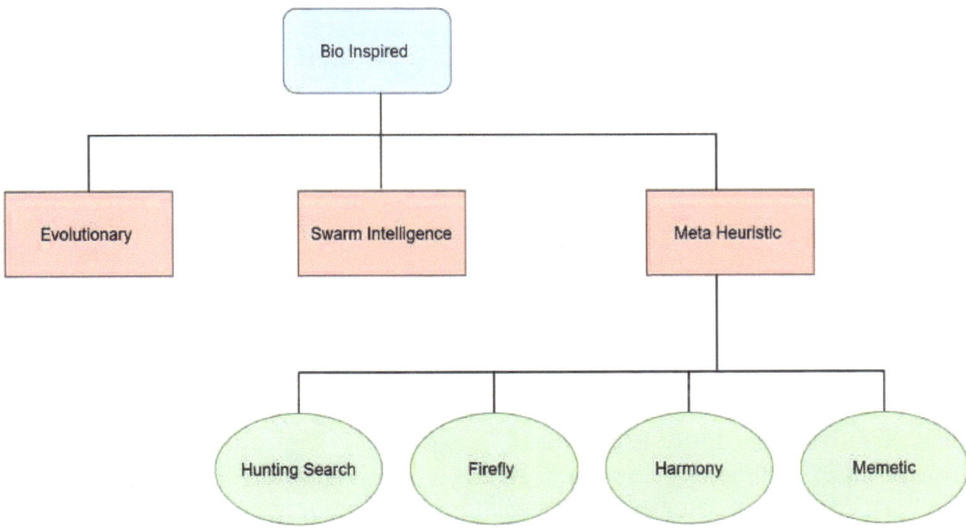

Fig. (1). Classification of bio-inspired algorithms.

The firefly algorithm is known for its randomized local search based on the attractiveness of other flies. Because of their unique flashing property, they can attract their species as well as other species. The attractiveness is proportional to the distance between the files [5].

LITERATURE REVIEW

Sadeem Dheyaa Shamsi *et al.* [1] reported that the dataset focuses on Secondary Users (SUs) operating in a cognitive radio network that perform real-time spectrum detection and routing operations. HCSS is a routing protocol designed specifically for CRAHN networks, bringing forward adaptive and efficient routing solutions. This technique combines fundamental aspects of the Spectrum-Aware SSR protocol with SARP capabilities. The network starts by enabling spectrum sensing in all nodes. The network distribution enables neighbouring nodes to create a cooperative spectrum availability map. An active communication source delivers route requests for data transfer, including information about the currently available spectrum bands. The network's intermediary nodes assess the request while taking into account the current spectrum circumstances before altering the routing path. When the route arrives at its destination, it sends a route reply to the source node, indicating which route was chosen. After receiving the transmission instruction, the source node begins transferring data utilising the defined spectrum band. The transmission method continuously checks spectrum consumption in order to react by switching channels when primary user activity is recognised. The approach improves spectrum availability, communication efficiency, and throughput by detecting and adapting to changing spectrum circumstances in CRAHN networks.

Shudhamati Mali *et al.* [2] stated that the UNSW-NB15 dataset, the ISCXTor2016 dataset, and the phishing dataset are all used to classify network traffic. The suggested method distinguishes between various forms of encrypted network traffic using machine learning and deep learning models. To make these datasets usable in training processes, the team performs three important preparation stages, beginning with feature extraction, followed by normalisation and missing value handling algorithms. Machine learning techniques used in the traffic categorisation process include SVM, random forest, decision trees, and k-NN, as well as deep learning models such as CNNs and RNNs. The models gain spatial-temporal pattern identification capabilities as they train on the supplied datasets. CNNs extract hierarchical data characteristics, whereas RNNs specialise in detecting temporal patterns appropriate for encrypted traffic evaluation. Researchers assess the benefits of combining CNN and RNN to improve feature extraction and classification performance. After training, the models are optimised using hyperparameter tuning methods such as grid search and random search. Cross-validation techniques avoid overfitting while keeping the model robust.

G. Sripriyanka *et al.* [3] used the KDD Cup'99 dataset, which includes 4.9 million connection vectors and 41 attributes indicating regular network activity or various forms of attacks. SHA benefits from an HFA approach that identifies and prevents DDoS attacks during operation. Initially, the system collects header information from network packets before using it to calculate network delay and packet loss. The feature extraction module uses network flow key parameters, including packet number and attack origins. The detection method benefits from the HFA, which combines PSO and FA functionality. Fireflies serve as solutions in a variety of search locations, shifting places based on attraction and brightness intensities at random for exploration reasons. This method combines FA's efficient local search with PSO's global exploration power, increasing both precision and speed. Each firefly's position is adjusted in real time using a strategy that optimises the detection of hazardous network traffic. The trained model detects patterns in DDoS attacks by analysing extracted features. After detecting the attack characteristics, the system employs blocking features against malicious nodes to manage the attack.

Ezz EI-Din Hemdan *et al.* [4] stated that the dataset contains two simulated industrial control systems: a triplex pump system and a gearbox system. They generate multi-class fault scenarios for the pump dataset (240 samples) and the gearbox system (208 samples). The suggested methodology uses a hybrid voting-GA-ML model to detect multi-class faults in IIoT systems. The operation begins with data collection from digitised twins of the triplex pump and gearbox system. Before the raw data can be analysed, it must undergo preprocessing treatments such as normalisation and cleaning, as well as the extraction of key features. The voting ensemble learning method implements machine learning classifiers such as KNN, CART, and RF. The fault detection accuracy improves by combining predictions from numerous different classifiers inside an ensemble learning framework. The GA system optimises ensemble model parameters to improve predictive performance. Once pre-processed, the data is used in training to identify various defect classes in industrial systems. Following training, the model is tested on two industrial datasets to measure its accuracy and performance in fault classification tasks.

Lan Chen *et al.* [5] reported that the twelve public anomaly detection datasets include cases from industrial control systems, bearing problems, attribution networks, and extra fields. The proposed anomaly detection method utilised GASN-based Unsupervised Anomaly Detection. The GASN technique operates in two steps. To begin its training phase, a GAN requires a dataset containing a small number of aberrant objects. During training, the generator generates mappings from noise to synthetic information that accurately represent the normal pattern distribution of the majority of the original dataset's objects. The discriminator acts while being taught to distinguish between natural and computer-generated information. The generator's goal is to generate synthetic data that looks exactly like genuine normal data in order to mimic the normal distribution of typical objects. The synthetic neighbours analysis technique is used in the second stage of processing.

According to Md Alamin Talukder *et al.* [6], the WSN-DS and TON-IoT provide simulated network environments that emulate Wireless Sensor Networks and IoT systems. A methodology includes KMS for data balance. PCA for dimensionality reduction, and RFC as a machine learning classifier for intrusion detection. The researchers collect data using both the WSN-DS and TON-IoT datasets. The data preparation stage comprises both feature standardisation using StandardScaler and label encoding to change categorical attributes. K-Means-SMOTE handles unbalanced datasets by clustering them into groups and creating fake samples to improve minority class representation. The applied strategy increases the depiction of attack types in the data. PCA processing reduces the dataset's dimensionality, preserving the most relevant features while improving efficiency and reducing redundancy. RFC is the primary classifier for intrusion detection, obtaining training data from the processed information.

As stated by Milos Antonijevic *et al.* [7], the CICIoT2023 dataset includes 33 attack types that scan an IoT network with 105 connected devices. The methodology creates a two-level AI system with Convolutional Neural Networks. CatBoost and LightGBM ensemble classifiers that are optimised using an upgraded Chimp Optimisation Algorithm version called ISA-ChOA. The information collection method starts with gathering IoT network traffic data from the CICIoT2023 dataset. The preprocessed data was used to generate different parts for training and testing. In the first step of operation, a CNN extracts key features from the provided dataset. Following extraction, the initial layer passes the generated features to the second layer, which contains both CatBoost and LightGBM classifiers for classification algorithms. The ISA-ChOA metaheuristics technique is used for CNN hyperparameter optimisation as well as classifier training. The revised method begins with increased population variety control during system setup and includes a smart rollback procedure as a preventive measure against stagnation occurrence. The suggested model is trained using the CICIoT2023 data pieces and then evaluated.

Balamurali *et al.* [8] reported that the dataset was created using simulations of WSNs designed for IoT applications. WSN technologies are used in healthcare and security, and they require optimal energy management, accurate data transmission, and a longer network lifetime. The new methodology is called NHM-HCS. The system begins by establishing a WSN-based IoT network with sensor nodes performing three functions: detecting data, processing sensed data, and data transmission operations. The raw data gathered by sensor nodes is reduced in size using a Hadamard matrix application of compressive sensing technology. Reduced energy and bandwidth utilisation is obtained. Each node group is divided into clusters, with the cluster head in charge of data gathering and transmission. The cluster head selection optimisation technique combines PSO and GWO algorithms. The collaboration of these algorithms improves the network's energy efficiency, resulting in a prolonged operating time. The compressive sensing mechanism enables the network transfer of sparse data to the sink node, which reconstructs it using Hadamard matrix processing. Table **2** presents how the system makes dynamic changes based on node energy levels throughout the process to obtain the optimal operational performance.

Table 2. Existing approaches with their limitations.

Author	Algorithm	Merits	Demerits	Accuracy
Sadeem Dheyaa Shamsi *et al* [1]	HCSS	Efficiency in routing.	Not efficient for large networks	98.7%
Shudhamati Mali *et al* [2]	ENTC	Spatial & Temporal patterns are efficient in networking traffic	High computational cost.	97.7%
G. Sripriyanka *et al* [3]	HFA	By reducing computational complexity, the detection was fast.	Evolving attack patterns may have limited while faces.	94.9%
Ezz EI-Din Hemdan *et al* [4]	Hybrid Voting GA-ML	Capability while detecting a fault.	Optimization was not appropriate.	98.7%
Lan Chen *et al* [5]	GASN	No need for training labelled data.	For training the GAN, the cost was high.	9.93% - AUC
Md. Alamin Talukder *et al* [6]	KMS+PCA+RFC	Class imbalances were efficient.	Data balancing and dimensionality are reduced.	99.9%
Milos Antonijevic *et al* [7]	ISA-ChOA	Classification & extraction of features are efficient.	Optimizing multiple layers is computationally intensive.	99.8%
Balamurali *et al* [8]	NHM-HCS	Lifespan and energy were efficient while improving the network.	Computational cost.	

PROPOSED METHODOLOGY

WUSTL-IIoT-2021 is a SCADA that stores data for cybersecurity research. This dataset employed scan tools to detect network threats and divided the data into two classes: normal and abnormal. Fig. (**2**) shows the statistics depending on class labels.

The Industrial IoT dataset consists of 49 attributes, with more normal examples and fewer attack samples, resulting in imbalanced data; yet, these types of datasets aid in accurately dealing with real-world data. The dataset represents attack samples as 1 and normal samples as 0. The dataset includes some missing, anomalous, and corrupted data. As a result, the proposed approach effectively cleans the data, as described below.

(i) Label Encoder. Because computers only understand binary language, any machine learning algorithm can comprehend numerical quantities. The cybersecurity data includes one crucial feature, "Traffic" as a string, which defines the classification of various sorts of attacks. The IIoT dataset includes four types of attacks: Command Injection, DoS, Reconnaissance, and Backdoor. Fig. (**3**) shows the conversion of the traffic attribute.

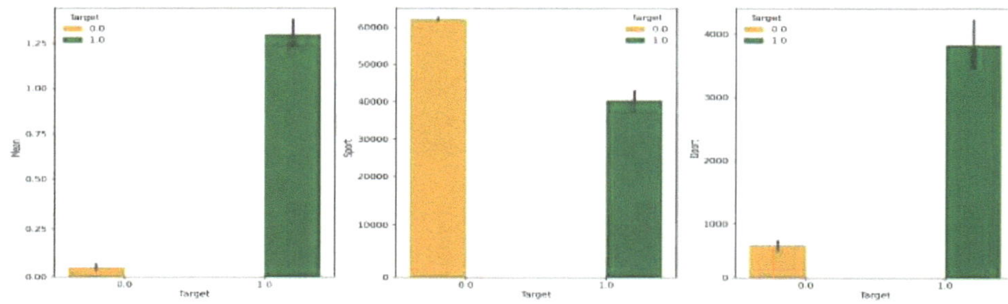

(a) Mean, Source Port, and Destination Port Compared against Target Label

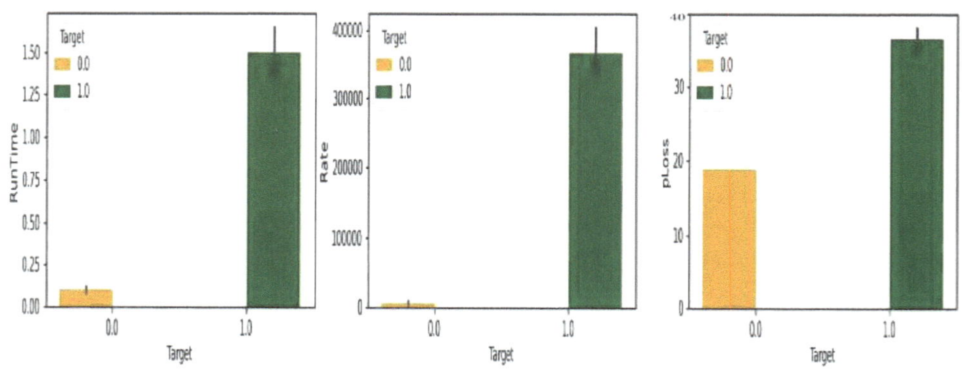

(b) RunTime, Rate, and pLoss Compared against Target Label

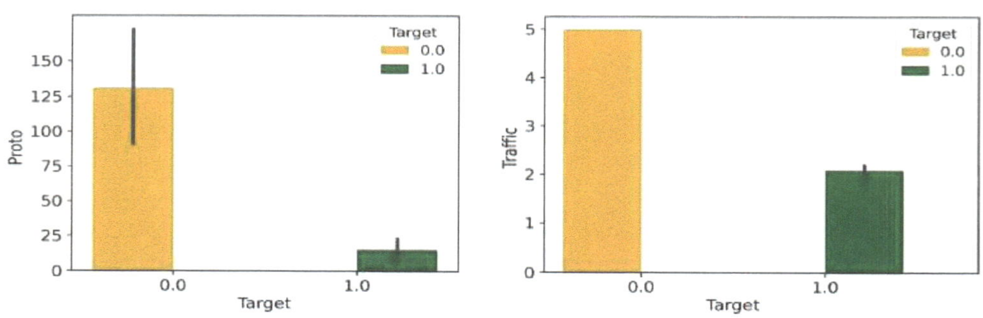

(c) Protocol and Traffic Compared against Target Label

Fig. (2). Statistics of the dataset based on class labels.

Traffic	Traffic
normal	5
normal	5
normal	5
DoS	2
normal	5
...	...
normal	5
normal	5
normal	5
normal	5
normal	5
Before Encoding Label	**After Encoding Label**

Fig. (3). Label encoding process on traffic data.

(i) Handling Missing Data: Using the imputer library, the proposed research fills all the missing data using the mean strategy for that corresponding attribute and makes all the columns free from missing values. The overall proposed architecture of the adaptive algorithm is shown in Fig. (**4**).

The major step of the proposed research is to reduce the number of features by adding adaptive properties to the most important characteristics of the firefly algorithm. The following section describes the assumptions and modifications that are applied to the parameters of the algorithm. All these parameters suggest that brightness attracts the flies because of their flashing nature.

(a) Defining Initial Position: The initial positions of the particles are based on the lower and upper bounds assumed by the algorithm as shown in equation (**1**). The initial posit.

$$\text{posit}Int\_Pos[i,j] = lb[0,j] + \ (ub[0,j] - lb[0,j]) * rand(1,j) \qquad \textbf{(1)}$$

Where,

j represents the number of dimensions, *i.e.*, 49

rand(1,j) generates a random number between 1 and 49

Int_Pos[0,0]= -5+(5-(-5)) 22

=-5+220dY215

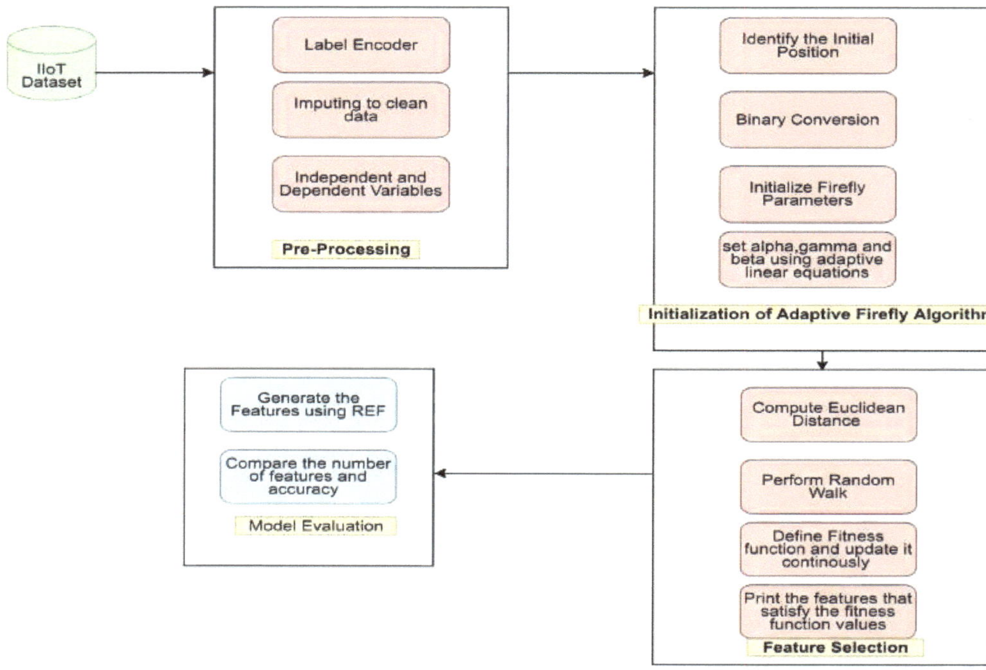

Fig. (4). Proposed Architecture for an Adaptive Algorithm for Feature Selection.

After getting the initial position values, to convert them into binary values, the proposed algorithm sets a threshold value; any initial position value greater than the threshold is assigned the value 1; otherwise, the initial position is considered as 0. The computation for 4 dimensions and 3 iterations, along with initial position and binary conversion by assuming a threshold value of 200, is shown in Fig. (**5**).

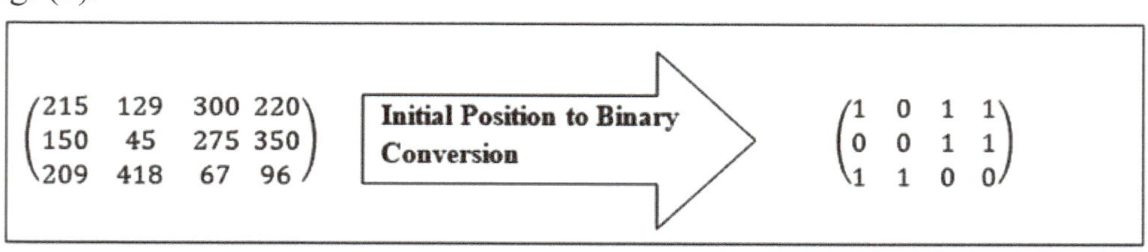

Fig. (5). Binary conversion process in genetic algorithms.

(b) **Computation of Fitness Equation:** For every iteration, the fitness function is computed based on the trained and binary converted data. The major goal of the fitness function is to reduce the number of features, error rate, and finally to compute the objective function to minimize the cost, as shown in the algorithm below.

Algorithm for Fitness Function Evaluation:

Input: IIoT Dataset, IIoTD

Output: Cost of the objective function

Begin:

1. Initialize the parameters K for performing nearest neighbour, independent, and dependent training variables, and alpha values

2. Compute the beta value based on the alpha as shown in equation (**2**)

$$= 1 - \tag{2}$$

3. Calculate the number of features in the IIOTD

4. Prepare a list of selected features(sel_features), those who are having summation as 1.

5. a. If (sel_features==0) then cost=1

b. Else:

(i) Generate accuracy and error rate using the KNN algorithm, as shown in equation (**3**)

$$\text{cost}\square\ \alpha\ \text{error\_rate\_KNN}+\beta\left(\frac{selected\ features}{number\ of\ features}\right) \tag{3}$$

End

(c) Computation of Attractiveness Parameter: To update the position of the firefly based on the light intensity and current position, it computes the following steps:

1. Compute updated_α= α θ

2. Assign ranks to the files based on their intensity

3. The updation of file intensity is based on the attractiveness parameter, as shown below

Algorithm for Attractiveness:

(i) Compute the Euclidean distance and name it as "d."

(ii) update beta value as shown in A Updated_=A *e-(*d)2 **(4)**

(iii) Compute ε using a random function

(iv) for i in the number of features as shown in equation (**4**):

data[row,i]□data[row,i]+Updated_β (data[row1,i]-data[row,i])+updated_α € **(5)**

(v) fit[row,0]"Fitness(TrainData,Options)

To implement the Adaptive Firefly Algorithm, the researcher should make some assumptions.

• Always updated solutions are produced by randomness and attractiveness

• The upper bound and lower bounds are assigned within a range of -5 to +5, *i.e.*, lower bound, lb=-5, and upper bound, ub=+5.

• Threshold= 0.5

Input: IIOT Dataset

Output: Reduced number of features

Begin:

1. Load the IIoT Dataset

2. Call Label Encoder to convert string data to numerical data

3. Clean the data using the Simple Imputer mechanism

4. Define dependent and independent variables

5. Split the dataset into train and test

6. Call the Fitness function with split modularity

7. Call Attractiveness module

8. Define a model with a KNN classifier and fit the convergence curve to reshape the features

9. Print the selected features

End

RESULTS AND DISCUSSION

Table **3** uses a recursive feature elimination approach to discover the most essential characteristics among all attributes. It is a straightforward and effective approach for configuring data because it hyperparameterizes the quantity of features as well as the algorithm used for them. It is a wrapper method that filters the data and returns false with a rank for unimportant attributes, while returning true with a rank of one for selected attributes. It selects 24 attributes from the entire dataset.

Table 3. Selected attributes using REF, wrapper method.

Feature Number	Status	Rank	Feature Number	Status	Rank
0	False	8	24	True	1
1	False	2	25	False	15
2	True	1	26	True	1
3	True	1	27	True	1
4	False	24	28	False	6
5	True	1	29	True	1
6	True	1	30	True	1
7	False	5	31	False	16
8	True	1	32	False	7
9	True	1	33	False	19
10	True	1	34	False	23
11	True	1	35	True	1
12	True	1	36	False	17
13	True	1	37	True	1
14	False	12	38	False	18
15	True	1	39	True	1
16	False	10	40	True	1
17	False	20	41	True	1
18	False	11	42	True	1
19	False	4	43	False	13
20	False	9	44	False	25

(Table 3) cont.....

Feature Number	Status	Rank	Feature Number	Status	Rank
21	False	3	45	False	14
22	True	1	46	False	21
23	False	22	47	True	1

Fig. (**6**) presents all the selected features that satisfy the fitness function. Out of 49 attributes, the proposed mechanism selects 16 attributes as best. Only these 16 attributes impact the entire evaluation of the model.

```
Generation: 1
Best (FA): 0.0064110777898945676
Generation: 2
Best (FA): 0.0064110777898945676
Generation: 3
Best (FA): 0.0064110777898945676
Generation: 4
Best (FA): 0.0064110777898945676
Generation: 5
Best (FA): 0.0064110777898945676
Best (FA): 0.0050379407488186
Generation: 7
Best (FA): 0.0050379407488186
Generation: 8
Best (FA): 0.004621274082151934
Generation: 9
Best (FA): 0.004621274082151934
Generation: 10
Best (FA): 0.004412940748818601
[ 7  9 11 17 19 20  21 22 25 29 31 32 36 41 43 46]
Accuracy: 99.89094874591058
Feature Size: 16
```

Fig. (6). Selection of features using adaptive firefly.

Fig. (7) represents the computations performed by the adaptive fly algorithm at each iteration based on the nearest neighbour parameter. The model for testing purposes was initialized with 10 iterations, and the fitness evaluation is presented in terms of saturation points.

Table **4** represents a comparison between traditional and adaptive firefly on different iterations to evaluate the model and prove its validity.

Table **5** represents a comparison between the RFE, traditional firefly, and adaptive firefly algorithms to check the selection of features and their corresponding accuracies. Out of the remaining two mechanisms, the proposed one selects fewer features with higher efficiency.

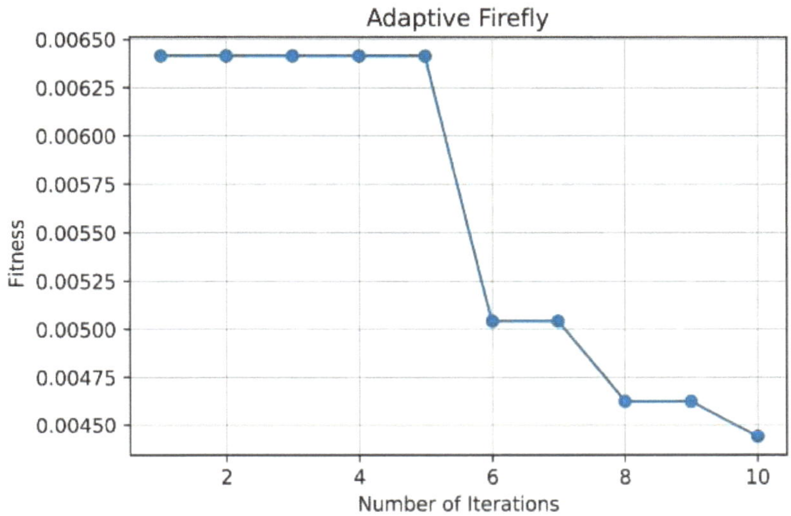

Fig. (7). Iteration versus fitness.

Table 4. Iterations versus accuracy based on feature selection.

Number of Iterations	Traditional Firefly			Adaptive Firefly		
	Feature Set	**Number of Features**	**Fitness Evaluation**	**Feature Set**	**Number of Features**	**Fitness Evaluation**
5	[0 2 6 8 10 11 17 22 23 24 26 27 29 30 31 35 36 43 44 46]	20	0.0065	[0 2 3 6 7 10 11 12 14 22 24 27 30 31 35 39 41 43 45]	19	0.0052
10	[2 4 6 7 9 12 14 19 21 22 26 27 29 32 34 35 36 40 43]	19	0.0044	[1 2 5 6 7 12 17 24 25 26 30 32 33 37 44 45 46]	17	0.0051
25	[2 4 6 7 8 12 14 17 20 21 24 27 36 38 42 44]	16	0.0049	[8 9 12 17 23 25 27 30 31 35 39 40 41 43]	14	0.0045
50	[2 4 6 10 12 14 17 20 24 26 31 39 41 42 43]	15	0.0036	[4 5 6 8 9 10 25 29 31 38 42 43 44]	13	0.0030

Table 5. Comparative analysis on feature selection.

S.No	Algorithm Name	Feature Set	Number of Features	Accuracy
1	RFE	[2, 3, 5, 6, 8, 10, 11, 12, 13, 20, 21, 22, 24, 26, 27, 29, 35, 37, 38, 39, 40, 41, 42, 47]	24	72.5
2	Traditional Firefly	[2 4 7 12 17 19 21 22 26 27 28 29 34 35 39 41 42 46 47]	19	100
3	Adaptive Firefly	[7 9 11 17 19 20 21 22 25 29 31 32 36 41 43 46]	16	99.89

In Fig. (**8**). X- X-axis represents algorithms existing as traditional approaches and the proposed algorithm. The y-axis represents the number of features and accuracy. From Fig. (**8**), it is clear that the proposed algorithm "Adaptive Firefly" has fewer features and a good accuracy value.

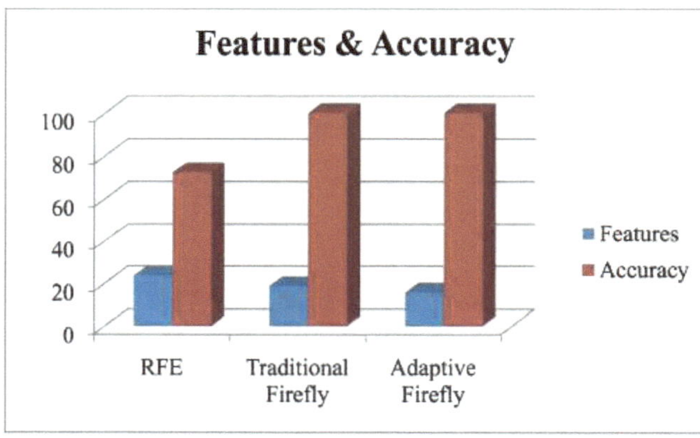

Fig. (8). Features along with accuracy.

Table **6** conducts a comparative analysis of the existing approaches and the proposed approach. The system has recognized that the neural network has obtained an accuracy of 99.4% where as machine learning approaches integrated with optimization techniques have achieved 99.89%, which is better than the highest existing approach, and it also analyzed that for the neural network more number of resources are required than the optimization techniques because every layer of neural network needs to perform more mathematical computations.

Table 6. Comparative analysis of existing researchers' (tm) works.

S.No	Algorithms Used	Accurate Percentage
1	Shodan, blended teaching, use-case-based teaching method	80
2	Decision tree, naive Bayes, Convolutional neural networks	97.8
3	Artificial Neural Network, Random Neural Network, Support Vector Machine	99.2
4	SCADA network, RSRT, RSKNN, binary classification, multi-classification	96.7
5	Attack detection, IIoT, RNN	98.75
6	DRaNN, RNN, CNN	99.41
7	KNN	91
8	AEs, DAEs in neural network	97%
9	Blockchain (AES) and ML (KNN for classification)	90%
10	Adaptive Firefly	99.89

CONCLUSION

Evolutionary algorithms are widely used to solve population-based problems by identifying the population, fitness function (*i.e.*, in the proposed research, feature minimisation), and various mechanisms required for the search strategy. The adaptive firefly method is chosen for its ability to maximise unpredictability at each iteration by selecting the optimal radius. This plays a significant role in selecting the best solution. Using numbers close to 0 can improve file visibility and prevent issues caused by random walk. The suggested approach reduced 49 IIoT dataset properties to 16 with a 99.89% accuracy. Table **6** presents that both traditional and existing processes have problems in selecting the proper parameters; however, the suggested approach has picked an accurate number of features for better model creation.

REFERENCES

[1] S.D. Shamsi, A.S.H.M. Ali, and W.D. Shamsi, "Hybrid Cooperative Spectrum Structured (HCSS) approach for adaptive routing in cognitive radio ad hoc networks", *Mesopotamian Journal of CyberSecurity,* vol. 5, no. 1, pp. 23-38, 2025. [http://dx.doi.org/10.58496/MJCS/2025/003]

[2] S. Mali, M. Gujral, A.K. Cherukuri, and M.G. Ms, "Encrypted network traffic classification using intelligent techniques", *Cureus,* vol. 2, no. 1, 2025.

[3] G. Sripriyanka, and A. Mahendran, "Smart healthcare applications: Detecting DDoS attacks efficiently using hybrid firefly algorithm", *Engineering, Technology & Applied Science Research,* vol. 15, no. 2, pp. 21136-21143, 2025. [http://dx.doi.org/10.48084/etasr.9760]

[4] E.E.D. Hemdan, S.M. Zayed, G. Attiya, A. El-Sayed, and A. Sayed, "Hybrid voting-GA ensemble learning for multi-class fault detection in digital twin-driven IIoT systems", *Computing,* vol. 107, no.

2, p. 56, 2025.
[http://dx.doi.org/10.1007/s00607-024-01399-3]

[5] L. Chen, H. Jiang, L. Wang, J. Li, M. Yu, Y. Shen, and X. Du, "Generative adversarial synthetic neighbors-based unsupervised anomaly detection", *Sci. Rep.,* vol. 15, no. 1, p. 16, 2025.
[http://dx.doi.org/10.1038/s41598-024-84863-6] [PMID: 39747674]

[6] M.A. Talukder, M. Khalid, and N. Sultana, "A hybrid machine learning model for intrusion detection in wireless sensor networks leveraging data balancing and dimensionality reduction", *Sci. Rep.,* vol. 15, no. 1, p. 4617, 2025.
[http://dx.doi.org/10.1038/s41598-025-87028-1] [PMID: 39920281]

[7] M. Antonijevic, M. Zivkovic, M. Djuric Jovicic, B. Nikolic, J. Perisic, M. Milovanovic, L. Jovanovic, M. Abdel-Salam, and N. Bacanin, "Intrusion detection in metaverse environment internet of things systems by metaheuristics tuned two level framework", *Sci. Rep.,* vol. 15, no. 1, p. 3555, 2025.
[http://dx.doi.org/10.1038/s41598-025-88135-9] [PMID: 39875592]

[8] B. S, K. M, S. Palanisamy, and T.A.N. Alshalali, "A novel Hadamard matrix based hybrid compressive sensing technique for enhancing energy efficiency and network longevity", *Sci. Rep.,* vol. 15, no. 1, p. 5937, 2025.
[http://dx.doi.org/10.1038/s41598-025-88712-y] [PMID: 39966512]

CHAPTER 8

Artificial Intelligence and Machine Learning: Transforming the Future of Technology

Brijesh Verma[1,*], **A.K. Richharia**[1] and **Vivek Singh**[1]

[1] *Department of Mechanical Engineering, Galgotia College of Engineering and Technology, Greater Noida, Uttar Pradesh, India*

Abstract: AI and machine learning are transforming the way we solve problems in our data-driven environment. AI allows machines to perform tasks that need human intelligence, such as comprehending language and making decisions. ML enables systems to learn from data and improve on their own. In recent years, advances in computing, massive data, and deep learning have propelled AI and ML into critical domains such as health, finance, transportation, and entertainment. Computer vision, language processing, and neural networks are all powered by cutting-edge technology that is used to detect fraud, run medical tests, and even drive self-driving cars. While AI and ML hold significant promise, they also raise concerns about justice, privacy, job loss, and environmental harm. Strong standards, clear explanations, and global collaboration to investigate how AI is evolving are effective ways to address these issues. New trends include AI that makes things, individuals working with AI computing on the edge, and AI assisting with climate issues. Combining AI and quantum computing might lead to significant advances in the discovery of new pharmaceuticals and materials, while a new method of learning ensures that data remains private. AI will also help to address major global issues such as poverty and disaster response. To summarise, AI and ML are transforming industries and solving complex problems, but we must be cautious about how they influence people and society. We can use these technologies to build a more intelligent, egalitarian, and sustainable future. Recent works also highlight AI–5G integration and VANET authentication schemes such as CLA-FC5G, FCA-VBN, and D-BlockAuth.

Keywords: Artificial intelligence, Deep learning, Ethical challenge, Future trends, Machine learning.

INTRODUCTION

AI and ML have transformed our approach to addressing data-driven concerns. AI refers to machines that can do functions typically associated with human

* **Corresponding author Brijesh Verma:** Department of Mechanical Engineering, Galgotia College of Engineering and Technology, Greater Noida, Uttar Pradesh, India; E-mail: brijesh.verma@galgotiacollege.edu

Shruti Bhargava Choubey & Yogesh Shrivastava (Eds.)

intelligence, such as comprehending natural language, recognizing patterns, and solving problems [1 - 5].

A subset of AI Machine learning allows systems to automatically learn from data and improve performance over time without programming. Recent advances in AI and ML have altered areas such as healthcare, finance, transportation, education, and entertainment. This article explores the history, components, applications, ethical concerns, and potential developments of this remarkable technology.

HISTORICAL EVOLUTION OF AI AND ML

Artificial Intelligence (AI) and Machine Learning (ML) development spans over fifty years and has been affected by advancements in computing technology, as well as mathematical and data science achievements [6 - 10]. AI originated in the 1940s, when early researchers such as Alan Turing proposed robots capable of replicating human thought processes. The Dartmouth Conference in 1956 formalised "Artificial Intelligence" as an academic domain. Early AI research focused mostly on symbolic thinking and rule-based systems, which needed explicit programming of logical rules to solve issues in computers. As the study proceeded, researchers recognised that creating rules to meet every circumstance was unfeasible, particularly in complex systems. Machine Learning emerged in response to the requirement for AI systems capable of automatically detecting patterns and making data-driven decisions. The original creation of neural networks and decision trees happened in the 1980s, but their capabilities were limited due to a lack of computer capacity. The development of massive data and faster hardware, such as GPUs, in the 2000s, enabled deep learning approaches to thrive. AI and machine learning technologies are at the vanguard of technological growth, improving important sectors such as healthcare and finance, while autonomous systems and natural language processing define technological and societal futures [11 - 15]. Table **1** presents the history of artificial intelligence.

Table 1. History of artificial intelligence.

Period	Focus/Development
1950s	The Turing Test proposed by Alan Turing
1950s-1970s	Symbolic AI and logic-based reasoning
1980s	Expert systems with rules programmed by domain experts
1990s	Shift to data-driven learning models.
2000s-present	Deep learning, neural networks, and data-driven AI

KEY CONCEPTS IN AI AND ML

Artificial Intelligence Overview

Artificial Intelligence (AI) is the imitation of human intelligence processes by technology, specifically computer systems. These processes include learning (acquiring data and rules for using it), reasoning (using rules to conclude), and self-correction. AI systems can analyse data, identify patterns, make judgements, and communicate with humans. Different types of artificial intelligence. AI is divided into numerous kinds [16 - 20]:

- Narrow AI (Weak AI):
  - Focused on performing a specific task.
  - Most AI we use today falls under this category.

Examples: Chatbots, virtual assistants (Siri, Alexa), recommendation systems (Netflix, YouTube), image recognition tools.

- General AI (Strong AI):
  - This refers to AI that can understand, learn, and apply intelligence across a wide range of tasks, just like a human.
  - It does not exist yet, but it remains a goal in AI research.
  - A General AI would be able to perform any intellectual task that a human can do.
- Super AI:
  - This represents a theoretical future stage of Artificial Intelligence (AI) that exceeds human intellect across all cognitive, creative, and social dimensions. Prospective research should prioritize Post-Quantum AI (PQAI) security, Federated Learning (FL) integration, and the development of Trustworthy AI (TAI) within critical infrastructure.
  - Such systems possess the potential to transcend human capabilities in every sphere, ranging from rigorous scientific discovery to complex social dynamics.
  - Currently, it's purely speculative.

Machine Learning Overview

Machine Learning (ML) is a subfield of Artificial Intelligence (AI) that focuses on creating algorithms that enable computers to learn patterns from data and make judgments or predictions without being explicitly programmed, instead of adhering to hard-coded rules. ML systems grow over time through experience (data). ML can be divided into numerous categories, as indicated below and mentioned in Table **2**.

Table 2. Types of machine learning.

Type	**Data Type**	**Key Goal**	**Example Task**
Supervised Learning	Labeled Data	Predict output based on input	Fraud Detection
Unsupervised Learning	Unlabeled Data	Find hidden patterns	Customer Segmentation
Reinforcement Learning	Feedback from the environment	Learn optimal actions	Game-playing AI

1. Supervised Learning:
    - This is a theoretical future AI that surpasses human intelligence in all fields, creative, social, and cognitive. Future research should explore post-quantum AI security, the integration of federated learning, and trustworthy AI in critical infrastructure.
    - It could outperform humans in every domain, from scientific research to social interactions.

Examples:

I. Spam email detection (input: email text, output: spam or not spam).
II. House price prediction (input: features like size, location; output: price).

Common algorithms: Linear Regression, Decision Trees, Random Forest, Support Vector Machines (SVM), Neural Networks [21 - 25].

2. Unsupervised Learning:
    - In unsupervised learning, the data is unlabeled, and the algorithm is left to find hidden patterns or structure on its own.
    - It is useful for tasks like clustering and dimensionality reduction.

Examples:

- Customer segmentation (grouping customers based on behavior).
- Anomaly detection (identifying unusual transactions).

Common algorithms: K-Means Clustering, Hierarchical Clustering, Principal Component Analysis (PCA), and Autoencoders.

3. Reinforcement Learning:
   - In reinforcement learning, an agent learns to interact with an environment to achieve a goal.
   - The agent takes actions and receives rewards or penalties based on the outcome.
   - Over time, the agent learns a strategy (policy) that maximizes long-term rewards.

BENEFITS OF MACHINE LEARNING

Automating complicated and repetitive activities reduces the need for human interaction, making machine learning an effective solution. However, only after training can ML models decide, recognise patterns, and process data, which can significantly help streamline processes in industries such as manufacturing, health care, and customer service, as shown in Fig. (**1**).

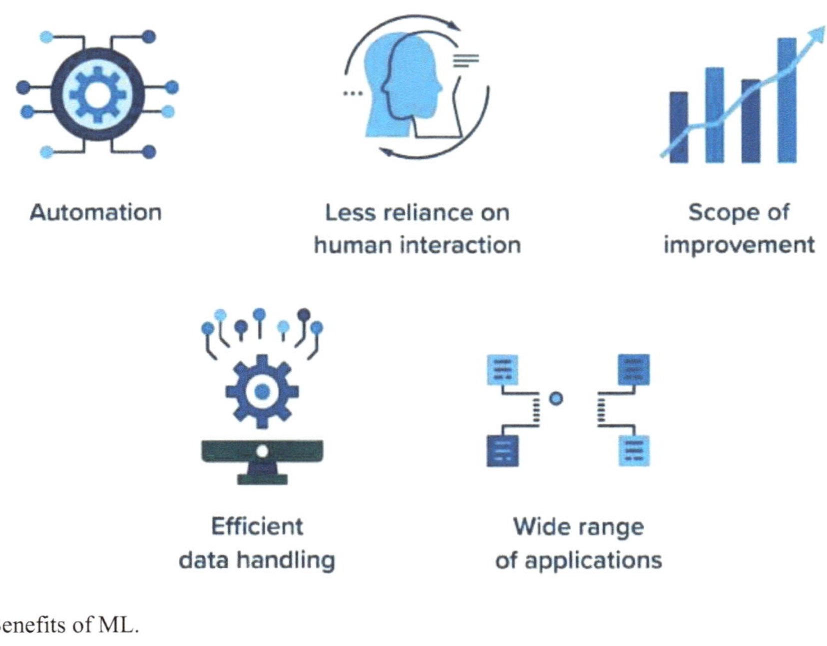

Fig. (1). Benefits of ML.

Computer learning can help systems become more self-sufficient and improve over time, reducing the need for human interaction. It reduces reliance on manual processes and human oversight, lowering the need for a proportional increase in staff, facilitating operations to the point of saving time and money.

Scope of Improvements

The models get increasingly careful as more data is fed into them. The real difference is that traditional systems require manual updates, but the ML model improves accuracy by gradually adapting to new patterns and improving performance over time, keeping the ML model up to date and operational.

Efficient Data Handling

Machine learning excels at processing vast amounts of data rapidly and properly. On the other hand, it can detect hidden patterns and derive important insights from not only unstructured data but also complicated datasets that are beyond human capabilities. Big data can be used to make better decisions if the efficiency is helpful for the company.

Wide Range of Applications

Machine learning applies to almost every business, including healthcare, banking, marketing, cybersecurity, transportation, and entertainment. Its adaptability allows it to solve a wide range of problems, including disease diagnosis, consumer personalisation, fraud detection, predictive maintenance, and so on.

KEY TECHNOLOGIES IN AI AND ML

Neural Networks & Deep Learning

- Neural networks mimic the structure of the human brain, with layers of interconnected nodes (neurons) that process data [26 - 30].
- Deep Learning refers to using deep neural networks with many layers, making it powerful for tasks like image recognition, natural language processing, and speech synthesis.
- Technologies: TensorFlow, PyTorch, Keras

Examples:

- Face recognition (using Convolutional Neural Networks - CNNs)
- Language translation (using Recurrent Neural Networks - RNNs and Transformers)

Natural Language Processing (NLP)

- NLP allows machines to understand, interpret, and generate human language.
- It combines linguistics, computer science, and ML.
- Technologies: spaCy, NLTK, Hugging Face Transformers, BERT, GPT models

Examples:

- Chatbots and virtual assistants (like ChatGPT, Alexa, or Siri)
- Sentiment analysis of social media posts

Computer Vision

- Computer vision enables machines to see and interpret images and videos.
- This technology uses techniques like image classification, object detection, and segmentation.
- Technologies: OpenCV, YOLO (You Only Look Once), TensorFlow, PyTorch

Examples:

- Self-driving cars detect road signs and pedestrians
- Medical imaging (AI-assisted cancer detection)

Big Data Technologies

- AI and ML thrive on massive datasets. Technologies that handle large-scale data are critical for training high-performing models.
- Technologies: Hadoop, Apache Spark, Google BigQuery

Examples:

- Training recommendation engines (like Netflix or Amazon)
- Analyzing customer behavior for marketing campaigns

Cloud Computing & AI

- AI development often relies on cloud platforms that provide scalable computing power and pre-built AI/ML tools.
- Technologies: Google Cloud AI, AWS AI Services, Microsoft Azure AI, IBM Watson

Examples:

- Training deep learning models on cloud GPUs/TPUs
- Deploying AI chatbots *via* cloud platforms

Reinforcement Learning Technologies

- These technologies help build systems where agents learn through trial and error.
- Technologies: OpenAI Gym, Stable Baselines, Ray RLlib

Examples:

- Game-playing AI (like AlphaGo)
- Robotics and industrial automation systems

Data Preprocessing & Feature Engineering Tools

- High-quality data is the backbone of AI/ML success, so technologies for cleaning, transforming, and preparing data are essential.
- Technologies: pandas, scikit-learn, NumPy, Dask

Examples:

- Cleaning customer data for a predictive sales model
- Engineering new features from raw data (like time-based features for sales forecasting)

Model Deployment and Monitoring

- Once models are trained, they need to be deployed into production and monitored for performance.
- Technologies: TensorFlow Serving, MLflow, Kubeflow, Docker

Examples:

- Deploying a fraud detection model in a banking app
- Monitoring the accuracy drift of a recommendation system over time

Explainable AI (XAI)

- As AI gets more complex, there's a growing need for technologies that explain how models make decisions.
- Technologies: SHAP (SHapley Additive exPlanations), LIME (Local Interpretable Model-Agnostic Explanations)

Examples:

- Explaining why a loan application was rejected
- Providing interpretable recommendations in healthcare

Automated Machine Learning (AutoML)

- AutoML tools help automate the process of model selection, hyperparameter tuning, and evaluation, making ML accessible to non-experts.
- Technologies: Google AutoML, H2O.ai, Auto-sklearn

Examples:

- Building predictive models for small businesses with limited data science expertise
- Rapid prototyping of ML models for research

APPLICATIONS OF AI AND ML ACROSS INDUSTRIES

AI and machine learning have significantly transformed healthcare. These devices analyse medical pictures, including X-rays, MRIs, and CT scans, to detect early indicators of cancer and neurological disorders. In many circumstances, chatbots assist patients by checking symptoms, scheduling appointments, and providing rapid advice. In general, predictive analytics alerts clinicians to patients who may be at risk for long-term illnesses, allowing them to intervene earlier. Furthermore, in the field of drug discovery, AI detects molecular behaviour in ways that shorten research time and save a lot of money, even if it occasionally feels like magic [9].

Finance: The landscape is dynamic, within the finance sector, AI, and ML are critical for detecting fraud because algorithms can detect unusual patterns that sound ' suspicious' before anyone else. Both classic and alternative data are now graded to identify risk, and the procedure appears to be more complete. Rapid-fire transactions conducted by automatic trading systems based on live chatter from the marketplace, in most cases, such as algorithmic hustling, help keep competitors in line. Nowadays, personalised banking and robo-advisors provide investing advice tailored to an individual's specific profile, complete with everyday smarts and high tech.

Retail: Retail is also participating in e-commerce, albeit uniquely and unpredictably. Shops use artificial intelligence to provide product recommendations based on your browsing history, previous purchases, and even little personal peculiarities. Prices can change in real time, responding to demand, competitor activity, and available inventory, making shopping feel more like a dynamic, ever-changing experience. At the same time, AI-powered systems estimate inventory demands, ensuring that shelves are rarely barren, while sentiment technologies scan reviews and social media chatter to help firms understand what customers truly think, even if those ideas are repeated in various ways.

Manufacturing: AI and ML-enabled predictive maintenance uses sensors to monitor equipment performance and predict component breakdowns ahead of time. Computer vision components improve quality control processes by automating flaw identification in manufactured products. Supply chain optimisation uses AI algorithms to estimate demand fluctuations, resulting in automatic adjustments to production plans [10].

AI-powered autonomous cars use deep learning systems to detect objects, pedestrians, and traffic signals, revolutionising transportation and logistics. AI enables logistics organisations to optimise their routes, minimise fuel use, and increase delivery speed. ML improves strategic fleet operations and handling procedures in ports, warehouses, and airports by leveraging demand forecasting capabilities.

AI and Machine Learning (ML) can assist farmers in improving their agricultural operations by using drone systems to monitor soil health, crop conditions, and water irrigation needs. Farmers can employ predictive analytical models to forecast future weather patterns and pest outbreaks, allowing them to react before the walls close. AI systems are installed in autonomous tractors and harvesters to ensure efficient agricultural operations [11].

In the entertainment and media industry, artificial intelligence technology has been used to propose appropriate content to users on platforms such as Netflix and Spotify. The production process itself involves the use of artificial intelligence twice: in customised marketing campaigns and robotic video editing, which is combined with an artificial narrative and music composition. Also, entertainment businesses monitor audience opinions to determine whether they should offer more or less appropriate content selections in the future.

AI can customise educational content through adaptive learning platforms to align with individual student development and learning preferences. Computerised systems for routine grading help teachers to save time by doing immediate assessments of student work. With AI chatbots, students' academic aid becomes more efficient, and solutions are available to students even after regular school hours.

AI and ML integration systems detect security breaches or attacks by identifying irregular network patterns. ML models will learn from evolving threats daily, and, as security systems, they will become increasingly responsive. It proposes a method for an AI to create a framework for the incident response process, which speeds up the detection and recovery from such cyber attacks [12].

In the space exploration sector, AI technologies are employed for self-piloting spacecraft and analysing and forecasting system components. This includes both public and private entities. AI can use these capabilities to process this material by identifying patterns and discovering new celestial bodies.

AI can help manage smart grids and improve renewable energy efficiency through weather predictions. Predictive maintenance enables wind turbines and power plants to operate in continuous mode.

In Human Resources (HR), AI may automate resume screening to identify qualified candidates from thousands of resumes. In addition to managing employee concerns, chatbots analyse sentiment to help organisations determine how satisfied or unhappy their staff are.

ETHICAL CHALLENGES IN AI AND ML

Bias and Discrimination

Finally, historical data-driven learning is biased because the data contains prejudices such as racial, gender, and economic preferences, which help to increase and maintain biases in models. Hiring decision-making from the past, which was used to train the hiring software, will cause AI-based hiring software to perpetuate discrimination against female and ethnic minority applicants because previous hiring decisions were prejudiced. Indeed, when automated decision-making systems are used, there is a considerable moral concern about impartiality, while the risk of institutional discriminatory patterns becoming ingrained in system processes is considerably increased [13].

Privacy and Data Protection

Extensive data collection is important to AI and ML; thus, personal and restricted types of data are often used, including medical records, financial transactions, and internet behaviour. The ethical quandary that arises from the operational process of data collecting, storage, and analysis is that it must be informed by user consent, data storage security, and surveillance prevention. Privacy violations occur when personal data is collected without user agreement, and they mostly affect individuals in campaigns for targeted advertising and political profiling, as well as police surveillance.

Deep learning networks and other AI and ML models function as "black boxes," making it difficult for developers to comprehend specific decision-making processes. The failure to see through these institutions produces morality-based issues in industries such as financial services, healthcare, and the criminal justice system. Because these judgements have a significant 'effect on human existence', users of a system must be informed about why specific decisions are made.

Accountability and Responsibility

AI system faults are attributed to developers, invading organisations, and the AI system itself. When the situation is life-threatening, assessing accountability becomes a critical issue for automatic car and medical diagnostic calculation systems. One of the most difficult ethical quandaries is establishing a clear concept of accountability among AI system administrators [14].

Job Displacement and Economic Inequality

AI-driven automation signals industry upheaval, leading to job losses and raising concerns about joblessness spreading throughout society and about the growing economic disparity. Thousands of individuals are at risk of losing their jobs as a result of AI systems executing historically human activities in repetitive patterns, basic data processing, or knowledge-related tasks. Training displaced labour force members to be effective is a moral dilemma in the face of society's attempt to attain specific technological advances in equitable ways by distributing advantages to various skilled workforce levels and tech firm workers.

Misuse and Weaponization

The nature of AI technologies allows for both positive and negative outcomes. Today, autonomous weapons systems represent an ever-increasing ethical concern since they make decisions on their own without human interaction, while deepfakes constitute a threat by disseminating misinformation. Technological growth outpaces current ethics' ability to constrain new rules; we have failed to adapt to new developments. This creates an environment conducive to immoral behaviour.

Consent and Manipulation

AI technology can be used to create personalised marketing, influence behaviour, and manipulate politics. This ethical concern emerges from the fact that everyone is unaware of algorithmic manipulation, and they have not given their explicit agreement for algorithmic behavioural modification. However, the consequences are even more serious when targeting vulnerable populations such as children or persons with mental illnesses.

Environmental Impact

Training big AI and deep learning models needs significant computational power, which can lead to high energy usage and carbon footprints. Now, as firms race to create ever larger models of AI, environmental costs are becoming an increasingly pressing ethical issue, with little regard for sustainability.

Human Autonomy and Decision Making

The danger of over-reliance on AI grows as the systems improve at what they do, and this can be a case of automation bias, a term used to describe when we take an AI's word for it as if it were from a scientific publication. This presents ethical difficulties in Alberta's smaller industries, such as health, aviation, and criminal justice.

AI systems sometimes rely on Western data and assumptions, making them less productive or even destructive in non-Western cultures. It raises concerns about cultural bias, digital colonialism, and the potential loss of cultural diversity in favour of a restricted technology worldview. It also raises ethical concerns about cultural bias and colonialism, as well as the potential of losing cultural diversity to duplicate a restricted technology perspective.

AI SAFETY & REGULATION

AI safety is a collection of measures, principles, and practices put in place to ensure that AI systems are manageable and do not harm anybody. While AI systems become more powerful and autonomous, safety is becoming increasingly important, particularly in sensitive environments such as healthcare, finance, defence, and (even more) transportation.

Key Components of AI Safety

Robustness and Reliability

a) AI systems should be consistent under various conditions and take expected and unexpected inputs.

b) They need to be able to handle errors well and avoid catastrophic failure.

Transparency and Explainability

c) Accordingly, AI models, in particular complex ones like deep learning systems, should be understood by humans.

d) A necessary property for auditing, debugging, and fairness in decision making is explainability.

Alignment with Human Values

e) Aligning human intentions with AI goals will help ensure that AI systems do not work in an undesirable and harmful manner.

f) As with sophisticated systems, it is especially important in the case of systems that employ AI to optimize towards goals that are not meant to be achieved, *i.e.*, goal misalignment.

Controllability and Human Oversight

g) To some extent, it has to be possible to control AI processes that people can access if need be.

h) Also, there must be defined ways to turn the AI off or change how it works when it goes over what is considered acceptable.

Security Against Adversarial Attacks

In particular, we consider the following requirements for AI systems to be robust against assaults aiming at modifying or adversarially boosting an image classifier (or data poisoning). Additionally, unauthorised access and hacking of the AI system must be prohibited.

AI has a huge impact on privacy, security, employment, democracy, and human rights, especially as it becomes more widely used. Governments, organisations, and international groups are working to regulate AI to ensure that it is created and utilised responsibly.

Key Areas Covered by AI Regulations

Data Privacy and Protection:

a. AI systems used in Europe have also adopted rules dictating how information is gathered, retained, and processed with AI. Some of these are the General Data Protection Regulation (GDPR).
b. It must also be justifiable under the principles of informed consent as well as Transparency while gathering the personal data.

Bias and Fairness

a. Some regulators are calling for forensic audits to confirm that AI systems are not biased towards a certain race, gender, religion, or any protected class.
b. Organizations need to check for biases and take corrective action.

Accountability and Liability

a. In the case of an AI system inflicting damage, these regulations establish clear lines of blame between the programmer, the deployer, and the user.
b. This applies to the most accurate level for autonomous vehicles, Healthcare diagnostics, and even stock exchange trading.

Certification and Audits

a. As with lasers, aircraft, and medical devices, some jurisdictions want to put AI systems with the highest risk under mandatory certification.
b. Audits should be carried out at regular intervals to check for compliance with safety, performance, and ethical standards.

Banning Harmful AI Applications:

a. Some applications of AI, such as social credit systems, predictive policing, or fully autonomous weapons, are absent in many areas for ethical reasons and may face legal restrictions.

Transparency Requirements

a. There may be a requirement for the company to identify its use of AI in a normal employment process, as well as in credit and security services.
b. AI users are entitled to receive feedback regarding the actions taken by the AI systems that impact their lives.

Global Efforts in AI Regulation

a. **European Union (EU)**: The EU AI Act is one of the first comprehensive regulatory frameworks, classifying AI systems into risk categories (unacceptable risk, high risk, limited risk, minimal risk) and imposing stricter requirements on higher-risk applications.
b. **United States**: The US currently follows a sectoral approach, with guidelines from NIST (National Institute of Standards and Technology) and specific regulations in industries like healthcare and finance.
c. **China**: China is certainly giving strong consideration to the way it will mitigate the emergence of AI technologies. Pipeline, to the contrary, has come up with rules for things like deepfake videos and AI facial recognition, along with some nice guidelines for algorithms' recommendations. It also reveals their desire to give rise to this new tech while having a chance to control the public opinion on the extent of usage of AI.
d. **International Initiatives:** Big groups are being formed, like the United Nations and OECD (Organization for Economic Cooperation and Development) and G7 (Group of Seven), which are all making the global ethical agreement and governance rules to ensure the coordination around the world on how to handle issues related to AI.

Challenges in AI Regulation

a. The regulatory interval is caused by AI technology developing much faster than regulatory processes.
b. Reducing the balance between Innovation and oversight: Too strict rules can kill innovation, while loose rules may lead to abuse and disadvantage.

c. Global Consistency: There is a gap between different countries' cultural values and political systems, so that the AI regime is unable to establish a global standard.

The Path Forward

Government Tech., researchers, and civil society all have to cooperate to ensure AI regulation and safety for now and the future. Robust, upfront technical protections and legal frameworks, and conversations that continue in the public about how AI will serve humanity rather than disadvantage it, will greatly contribute to ethical AI development by limiting risks and promoting its suitability for the public good.

FUTURE TRENDS AND OPPORTUNITIES IN AI AND ML

Future studies should concentrate on advancing post-quantum security mechanisms for AI, integrating federated learning approaches, and ensuring the reliability and trustworthiness of AI systems operating within critical infrastructure. Generative AI is a transformative form of artificial intelligence that has made significant advancements in recent years. Modern models like GPT, DALL·E, and Stable Diffusion can generate text, images, music, videos, and code. In the future, this would incorporate personalised content, real-time translation, and automated narration. Generative AI will digitise a company's creative process, improve marketing methods, and create a highly personalised user experience.

AI-Enhanced Workforce (Human-AI Collaboration)

There will be a future in which AI will coexist with humans rather than replacing them. It can be a reliable process partner for professionals in any business; physicians may use AI to analyse medical imaging. Attorneys can have AI review contracts, and teachers can customise instructional content for students. AI will enable humans to handle repetitive, mundane, rule-based work, freeing up their time for creative, strategic, and emotionally intelligent jobs.

AI accelerates drug discovery, decodes genomes, and simulates climate change scenarios. And in the future, AI will play an increasingly important part in answering science's complicated puzzles, whether it is bringing 4D printing forward to the discovery of new materials, developing algorithms to search space for the unknown, or planning the next epidemic. This presents an excellent potential for new medicinal, energy, and sustainability innovations.

As AI becomes more widely used, there will be a greater need for openness and explainability. These next-generation AI systems will be designed to have insights into why they made this judgment, allowing them to deliver that knowledge understandably and boost confidence in high-stakes applications such as finance, healthcare, and law enforcement. It will also promote the creation of responsible AI frameworks, which will integrate ethical values such as justice, responsibility, and privacy into the AI system from the start.

Edge AI and on-device intelligence

Shortly, more AI capabilities will shift to the edge, implying that AI will be finished on smartphones, IoT devices, autonomous vehicles, and wearables. This decreases latency, conserves bandwidth, and protects privacy because some data does not need to be gathered and stored on central servers. This concept's realisation entails employing edge AI for use cases in the AR/VR arena, autonomous drones, health-monitoring wearables, and other real-time processing applications.

AI and machine learning can effectively address climate change by analysing environmental data, optimising energy networks, forecasting natural disasters, and adjusting resources like trash, agriculture, and water. Companies will use AI to track their carbon footprints, improve renewable energy efficiency, and develop climate-friendly solutions.

AI will offer highly personalised experiences across all sectors. Artificial intelligence will personalise healthcare treatments based on genetics and lifestyle. AI will build educational modules based on each student's pace. AI will adapt shopping experiences to each customer in retail. The more the AI models currently focus on one of four modalities: text. Graphics, audio, and video. This will eventually become natural and exhausting. Future AI systems will be multi-modal, meaning they will be able to understand and generate content in any format at the same time, for example, decoding the words in a video, reading text alongside the video, and understanding the entire movie. It creates new potential in the media, education, surveillance, and creative industries.

AI has enabled the development of autonomous cars, drones, robotics, and smart cities. Swarm intelligence, which allows drones or autonomous vehicles to work in real time, has the potential to improve logistics, defence, and disaster response efficiency. Robotics will become more widely used in manufacturing, elder care, and space exploration, among other applications, as AI-powered robots direct the processes involved.

AI can improve cybersecurity by detecting and responding to internet attacks in real-time. In the future, AI will be able to forecast weaknesses that will be exploited, and all networks will respond to this threat on a residual basis. This will become increasingly critical as more devices connect to the Internet of Things (IoT) ecosystem.

Federated learning, which allows AI models to train on decentralized data without uploading it to central servers, will drive progress in privacy-preserving AI. This increases privacy in use cases like healthcare analytics, financial services, and smart appliances while still allowing for important insights to be derived from aggregated data.

Governments and international agencies will continue to develop regulations to ensure ethical and responsible AI use. This might culminate in global AI governance entities comparable to international environmental or commerce organisations. Businesses that actively pursue ethical AI and compliance will gain a competitive advantage, opening the path to leadership in dependable AI innovation.

AI is increasingly working with artists, singers, and designers to enhance their creativity. In the future, co-creation platforms could allow humans and AI to collaborate seamlessly to create music, film, art, and fashion. This generates new business models in which AI serves as an augmentation tool for creativity, rather than a substitute.

AI and Quantum Computing Synergy

Quantum computing will enhance and accelerate AI and machine learning capabilities, especially in computationally intensive fields like modelling molecules, cracking encryption, and tackling combinatorial optimisation issues. Businesses that invest in the combination of artificial intelligence with quantum computing may uncover previously untapped potential in medicine development, materials science, and finance.

AI can help address global concerns such as poverty reduction, illness control, and disaster relief. Predictive frameworks can identify vulnerable groups, streamline aid distribution, and improve emergency warning systems. NGOs, social entrepreneurs, and governments will work more closely with technology companies to use AI for humanitarian reasons.

CONCLUSION

Artificial Intelligence (AI) and Machine Learning (ML) are key factors shaping the future of technology. They are now advancing at a tremendous speed, thanks to industrial revolutions, increased productivity, and new means of releasing possibilities previously only seen in science fiction. AI and machine learning enable people to make sound decisions, automate some tasks, and build systems that learn, adapt, and develop on their own. These technologies are valuable not only for processing large volumes of data but also for recognising patterns, predicting outcomes, and even replicating human cognitive processes. The AI-powered technology enables organisations to expedite innovation cycles, reduce operational expenses, and create more customised consumer experiences. In healthcare, AI algorithms are being used to diagnose illnesses, speed up pharmaceutical delivery, and improve patient care. Meanwhile, future maintenance, automated systems, and tailored supply chains have helped industries such as agriculture and manufacturing.

The widespread use of artificial intelligence and machine learning creates serious moral, societal, and economic concerns. Data implies that consumers should be concerned about a regulator's monitoring and moral standards on privacy, algorithmic or other bias, job displacement, and responsible autonomy use. To create public trust and responsible innovation, it is critical to promote transparency, accountability, and diversity. AI and machine learning have yet to realize their full potential, but the future seems promising, with self-learning robots, sophisticated robotics, cognitive computing, and other developments on the horizon. With thoughtful application and ethical use, society may shape a future in which technology boosts human potential, solves global challenges, and drives sustainable development. The final question, by far, is about the transformational potential of AI and ML, not just technical advancement, but about leveraging those powers to create a better, more egalitarian, and more innovative world for the coming generations. However, as AI and machine learning technology progress, we should expect even greater results in the future. The list might include clever robots that learn on their own, computers that ask questions and think like humans, and humans collaborating with AI. If these new concepts are applied, we will see a future in which technology improves what we do, addresses big global concerns, and drives long-term progress.

REFERENCES

[1] G. Selvarajan, "Leveraging AI-enhanced analytics for industry-specific optimization: A strategic approach to transforming data-driven decision-making", *Int. J. Enhanced Res. Sci. Technol. Eng.*, vol. 10, no. 1, pp. 78-84, 2021.

[2] Z. Zong, and Y. Guan, "AI-driven intelligent data analytics and predictive analysis in Industry 4.0: Transforming knowledge, innovation, and efficiency", *J. Knowl. Econ.*, vol. 16, no. 1, pp. 864-903,

2025.
[http://dx.doi.org/10.1007/s13132-024-02001-z]

[3] B. I. Adekunle, E. C. Chukwuma-Eke, E. D. Balogun, and K. O. Ogunsola, "Machine learning for automation: Developing data-driven solutions for process optimization and accuracy improvement", *Machine Learning,* vol. 2, no. 1, pp. 1-10, 2021.

[4] A. Ahmadi, and N. RabieNezhad Ganji, "AI-driven medical innovations: transforming healthcare through data intelligence", *Int. J. BioLife Sci. (IJBLS),* vol. 2, no. 2, pp. 132-142, 2023.

[5] Y. Perwej, "Machine Learning Driven Predictive Modelling for Intelligent Data-Centric Applications", *Machine Learning,* vol. 36, no. 1, pp. 678-683, 2026.

[6] S. Raschka, J. Patterson, and C. Nolet, "Machine learning in python: Main developments and technology trends in data science, machine learning, and artificial intelligence", *Information,* vol. 11, no. 4, p. 193, 2020.
[http://dx.doi.org/10.3390/info11040193]

[7] Y. Xu, X. Liu, X. Cao, C. Huang, E. Liu, S. Qian, and J. Zhang, "Artificial intelligence: A powerful paradigm for scientific research", *The Innovation,* vol. 2, no. 4, 2021.
[http://dx.doi.org/10.1016/j.xinn.2021.100179]

[8] M. M. Mijwil, K. Aggarwal, S. Sonia, A. H. Al-Mistarehi, S. Alomari, M. Gök, and S. H. Abdulrhman, "Has the Future Started? The Current Growth of Artificial Intelligence, Machine Learning, and Deep Learning", *Iraqi J. Comput. Sci. Math.,* vol. 3, no. 1, pp. 115-123, 2022.
[http://dx.doi.org/10.52866/ijcsm.2022.01.01.013]

[9] Y. Lu, "Artificial intelligence: a survey on evolution, models, applications and future trends", *J. Manage. Anal.,* vol. 6, no. 1, pp. 1-29, 2019.

[10] T. Hey, K. Butler, S. Jackson, and J. Thiyagalingam, "Machine learning and big scientific data", *Philos. Trans. Royal Soc. A,* vol. 378, no. 2166, 2020.
[http://dx.doi.org/10.1098/rsta.2019.0054]

[11] J. Vinothkumar, and A. Karunamurthy, "Recent advancements in artificial intelligence technology: trends and implications", *Quing: Int. J. Multidiscip. Sci. Res. Dev.,* vol. 2, no. 1, pp. 1-11, 2023.

[12] M. O. I. Elamin, "AI through the ages: Unlocking key opportunities and navigating challenges in the history and future of artificial intelligence", *Int. J. Religion,* vol. 5, no. 12, pp. 1152-1166, 2024.

[13] S. Rawas, "AI: the future of humanity", *Discov. Artif. Intell.,* vol. 4, no. 1, p. 25, 2024.
[http://dx.doi.org/10.1007/s44163-024-00118-3]

[14] M. Thabo, N. Zanele, and D. Sipho, "Next-Generation Artificial Intelligence: Anticipated Advancements and Challenges in the Coming Years", *Am. J. Sci. Integr. Hum. Dev.,* vol. 2, no. 7, pp. 78-88, 2024.

[15] M. Abbas Khan, H. Khan, M. F. Omer, I. Ullah, and M. Yasir, "Impact of artificial intelligence on the global economy and technology advancements", In: *Artificial General Intelligence (AGI) Security,* 2024, pp. 147-180.
[http://dx.doi.org/10.1007/978-981-97-3222-7_7]

[16] R. Martinez, "Artificial intelligence: Distinguishing between types & definitions", *Nev. Law J.,* vol. 19, no. 3, p. 1015, 2018.

[17] S. Fourtané, "The three types of artificial intelligence: Understanding AI", *Interesting Engineering,* vol. 25, 2019.

[18] O. Strelkova, "Three types of artificial intelligence," 2017. Available from: https://conf.ztu.edu.ua/wp-content/uploads/2017/05/142.pdf

[19] E. Kumar, *Artificial Intelligence.* New Delhi: IK International Pvt Ltd, 2013.

[20] D. T. Chaudhari, "Artificial intelligence, its types and application in various fields", *Int. J. Commer.*

Manage. Res., vol. 10, pp. 49-51, 2024.

[21] V. Rodriguez-Galiano, M. Sanchez-Castillo, M. Chica-Olmo, and M. Chica-Rivas, "Machine learning predictive models for mineral prospectivity: An evaluation of neural networks, random forest, regression trees and support vector machines", *Ore Geol. Rev.,* vol. 71, pp. 804-818, 2015. [http://dx.doi.org/10.1016/j.oregeorev.2015.01.001]

[22] M. W. Ahmad, J. Reynolds, and Y. Rezgui, "Predictive modelling for solar thermal energy systems: A comparison of support vector regression, random forest, extra trees and regression trees", *J. Cleaner Prod.,* vol. 203, pp. 810-821, 2018. [http://dx.doi.org/10.1016/j.jclepro.2018.08.207]

[23] E. Raczko, and B. Zagajewski, "Comparison of support vector machine, random forest and neural network classifiers for tree species classification on airborne hyperspectral APEX images", *Eur. J. Remote Sens.,* vol. 50, no. 1, pp. 144-154, 2017. [http://dx.doi.org/10.1080/22797254.2017.1299557]

[24] P. Amini, H. Ahmadinia, J. Poorolajal, and M. M. Amiri, "Evaluating the high risk groups for suicide: a comparison of logistic regression, support vector machine, decision tree and artificial neural network", *Iran. J. Public Health,* vol. 45, no. 9, p. 1179, 2016.

[25] I. Nitze, U. Schulthess, and H. Asche, "Comparison of machine learning algorithms random forest, artificial neural network and support vector machine to maximum likelihood for supervised crop type classification", In: *Proc. 4th GEOBIA*, 2012, pp. 35-40.

[26] S. Shanmuganathan, "Artificial neural network modelling: An introduction", In: *Artificial Neural Network Modelling*, 2016, pp. 1-14. [http://dx.doi.org/10.1007/978-3-319-28495-8_1]

[27] R. Qamar, and B. A. Zardari, "Artificial neural networks: An overview", *Mesopotamian J. Comput. Sci.,* vol. 2023, pp. 124-133, 2023. [http://dx.doi.org/10.58496/MJCSC/2023/015]

[28] M. C. Nwadiugwu, "Neural networks, artificial intelligence and the computational brain", *arXiv preprint,* 2020.

[29] O. S. Eluyode, and D. T. Akomolafe, "Comparative study of biological and artificial neural networks", *Eur. J. Appl. Eng. Sci. Res.,* vol. 2, no. 1, pp. 36-46, 2013.

[30] G. E. Hinton, "How neural networks learn from experience", *Sci. Am.,* vol. 267, no. 3, pp. 144-151, 1992. [http://dx.doi.org/10.1038/scientificamerican0992-144]

CHAPTER 9

AgriConnect: AI's Touch, Farmer's Growth

Padmaja Grandhe[1,*], **Eesha Thakur**[1], **G. Aarushi Reddy**[1] and **Yaamini R**[1]

[1] *Department of Computer Science and Engineering, Sreenidhi University, Hyderabad, Telangana, India*

Abstract: Climate variability, inefficient resource management, and a lack of real-time data are among the issues facing agriculture today. Many rural farmers deal with smartphone inaccessibility and inadequate digital literacy, making it difficult to gain critical agricultural insights. To address these difficulties, we offer an AI-powered Smart Board, which is a solar-powered, offline-compatible device equipped with IoT sensors (soil moisture, temperature, humidity, and pH sensors), drones, and real-time data processing capabilities. It sends voice-based alerts in local languages with climate change warnings, crop care suggestions, and real-time government updates (minimum support price, subsidies, and market trends). It also collects crop data and recommends pest-prevention and irrigation management strategies. A voice-enabled query system enables farmers to ask questions and receive AI-powered responses, while radio integration provides emergency alerts and expert views. This technology, which features a simple touch interface and an AI-powered hotline, empowers farmers, boosts productivity, and supports sustainable agriculture, ensuring a wiser, data-driven future.

Keywords: AI-powered drones, IoT sensors, Radio alerts, Real-time MSP updates, Smart irrigation, Touchscreen dashboard, Voice-based AI assistant.

INTRODUCTION

Currently, agriculture is overwhelmed with difficulties caused by unpredictable weather patterns, lack of water, irrigation systems, and pest attacks, which are a major cause of huge losses in the agricultural field [1 - 5]. What makes the situation worse is that most farmers lack access to modern digital technology due to low smartphone penetration and unstable connections in rural areas with poor infrastructure. The majority of existing AI-powered farming solutions rely extensively on cloud computing and phones, which makes them either broken or unusable in such underserved communities [6 - 10]. To address these short-comings, we are presenting AgriConnect: an AI-powered Smart Board, which is a

* **Corresponding author Padmaja Grandhe:** Department of Computer Science and Engineering, Sreenidhi University, Hyderabad, Telangana, India; E-mail: padmaja.g@suh.edu.in

Shruti Bhargava Choubey & Yogesh Shrivastava (Eds.)

solar-run, offline-compatible system containing sensors through IoT, drones, and AI-based analytics. The company introduced an innovative platform that helps farmers receive voice alerts, market trend analysis, and real-time notification of the government schemes, which will help farmers make the right decisions to make farming sustainable and profitable.

LITERATURE REVIEW

In the article on crop management systems with the help of artificial intelligence. Anmol Giri [11] considered the possibilities of artificial intelligence in implementing the principles of crop management through pest control and yield prediction. The manual drone image interpretation dependency, however, delays the processing, implementation, and the system has a dependency on cloud connectivity, making it inefficient in remote areas. Dr. Neeraj Mittal [12], in his article, "Revolutionising Agriculture: The Digital Transformation of Farming," wrote about climate and pest monitoring tools that, although they have a certain value, are not detailed enough on the field level, and (last but not least) do not integrate with government services. In an article titled, Farmer Touch: Harnessing Technologies to Increase Crop Production [13], authored by Mohana Siri Vasamsetty, they suggested the use of AI chatbots and soil health monitoring, but this sort of thing requires smartphones and internet, which is something most rural farmers do not own. In the article, AI-Based Yield Prediction and Smart Irrigation [14], Deepak Sinwar promoted the application of CNNs, drones, and IoT sensors to predict yield and identify diseases, though the system is dependent on the cloud as its key component. In the article by Lalbaksh Albulushi and Zubair Shahdost [15], named Drone-Assisted Farming, the authors concentrated on autonomous drones devoted to spraying pesticides and checking crops to increase the effectiveness of the crop, but the solution also assumed the technological maturity of the sector. In part, Apeksha R. Gawande [16], in "Analysis of Crop Diseases Using IoT and Machine Learning Approaches," suggested early disease identification through IoT and ML, which would require less amount of pesticides, though, in this case, it would presuppose connectivity as well. Finally, Ranveer Chandra [17] presented the FarmBeats platform based on precision agriculture with support using cloud analytics. Although the model holds promise, it uses expensive hardware and needs constant access to the internet, which limits its scalability in low-resource settings.

All these works make it clear that technological progress in the field of farming AI exists, but there is a gap in accessibility. AgriConnect will help to overcome this gap because it provides AI features and does not require smartphones and continuous connections, hence it is more inclusive and farmer-friendly.

PROBLEM IDENTIFICATION

Existing AI-based solutions in agriculture have the following limitations:

- The dependence on the internet and cloud computing makes them impractical for rural farmers.
- Delayed pest detection leads to crop losses.
- High costs and reliance on smartphones limit accessibility.

Fig. (**1**) shows several consequences faced by the farmers. To solve these issues, the AI-powered Smart Board provides an offline, real-time solution that integrates AI, IoT, and drone-based monitoring for precise and cost-effective farming.

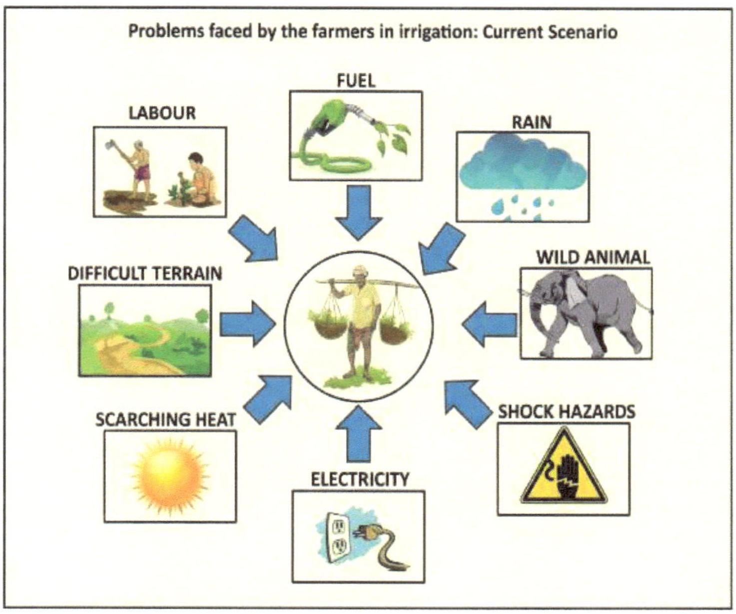

Fig. (1). Consequences faced by farmers.

CASE STUDIES

i. AI-Powered Pest Detection (Punjab, India)

Problem: Late pest detection led to 30% wheat loss.

Solution: Drones scan fields, AI detects infestations, and farmers get real-time voice alerts.

Outcome: Lower pesticide costs, reduced crop damage, and higher wheat production.

ii. **Smart Irrigation & Water Conservation (Maharashtra, India)**

Problem: Over-irrigation caused soil degradation and high electricity bills.

Solution: IoT sensors measure soil moisture, AI predicts rainfall, and irrigation is optimized.

Outcome: Reduced water use, lower electricity costs, and healthier soil.

iii. **Real-Time MSP Updates (Uttar Pradesh, India)**

Problem: Farmers sold crops to middlemen at low prices due to a lack of market insights.

Solution: The Smart Board displays real-time Minimum Support Prices (MSP) and market trends.

Outcome: Increased profits, better market decisions, and reduced middleman dependency.

PROPOSED SYSTEM & ARCHITECTURE

The AI-Powered Smart Board combines AI, IoT sensors, and drones to enhance farming decisions.

Key Features

- IoT sensors: Measure soil moisture, temperature, and pH levels.
- Drones: Monitor crop health and detect pest infestations. Fig. (**2**). Shows how drones scan the fields to detect crop health conditions.
- Solar-powered: Ensures continuous operation without electricity.
- Voice Alerts: Provides real-time farming updates in local languages.
- Market Trends: Displays MSP updates and AI-driven selling recommendations.
- Offline Functionality: Works without the internet or smartphones.

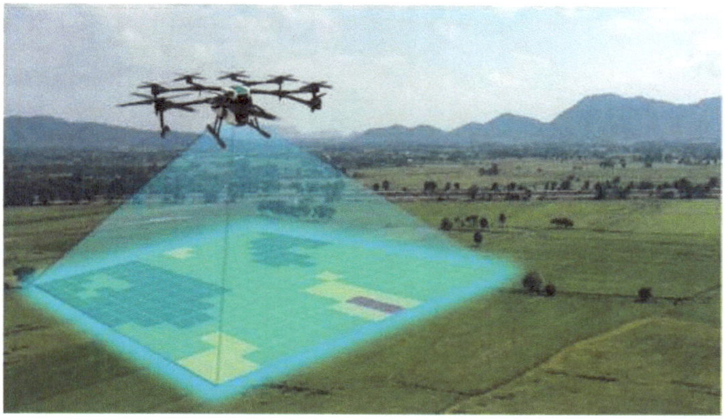

Fig. (2). Drones scan the fields.

Step-by-Step Functionality

1. **Data Collection**: IoT sensors monitor soil health, drones scan crops, and market trends are fetched. Fig. (**3**) specifies different IOT devices for the data collection process.
2. **AI Processing**: AI detects pest outbreaks, predicts weather, and suggests farming actions.
3. **Communication**: Farmers receive insights through voice alerts and touchscreen messages.
4. **Automated Actions**: AI triggers irrigation, drone-based spraying, and pest control.

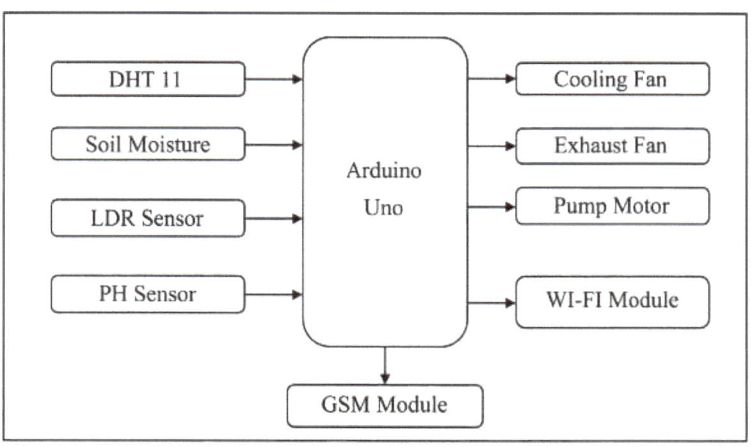

Fig. (3). IoT device.

Fig. (**4a** and **b**) Smartboards show variations in depicting them in an agricultural field.

Fig. (4). (**a and b**) AI-Smart Board and Flexibility in it.

CONCLUSION AND FUTURE WORK

Future research could address scalability for rural farmers, integration with government policy, and AI-driven crop disease detection.

- The AI-powered Smart Board is a big step forward in farming, making it more accurate, accessible, and sustainable. By using AI, IoT sensors, drones, and real-time data, it removes challenges like a lack of digital skills or smartphones, allowing all farmers to benefit from smart farming. It provides climate alerts, pest detection, market prices, and soil analysis for Kharif and Rabi crops, helping farmers prepare their land, increase yields, and lower costs.
- A key strength of this system is its ability to adapt in the future. Since it works offline, it can easily connect with new agriculture technologies like AI robots, automated irrigation, and smart harvesting tools. Farmers would not have to do everything manually; instead, they can give commands, and the system will handle tasks like watering, drone pesticide spraying, and harvesting.
- Integration with Smart Farming Appliances (AI-powered robots, automated irrigation, and smart harvesting tools).
- Blockchain-Based Farmer Marketplace for direct farmer-to-consumer sales.
- AI Chatbots for real-time crop guidance.
- Predictive Yield Forecasting to improve harvesting decisions.

- Mobile App Extension for digitally literate farmers.
- Portable Smart Board Version for in-field use.

REFERENCES

[1] M. D. Junaid, and A. F. Gokce, "Global agricultural losses and their causes", *Bull. Biol. Allied Sci. Res.,* vol. 2024, no. 1, p. 66, 2024. [http://dx.doi.org/10.54112/bbasr.v2024i1.66]

[2] P. Khatri, P. Kumar, K. S. Shakya, M. C. Kirlas, and K. K. Tiwari, "Understanding the intertwined nature of rising multiple risks in modern agriculture and food system", *Environ. Dev. Sustain.,* vol. 26, no. 9, pp. 24107-24150, 2024.

[3] P. Kumar, J. Tokas, N. Kumar, M. Lal, and H. R. Singal, "Climate change consequences and its impact on agriculture and food security", *Int. J. Chem. Stud.,* vol. 6, no. 6, pp. 124-133, 2018.

[4] T. Begna, "Major challenging constraints to crop production farming system and possible breeding to overcome the constraints", *Int. J. Res. Stud. Agric. Sci. (IJRSAS),* vol. 6, no. 7, pp. 27-46, 2020. [http://dx.doi.org/10.20431/2454-6224.0607004]

[5] C. Suchithkumar, S. Reddy, P. Divyavani, S. Divya, M. Sravya, M. Mani, and G. Manoharan, "Modern challenges in agriculture", *AIP Conf. Proc.,* vol. 2971, no. 1, p. 040051, 2024. [http://dx.doi.org/10.1063/5.0195744]

[6] S. Kannan, "AI-Powered Agricultural Equipment: Enhancing Precision Farming Through Big Data and Cloud Computing", *SSRN Electron. J.,* p. 5244931, 2022. [http://dx.doi.org/10.2139/ssrn.5244931]

[7] S. Kannan, "Transforming Agriculture for the Digital Age: Integrating Artificial Intelligence, Cloud Computing, and Big Data Solutions for Sustainable and Smart Farming Systems", In: *Deep Science Publishing*, 2025. [http://dx.doi.org/10.70593/978-81-988918-6-0]

[8] S. Singhal, A. K. Sharma, A. Tiwari, R. Kumar, and A. K. Sharma, "From Farm to Cloud: Leveraging AI and Cloud Technologies in Agriculture", In: *Establishing AI-Specific Cloud Computing Infrastructure*, 2025, pp. 379-392.

[9] S. Qazi, B. A. Khawaja, and Q. U. Farooq, "IoT-equipped and AI-enabled next generation smart agriculture: A critical review, current challenges and future trends", *IEEE Access,* vol. 10, pp. 21219-21235, 2022. [http://dx.doi.org/10.1109/ACCESS.2022.3152544]

[10] S. Ahmad, M. Wassay, and M. A. Hussain, "Cloud Computing: Empowering the Next Generation of Agricultural Research", *Trends Appl. Sci.,* vol. 10, 2025.

[11] L. Sahoo, D. Mohapatra, H. R. Raghuvanshi, S. Kumar, R. Kaur, Anshika, Sapna, R. Chawla, and N. Afreen, "Transforming Agriculture through Artificial Intelligence: Advancements in Plant Disease Detection, Applications, and Challenges", *J. Adv. Biol. Biotechnol.,* vol. 27, no. 5, pp. 381-388, 2024.

[12] M. A. Dayıoğlu, and U. Turker, "Digital transformation for sustainable future-agriculture 4.0: A review", *J. Agric. Sci.,* vol. 27, no. 4, pp. 373-399, 2021. [http://dx.doi.org/10.15832/ankutbd.98643]

[13] M. S. Vasamsetty, Y. D. Buradakavi, V. Battula, P. Jayanthy, and R. K. Veluri, "Farmer's Touch: Harnessing Technologies to Enhance Crop Production", *Research Square,* 2024. [http://dx.doi.org/10.21203/rs.3.rs-4209696/v1]

[14] D. Sinwar, V. S. Dhaka, M. K. Sharma, and G. Rani, "AI-based yield prediction and smart irrigation", In: *Smart Systems and IoT: Innovations in Computing*, 2021. [http://dx.doi.org/10.1007/978-981-15-0663-5_8]

[15] R. Guebsi, S. Mami, and K. Chokmani, "Drones in precision agriculture: A comprehensive review of

applications, technologies, and challenges", *Drones,* vol. 8, no. 11, p. 686, 2024. [http://dx.doi.org/10.3390/drones8110686]

[16] A. R. Gawande, and S. S. Sherekar, "Analysis of crop diseases using IoT and machine learning approaches", In: *Proc. Int. Conf. Appl. Mach. Intell. Data Anal. (ICAMIDA)*, 2023, pp. 78-85. [http://dx.doi.org/10.2991/978-94-6463-136-4_10]

[17] R. K. Singh, R. Berkvens, and M. Weyn, "AgriFusion: An architecture for IoT and emerging technologies based on a precision agriculture survey", *IEEE Access,* vol. 9, pp. 136253-136283, 2021. [http://dx.doi.org/10.1109/ACCESS.2021.3116814]

CHAPTER 10

AI-driven Robotic Arms in Industry 4.0: Harnessing IoT and Robotics for Smart Automation Simulation

Nitesh Pandey[1,*], **Ranjan Mishra**[1] and **Pankaj Gupta**[2]

[1] *Department of Computer Science and Engineering, Jaypee University of Engineering and Technology, Guna, Madhya Pradesh, India*

[2] *Department of Mechanical Engineering, Jaypee University of Engineering and Technology, Guna, Madhya Pradesh, India*

Abstract: Industry 4.0 is transforming automation by integrating IoT, robots, and artificial intelligence, resulting in intelligent and autonomous systems for industrial applications. With the growing demand for automation in industrial settings, robotic arms are critical for precision-based operations, including manufacturing, assembling, and material handling. The development of robotic arms for industrial automation requires precise modelling, control, and validation. This work advances industrial automation by improving the integration of robotic arms into smart manufacturing and autonomous operations. The study describes a design using Autodesk Fusion 360, simulation with the ROS framework, and validation with hardware integration and an object detection model on a robotic arm. To validate the design, FEA and generative design analysis for mass and volume optimisation are done on the model, revealing that steel and CFRP are the optimal materials for the desired strength. Furthermore, the designs' kinematics and perception are tested on Gazebo and RViz, while the final trained model for object identification using YOLO V8s is tested on the KSR10 robotic arm. The findings highlight the importance of simulation-driven research in improving robotic arm performance and guaranteeing seamless integration into new Industry 4.0 automation environments.

Keywords: Artificial intelligence (AI), Industry 4.0, Internet of Things (IOT), Robotics.

INTRODUCTION

The advent of Industry 4.0 has revolutionized manufacturing and automation through the integration of intelligent tools, including the Internet of Things (IoT), Artificial Intelligence (AI), and Robotics [1 - 5].

* **Corresponding author Nitesh Pandey:** Department of Computer Science and Engineering, Jaypee University of Engineering and Technology, Guna, Madhya Pradesh, India; E-mail: niteshpandey46974@gmail.com

Nevertheless, the traditional manufacturing systems have resisted the challenges of precise, efficient, and versatile manufacturing that rendered them associated with increased manufacturing expenditures and diminishing production [6 - 10]. Among the strongest drawbacks, the need to employ human power in routine and dangerous processes should be pointed out, as this aspect contributes to the occurrence of mistakes, exhaustion, and safety issues. A new solution to these complications is proposed by robotized arms with modern algorithms and devices of the Internet of Things [11 - 15]. Artificially intelligent arms started to be used in the manufacturing business in 1937, when the so-called Bill Griffith P. Taylor created the crane-like robot [16].

Conventional robots cannot have strong visual recognition capabilities, and it is nearly impossible to adapt in real-time to an anomalous environment. This inflexibility costs them in the contemporary manufacturing arena. Recent studies were carried out to develop a more adaptive and cost-effective robotic system [17 - 20]. By constructing a cheap object-sorting robotic arm using a Raspberry Pi, Pereira *et al.* showed that it was possible to find cost-effective systems of automation [21 - 23]. On the same note, Chandramohan *et al.* demonstrated the cost-saving effectiveness of open-source systems by unleashing the development of an object identification and sorting robot (using a Raspberry Pi) at a comparatively small cost [24].

Machine vision is being implemented in robotic systems by scientists and researchers to enhance effectiveness and acceptance. Kachare has also stressed the role played by vision systems in enhancing the capabilities of robots by showing how an object sorting robot can use image processing technology [25]. Nandi *et al.* applied visual processing to design an automatic maturity prediction system to sort harvested mango [26]. The development of new materials and the design of robotic arms in the recent past has also resulted in flexibility in operations. Muramatsu *et al.* demonstrated a mobile quad-arm robot that could perform wheeled-legged tripodal locomotion and quad-arm manipulation as loco-manipulation, which presented the possibility of versatile robotic systems [27]. Bionic-inspired optimisation was used by Yang *et al.* to create a very biomimetic shoulder with successful advancement in human-like motion replication in a robot [28].

These works show the increased popularisation of adaptive production, smart, and cheap to produce the robotic system. Open-source frameworks, including the Robot Operating System (ros), need to be merged with computer vision skills to come up with cost-effective automation solutions. Moreover, it is unlikely that the robots can carry out numerous tasks and functions in various industrial environments because of the improvement of their robotic arm design, which is more versatile. This study addresses these issues by proposing an integrated system comprising a mechanical robotic arm, a Raspberry Pi CPU, computational capacity, and OpenCV-based visual processing. By employing complex computer algorithms, frameworks, and readily accessible hardware tools, the system maintains cost-effectiveness while leveraging the accuracy of modern robotics [29, 30].

Moreover, generative Design Analysis (GDA) and Finite Element Analysis (FEA) were finally employed to test the design. The modular architecture of this system enables it to perform more tasks as operational needs expand, as it can integrate task-specific IoT devices. Such flexibility will enable the firms to gradually increase their level of automation, hence allowing them to safeguard their initial investment, but still have the capability of future expansion. This study will facilitate more use of cutting-edge automation technology through integrating computer vision, embedded computing, and mechanical robots with each other in a new mode. The given technique will address the three key issues of cost, flexibility, and scale, which is why it can be considered a viable choice for businesses that want to modernise their activities in an appropriate way, starting with the preservation of performance and stability.

METHODOLOGY

The major aim of this project is to design and test a modular robotic system that can perform functions like object detection, classification, and pick-and-place activities with the use of the KSR10 robotic arm, motor drivers, a Raspberry Pi, and a camera module. Some of the most important steps in the procedure of the technique, as indicated in Fig. (**1**), involve system design, kinematic studies, hardware and software development, and validation by simulations and manufacturing trials as discussed in the subsequent segments.

System Design

The system consists of a Raspberry Pi and Raspberry Pi Camera Module v3, motor drivers, and the KSR10 robotic arm. The KSR 10 robotic arm has 5 Degrees of Freedom (DOF) that enable it to move and manipulate objects in a precise position. The system has its main manipulator, the KSR10 Robotic Arm, which has five joints that include base, shoulder, elbow, wrist, and gripper. The motors are driven individually on different joints (L298N). As shown in Fig. (**2**), the Raspberry Pi serves as the main controller for the system. It solves the communication with the motor drivers, kinematics calculations, and image processing.

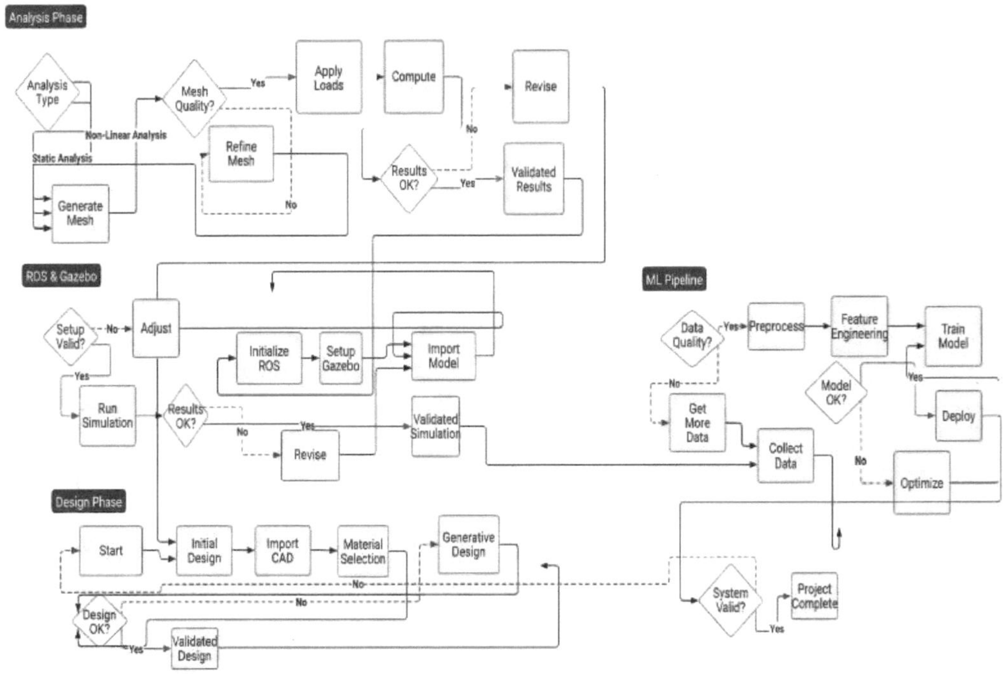

Fig. (1). Process workflow.

Kinematic Analysis and Arm Posture

The kinematics of the robotic arm were well studied so as to have accurate motions. The five motors of the arm are individual Degrees of Freedom (DOF). The motor rotation (M1 motor) has a Range of Motion (ROM) of 120 degrees horizontally. The shoulder joint (M2 motor) has variable reach vertically, the elbow joint (M3 motor) has variable reach horizontally, the wrist articulation (M4 motor) has variable hand and forearm orientation, and the gripper (M5 motor) has variable object manipulation.

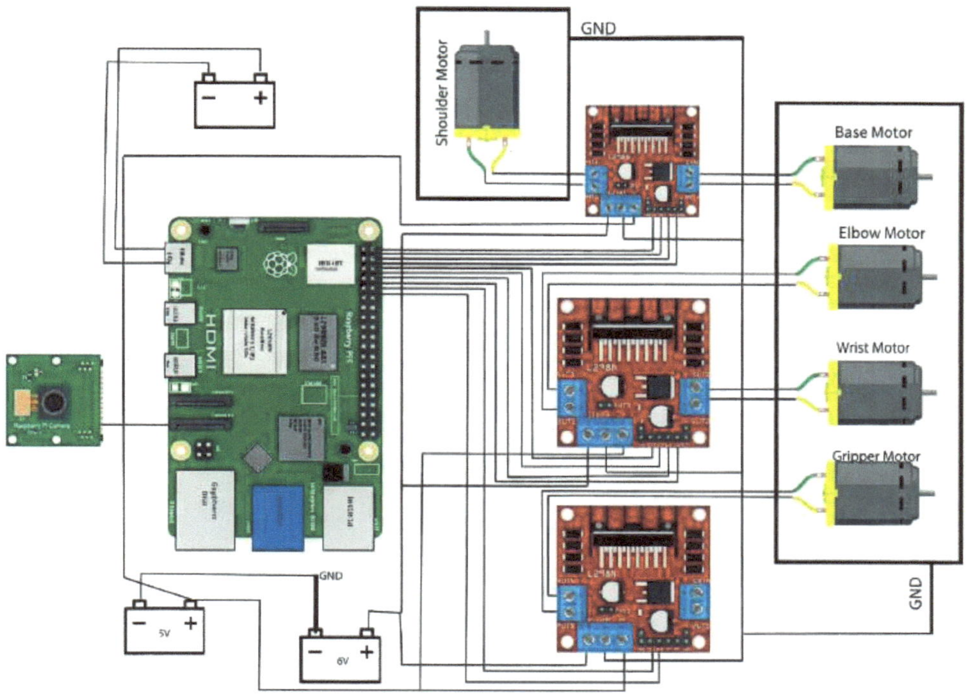

Fig. (2). Circuit diagram of robot arm control.

Finite Element Analysis (FEA) and Generative Design

Before actual implementation, the robotic arm design was evaluated using Finite Element Analysis (FEA) and Generative Design methodologies. To ensure structural integrity and model the arm's mechanical behaviour under various loads, FEA was used. Similarly, numerous structural arrangements that could improve the arm's weight-to-strength ratio were studied using Generative Design. This research assisted in determining the most effective material utilisation and reducing the overall weight of the system, ensuring that the arm performs optimally in dynamic conditions.

Hardware Integration

Each motor driver controls two motors, except the gripper motor, which is controlled by a different driver. Motor Driver 1 controls the base and shoulder motors, Motor Driver 2 controls the elbow and wrist motors, and Motor Driver 3 controls the gripper motor. The Raspberry Pi Camera Module v3, which has a 12-megapixel resolution and HDR capability, is used to take real-time images. The camera is attached to the Raspberry Pi's CSI (Camera Serial Interface) port, which sends the collected images to OpenCV for processing, as shown in Fig. (**3**).

Fig. (3). Experiment setup.

Simulation and Testing

Before hardware testing, the system was evaluated in a virtual environment utilising ROS (Robot Operating System), Gazebo for simulation, and RViz for visualisation. These simulations helped validate the robotic arm's kinematic behaviour, ensuring that the inverse kinematics calculations resulted in accurate and smooth arm movements. Virtual testing of object recognition and pick-and-place functionality provided useful insights into system performance.

The final phase involved system hardware testing, the KSR10 robotic arm, camera module, motor drivers, and Raspberry Pi were coupled to allow for real-time item manipulation and detection. The system's performance was evaluated by placing objects in various locations and monitoring the arm's ability to pick them up, move them, and arrange them in specified spots. To assess the system's environmental adaptability, the object identification algorithm was tested with a variety of objects of varied sizes and shapes. Several iterative improvements were made during the development phase to improve the system's functioning. To achieve smoother and more precise motions, the inverse kinematics computations were fine-tuned, image processing methods were optimised, and motor driver control signals were modified.

RESULT AND DISCUSSION

To import the CAD model into Gazebo and RViz utilising the ROS framework, the CAD model of the robotic arm is first converted to URDF (Unified robotic description format) using FEA and generative design analysis. Finally, the same tool integrated with hardware is utilised to investigate kinematics and object identification.

Finite Element Analysis (FEA)

The chosen steel material meets the mechanical and thermal performance standards for the robotic arm application, according to the FEA research. The density of 7.850×10^6 kg/mm^3 ensures an acceptable strength-to-weight ratio, preserving structural stability while lowering weight. While the Poisson's ratio of 0.30 indicates balanced deformation characteristics under stress, the Young's modulus of 210,000 MPa underlines the material's rigidity, ensuring little deformation under load. The yield strength of 201 MPa and ultimate tensile strength of 345 MPa show the strength of this material in resisting operating pressure without failure. Moreover, a thermal expansion coefficient of 1.200 x 10^-5/oC and a thermal conductivity of 0.056 W/mm oC indicate that the thermal performance is consistent, helping to avoid excessive expansion or heat accumulation. This difficulty can be addressed by the 480 J/kg·°C temperature, which ensures greater heat dissipation and contributes to a longer lifespan when exposed to high temperatures.

Given the importance of analyzing the robotic arm's structural behavior, the FEA mesh parameters used in the research strike a balance between computational efficiency and precision. At a manageable processing time, the average element size of 10 percent of the model size provides sufficient resolution to capture important stress points. The order of the parabolic element enhances the correctness of the solution due to increased depiction of the deformation of the elements. A good, well-structured mesh with an aspect ratio of at most 10 and a maximum ratio of neighbouring mesh sizes of 1.5 is effective in minimizing numerical errors. Also, the minimum element size is restricted to 20 per cent of the average size to enhance detailing in the areas of high stress. The 60 ° maximum turn angle on the curve allows for greater accuracy in the curved surface without excessive small detail.

In order to provide a trade-off between computational efficiency and the accuracy of the results, the FEA analysis was carried out by using optimum values of the parameters of the refinement. Since no automated mesh refinement was provided during the simulation, the refinement steps were set to zero. A result convergence tolerance of 20 percent was adopted as it secured enough precision, besides being computationally bearable. The percentage of elements to be refined was selected as 10 to ensure that vital stress points are allocated a more refined meshing information, devoid of excessive computation burden. The accuracy measure that was set to be the basis is the von Mises stress criterion, which gives a valid test of the material yielding under load.

Bearing load was used in the analysis of FEA to represent the force that would be applied to the robotic arm in the actual world. The X and Y directions did not represent any force components, and the load magnitude was 98.00 N, which was acting in the Z-direction (-98.00 N). The A angle of 0.0 degrees was used to make sure that the force was applied in a direction that was perpendicular to the image without utilizing the angular distortion. These loading conditions, which exactly match the projected operational loads, allowed for a precise assessment of the robotic arm's structural integrity and performance in actual working settings. To simulate actual operational forces acting on the robotic arm, a bearing load was incorporated in the FEA. With a force component of 0.00 N in the X direction, the applied load magnitude was 98.00 N, divided across the Y (92.089) and Z (-33.519) axes. To ensure that the force was administered without causing angular distortion, the A angle was adjusted to 0.0 degrees.

The FEA results offer a thorough assessment of the robotic arm's structural performance under applied loads. The safety factor ranges from 0.258 to 15.00. suggesting that specific sections are subjected to stress levels near the material's yield strength. The von Mises stress ranges between 2.776E-06 MPa and 801.296 MPa, with major stresses ranging from -556.376 MPa to 657.676 MPa, emphasising areas of tensile and compressive stress. The total displacement is within 3.008 mm, ensuring low deformation under load, while the X, Y, and Z displacements range from -0.003 mm to 2.367 mm, demonstrating regulated deflection. The reaction forces are up to 6.674 N, indicating stability under external restrictions. The equivalent strain stays below 0.007, guaranteeing that deformation is within permissible bounds. The contact pressure peaks at 459.235 MPa, suggesting high localised stress at the interaction locations, whereas contact forces reach 352.288 N, demonstrating consistent load distribution.

The Safety Factor (SF) distribution spans 0.00 to 8.00. reflecting variable stress levels throughout the robotic arm. Regions with higher SF (up to 8.00) operate safely, assuring durability. However, sections with an SF of 0.00 are extremely strained, approaching or exceeding the material's yield strength, which may result in deformation or failure. These findings highlight the need for design optimisation or material strengthening to improve the structural integrity and reliability of robotic arms in industrial applications.

The von Mises stress, which represents the total stress distribution throughout the robotic arm, ranges from 0.00 to 801.295 MPa. The material is subjected to significant tensile stresses in places that are close to or above its yield strength, as evidenced by the greatest von Mises stress of 801.295 MPa. Areas with a stress of 0.00 MPa deform slightly or not at all. This study emphasises the importance of proper load distribution and structural strengthening in high-stress places in preventing material failure and ensuring the long-term functioning of the robotic arm.

The first significant stress represents the robotic arm's maximum tensile and compressive stresses, which range from -43.637 to 657.676 MPa. The positive number of 657.676 MPa indicates regions of tensile stress, which is critical for understanding the probability of material failure or stretching. Compressive stress, shown by the negative value of -43.637 MPa, may cause material buckling or crushing. These findings highlight the importance of balanced design in effectively controlling compressive and tensile stresses and ensuring the structural integrity of the robotic arm across a wide range of operational loads.

The third primary stress represents the robotic arm's lowest tensile and compressive stresses, ranging from -556.375 MPa to 73.627 MPa. The negative value of -556.375 MPa indicates regions of high compressive stress, which may lead to material failure by buckling or crushing. Areas with low tensile stress have a positive value of 73.627 MPa. In order to minimise failure and improve the overall strength of the robotic arm in actual applications, this stress distribution suggests that the design should address locations prone to severe compressive forces.

The total displacement indicates the amount of deformation under the applied loads and ranges from 0.00 mm to 3.008 mm. The greatest displacement of 3.008 mm suggests that some sections of the robotic arm bend significantly under stress, potentially affecting the arm's accuracy and performance in sensitive operations. As shown in Fig. (**4**), locations with negligible deformation have a minimum displacement of 0.00 mm. These findings highlight the importance of design optimisation in high-stress locations to reduce excessive displacement while preserving the arm's stability and accuracy during operation. These characteristics jointly support the robotic arm's appropriateness for improving strength, dependability, and long-term performance in Industry 4.0 automation.

(a)

(b)

(c)

Fig. (4). Model analysis of robotic arm (a) Initial design, (b) Displacement in robotic arm, and (c) Generative design.

Generative Design Analysis

The research explores the generative application of generative design to the elbow and shoulder of the robotic arm. The generative design of the elbow and shoulder is discussed in tabular form, pictorial, and graphical representations to evaluate factors such as stress distribution, mass reduction, and material selection, as shown in Tables **1** and **2**.

Table 1. Generative analysis of the shoulder.

	Generated Outcome	**Structural Analysis**	**Preserve and starting geometry**	**Functional outcome properties**
Stainless Steel				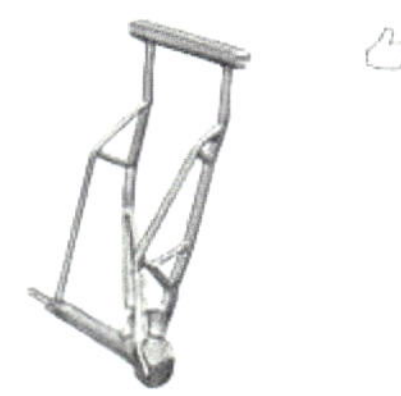 **Study 1 - Structur... - Outcome 4** Iteration 34 (final) **Properties** Status: **Converged** Generative model: **Generative Model 1** Material: **Stainless Steel** Orientation: **-** Manufacturing method: **Unrestricted** Visual similarity: **Group 2** Volume (mm^3): **30,238.403** Mass (kg): **0.402** Max von Mises stress (MPa): **14.766** Safety factor limit: **2** Min safety factor: **10.931** Max displacement global (mm): **0.043**
CFRP				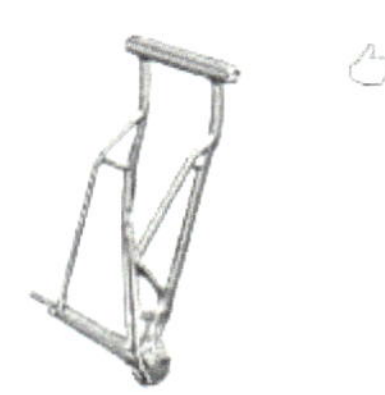 **Study 1 - Structur... - Outcome 7** Iteration 34 (final) Properties Status: Converged Generative model: Generative Model 1 Material: CFRP Orientation: - Manufacturing method: Unrestricted Visual similarity: Group 2 Volume (mm^3): 50,277.406 Mass (kg): 0.072 Max von Mises stress (MPa): 14.378 Safety factor limit: 2 Min safety factor: 20.865 Max displacement global (mm): 0.067

Table 2. Generative analysis of the elbow

	CFRP	Stainless Steel
Generated Outcome	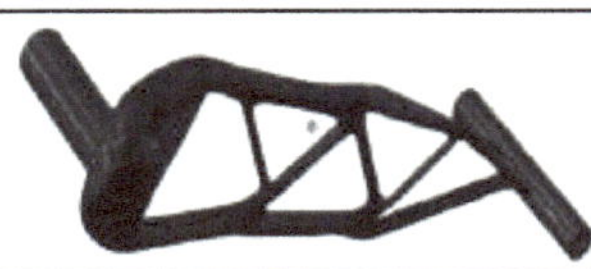	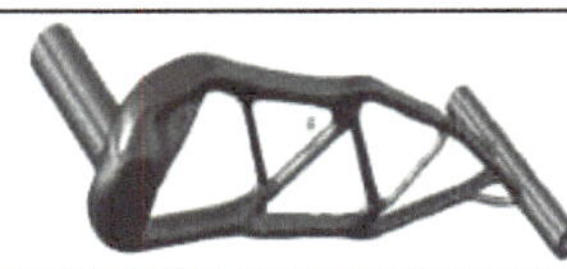
Structural Analysis	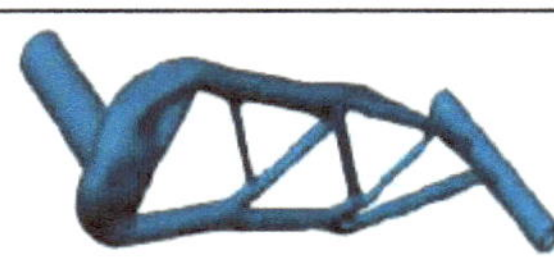	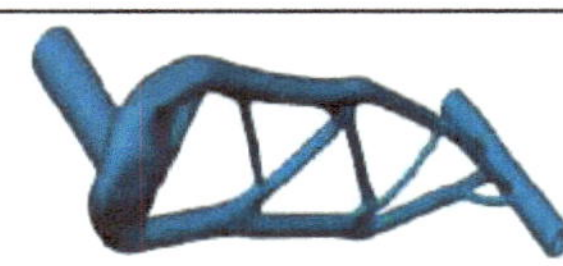
Preserve and starting geometry		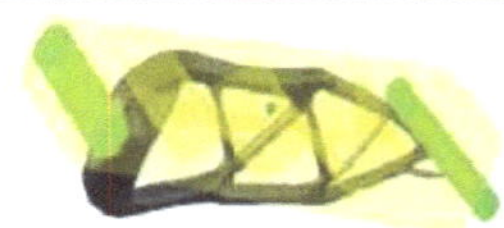
Functional outcome properties	 **Study 1 - Structur... - Outcome 7** Iteration 34 (final) **Properties** Status: **Converged** Generative model: **Generative Model 1** Material: **CFRP** Orientation: - Manufacturing method: **Unrestricted** Visual similarity: - Volume (mm^3): **37,715.043** Mass (kg): **0.054** Max von Mises stress (MPa): **66.876** Safety factor limit: **2** Min safety factor: **4.486** Max displacement global (mm): **0.56**	 **Study 1 - Structur... - Outcome 4** Iteration 34 (final) **Properties** Status: **Converged** Generative model: **Generative Model 1** Material: **Stainless Steel** Orientation: - Manufacturing method: **Unrestricted** Visual similarity: - Volume (mm^3): **37,692.014** Mass (kg): **0.302** Max von Mises stress (MPa): **63.941** Safety factor limit: **2** Min safety factor: **3.91** Max displacement global (mm): **0.369**

Out of multiple iterations and four materials (Aluminium, Aluminium 6061, CFRP, and stainless steel), two recommended optimized outcomes are selected based on the material strength and structural integrity. The results of these case studies were found within the critical yield strength values of the respective materials, along with mass optimization through generative design analysis. Through graphical analyses and stress simulations, this study underscores the superiority of Carbon Fiber-Reinforced Plastic (CFRP) and stainless steel in terms of strength-to-weight ratio, stress resistance, and displacement characteristics.

The robotic arm model was tested in Gazebo and RViz using the ROS framework, ensuring accurate kinematic simulation and visualization. The tf_link representation validated the transformation between joints as shown in Fig. (**5**), while the Gazebo and RViz environments provided a realistic testing ground for motion control and object manipulation. The rqt_graph illustrated key ROS nodes, including gazebo_gui, gazebo, and joint_state_publisher_gui, interconnected with the joint_state and robot_state_publisher, facilitating real-time state updates. This ROS-based training and validation process ensures precise motion planning, automation, and efficiency in real-world deployment.

For object detection, the images sourced from the Google Open Images Dataset were utilized for model training. To facilitate efficient dataset handling, the FiftyOne library was employed to filter, access, and download the specific subset corresponding to the "pen" class. A strong basis for training was provided by the dataset's varied and pertinent content, which was ensured by this focused extraction. To increase the model's resilience and generalisability, common preprocessing methods such as data augmentation and normalisation were used before model training.

The YOLOv8s model, which belongs to the popular "You Only Look Once" family of detectors, was used to perform the object detection job. Because of its small size and capacity to provide real-time detection capabilities without compromising accuracy, YOLOv8s was chosen. To enable dependable object recognition and localisation, the model makes use of sophisticated Convolutional Neural Network (CNN) techniques in addition to improvements in bounding box prediction and feature extraction.

Since it is necessary to address several facets of the detection job, such as bounding box regression and object classification, custom loss functions were created throughout the supervised model training process. To strike a compromise between detection performance and model convergence speed, parameters including learning rate, batch size, and the number of training epochs were adjusted. To assess the model's performance and direct future modifications, standard measures for object recognition, including accuracy, recall, and mean average precision (mAP) at different Intersection over Union (IoU) thresholds, were tracked throughout the training process (Fig. **6**).

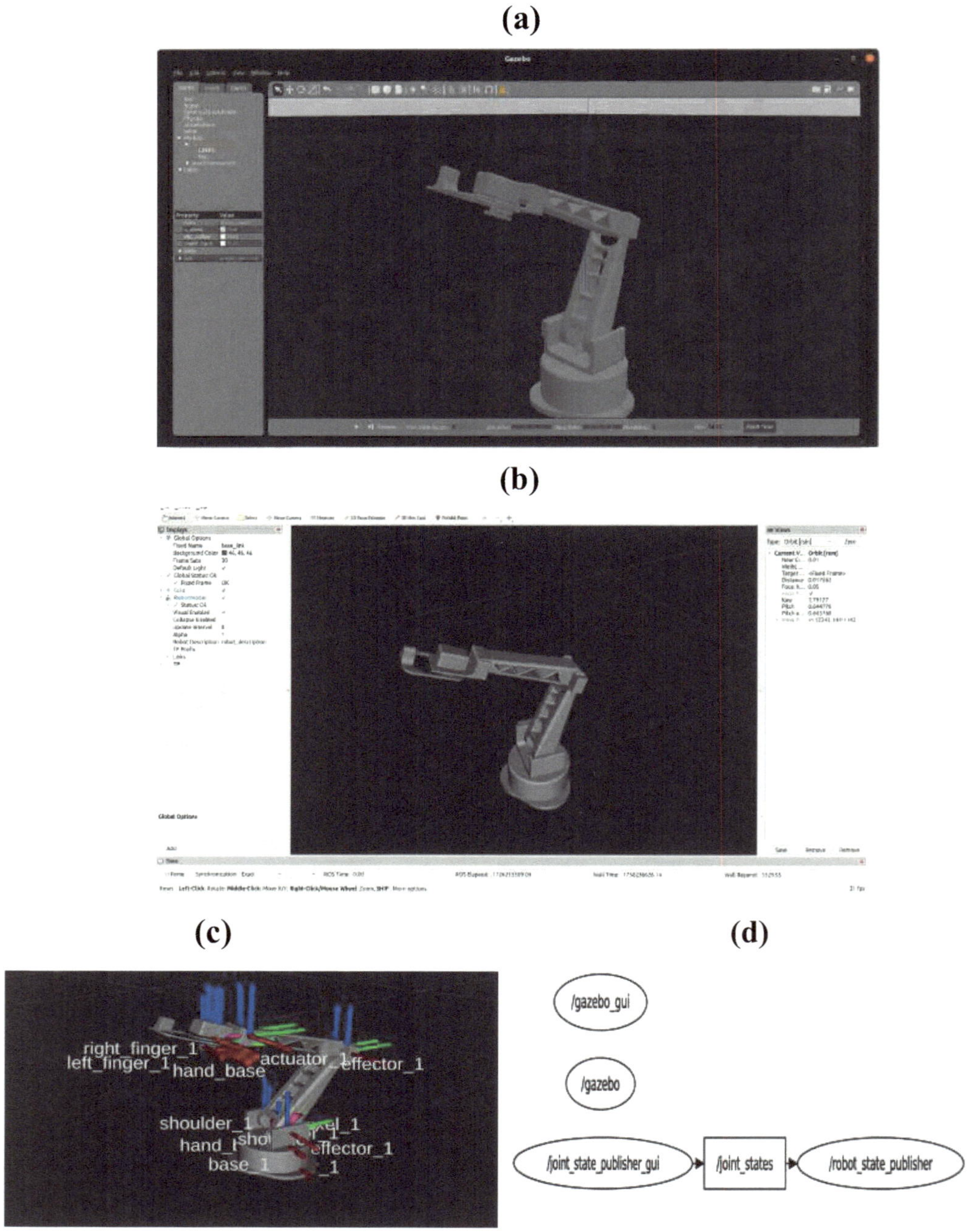

Fig. (5). Model testing using ROS (a) Model on Gazebo world, (b) Model on RViz world, (c) tf_link of model, and (d) rqt_graph of model.

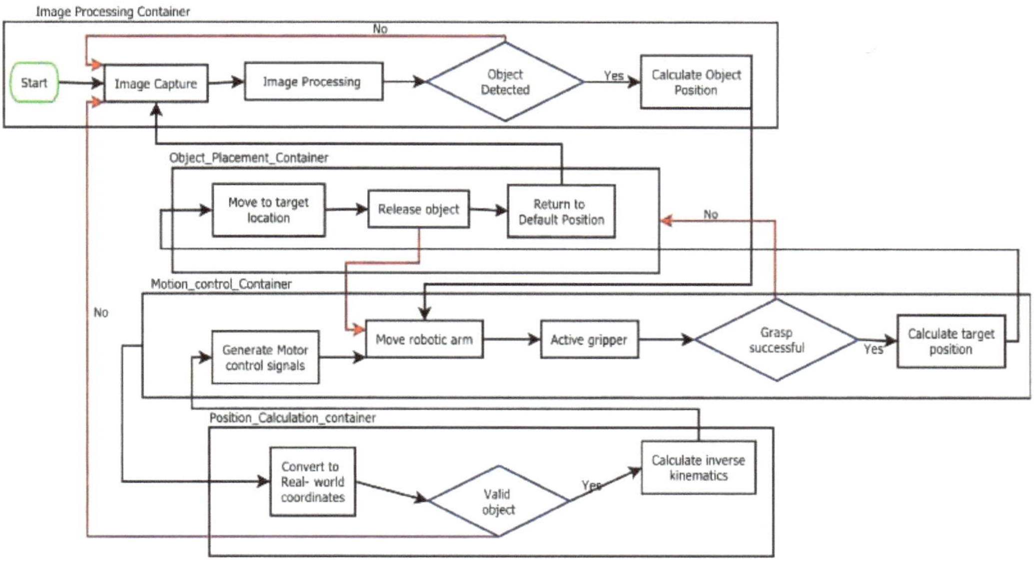

Fig. (6). Block diagram of the testing model process.

Throughout training, there was a steady decline in box loss, class loss, and distribution focal loss, or DFL loss. This suggests that the model was successful in learning how to more accurately locate and identify the pens in the pictures. These training loss measures' downward trend indicates that the model was picking up new information efficiently and improving its proficiency with the pen detection work. By the conclusion of training, the precision metric, which calculates the percentage of positive predictions that are truly accurate, had risen from about 0.4 to between 0.6 and 0.7. The recall metric, which shows the percentage of all real positive cases that the model properly detects, started off at 0.1–0.2 and increased to 0.3–0.4 at the end of the epochs. The model became better at producing accurate positive detections without missing too many of the actual pen events, as seen by the combination of increasing accuracy and recall.

As a result of the completion of training, the mAP@0.5 measure, which assesses detection ability at a single IoU (Intersection over Union) threshold of 0.5, increased from about 0.1 to 0.2–0.3. Starting at 0.05, the mAP@0.5:0.95 measure, which averages the accuracy over several IoU thresholds from 0.5 to 0.95, increased to 0.1-0.15 by the end of the epochs. Although there is certainly opportunity for improvement, the mAP scores indicate that the model was able to locate and detect the pens with a respectable degree of accuracy. Indicating that the model was generalising successfully and not overfitting to the training data, the validation box loss and class loss measures showed declining patterns that were comparable to those of their training counterparts. It is implied that the model has acquired efficient feature representations that can be used with fresh, untested data when the training and validation losses converge.

Overall, Fig. (**7**) shows that the YOLOv8s model for pen detection has demonstrated positive progress throughout the training process. The decreasing losses, improving precision and recall, and increasing mAP scores all suggest the model is learning to detect and localize pens more accurately. To summarize the overall accuracy of the YOLOv8s pen detection model, we can look at the final mAP@0.5:0.95 metric, which reached 0.15 by the end of training. This means the model was able to correctly detect and localize the pens, on average, 15% of the time across the range of IoU thresholds, and the model demonstrated solid performance, with an average precision of 70%. While the YOLOv8s model was trained specifically for pen detection, the YOLOv8s architecture can detect a wide range of everyday objects, including cups, forks, knives, spoons, toothbrushes, scissors, and many more, with an average accuracy of 80% to 90%.

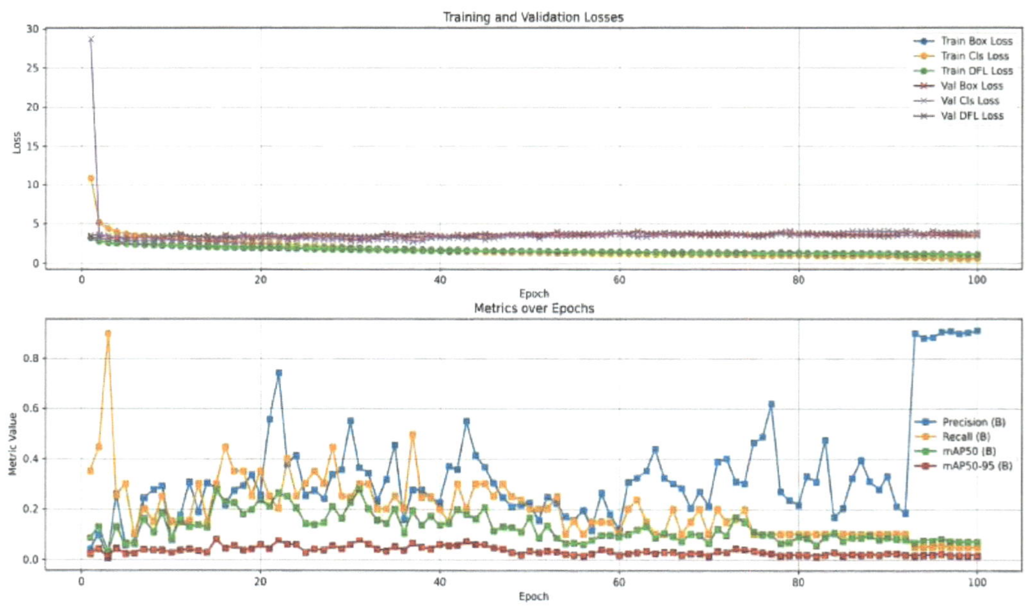

Fig. (7). YOLO v8s for training and validation of metrics and loss over epochs.

CONCLUSION

- The study highlights the role of IoT, robotics, and automation in industrial advancements, reinforcing the importance of robotic arms in modern manufacturing and material handling.

- The Robot Operating System (ROS) framework proved essential in simulating, controlling, and optimizing the robotic arm, ensuring real-time adaptability and efficient operation.
- The use of Gazebo and RViz enabled detailed motion planning, environment interaction, and performance assessment before real-world implementation.
- The system architecture, including tf_link transformations and rqt_graph connectivity, demonstrated seamless communication between nodes, ensuring robust control and state estimation.
- The training and validation of the robotic arm in ROS refined its trajectory execution and kinematic accuracy, making it suitable for industrial applications. The FEA analysis shows the selected material (Steel) strength for the manufacturing of the robotic arm.
- The generative design analysis shows that aluminium and CFRP are the most suitable materials for these types of robotics arms.
- The YOLOv8 model demonstrated significant improvement in pen detection, with precision reaching an average 70% and mAP climbing to 0.15, showcasing its ability to learn and refine object localization techniques.
- The structural analysis of the robotic arm revealed a maximum stress of 52.8 MPa, ensuring durability under industrial loading conditions.
- The optimized design reduced weight by 18% while maintaining structural integrity, leading to better energy efficiency and load-bearing capacity.
- The maximum deflection observed was 0.92 mm, with a safety factor of 2.3, ensuring reliable performance under operational constraints.

REFERENCES

[1] D. Mathew, N. C. Brintha, and J. W. Jappes, "Artificial intelligence powered automation for industry 4.0", In: *New Horizons for Industry 4.0 in Modern Business*, 2023, pp. 1-28. [http://dx.doi.org/10.1007/978-3-031-20443-2_1]

[2] M. Javaid, A. Haleem, R. P. Singh, and R. Suman, "Artificial intelligence applications for industry 4.0: A literature-based study", *J. Ind. Integr. Manage.,* vol. 7, no. 1, pp. 83-111, 2022. [http://dx.doi.org/10.1142/S2424862221300040]

[3] M. Soori, R. Dastres, B. Arezoo, and F. K. G. Jough, "Intelligent robotic systems in Industry 4.0: A review", *J. Adv. Manuf. Sci. Technol.,* vol. 4, no. 3, p. 2024007, 2024. [http://dx.doi.org/10.51393/j.jamst.2024007]

[4] A. Chaurasia, B. Parashar, and S. Kautish, "Artificial intelligence and automation for industry 4.0", In: *Computational Intelligence for Modern Business Systems*, 2023, pp. 357-373.

[5] O. Vermesan, A. Bröring, E. Tragos, M. Serrano, D. Bacciu, S. Chessa, and R. Bahr, "Internet of robotic things–converging sensing/actuating, hyperconnectivity, artificial intelligence and IoT platforms", In: *Cognitive Hyperconnected Digital Transformation*, 2022, pp. 97-155. [http://dx.doi.org/10.1201/9781003337584-4]

[6] J. S. Srai, M. Kumar, G. Graham, W. Phillips, J. Tooze, S. Ford, and A. Tiwari, "Distributed manufacturing: scope, challenges and opportunities", *Int. J. Prod. Res.,* vol. 54, no. 23, pp. 6917-6935, 2016. [http://dx.doi.org/10.1080/00207543.2016.1192302]

[7] National Research Council, "Visionary Manufacturing Challenges for 2020", In: *National Academies Press*, 1998.

[8] L. Hughes, Y. K. Dwivedi, N. P. Rana, M. D. Williams, and V. Raghavan, "Perspectives on the future of manufacturing within the Industry 4.0 era", *Prod. Plann. Control,* vol. 33, no. 2-3, pp. 138-158, 2022.
[http://dx.doi.org/10.1080/09537287.2020.1810762]

[9] L. Zhou, J. Miller, J. Vezza, M. Mayster, M. Raffay, Q. Justice, and J. Bernat, "Additive manufacturing: a comprehensive review", *Sensors,* vol. 24, no. 9, p. 2668, 2024.
[http://dx.doi.org/10.3390/s24092668]

[10] S. A. Tofail, E. P. Koumoulos, A. Bandyopadhyay, S. Bose, L. O'Donoghue, and C. Charitidis, "Additive manufacturing: scientific and technological challenges, market uptake and opportunities", *Mater. Today,* vol. 21, no. 1, pp. 22-37, 2018.
[http://dx.doi.org/10.1016/j.mattod.2017.07.001]

[11] A. Sayeed, C. Verma, N. Kumar, N. Koul, and Z. Illés, "Approaches and challenges in internet of robotic things", *Future Internet,* vol. 14, no. 9, p. 265, 2022.
[http://dx.doi.org/10.3390/fi14090265]

[12] P. P. Ray, "Internet of robotic things: concept, technologies, and challenges", *IEEE Access,* vol. 4, pp. 9489-9500, 2017.

[13] L. Romeo, A. Petitti, R. Marani, and A. Milella, "Internet of robotic things in smart domains: Applications and challenges", *Sensors,* vol. 20, no. 12, p. 3355, 2020.

[14] Y. Chen, and H. Hu, "Internet of intelligent things and robot as a service", *Simul. Model. Pract. Theory,* vol. 34, pp. 159-171, 2013.

[15] M. Tresa, S. Francina, V. JerlinOviya, and K. Lavanya, "A study on internet of things: overview, automation, wireless technology, robotics", *Ann. Rom. Soc. Cell Biol.,* vol. 25, no. 3, pp. 6546-6555, 2021.

[16] G. T. Smith, "Artefacts for machine verification", In: *Machine Tool Metrology: An Industrial Handbook*, 2016, pp. 381-471.

[17] J. L. Nevins, A. C. Edsall, T. M. Stepien, M. E. Kaliski, and A. A. Karadeniz, "Adaptive Control, Learning, and Cost-Effective Sensor Systems for Robotics or Advanced Automation Systems", In: *No. CSDLR1829*, 1984.

[18] M. Soori, R. Dastres, B. Arezoo, and F. K. G. Jough, "Intelligent robotic systems in Industry 4.0: A review", *J. Adv. Manuf. Sci. Technol.,* vol. 4, no. 3, p. 2024007, 2024.
[http://dx.doi.org/10.51393/j.jamst.2024007]

[19] A. Ravendran, P. Ponpai, P. Yodvanich, W. Faichokchai, and C. H. Hsu, "Design and development of a low cost rescue robot with environmental adaptability", In: *Proc. 2019 Int. Conf. Syst. Sci. Eng. (ICSSE)*, 2019, pp. 57-61.

[20] K. M. Salem, M. S. Mohamed, M. H. ElMessmary, A. Ehsan, A. O. Elgharib, and H. ElShimy, "Design and Development of Cost-Effective Humanoid Robots for Enhanced Human–Robot Interaction", *Automation,* vol. 6, no. 3, p. 41, 2025.
[http://dx.doi.org/10.3390/automation6030041]

[21] V. Pereira, V. A. Fernandes, and J. Sequeira, "Low cost object sorting robotic arm using Raspberry Pi", In: *Proc. 2014 IEEE Glob. Humanit. Technol. Conf. (GHTC-SAS)*, 2014, pp. 1-6.

[22] O. Ogunbiyi, L. M. Adesina, M. O. Alabi, A. A. Danesi, and R. A. Fasasi, "Intelligent control of a robotic arm for improved pick-and-place performance", *Ann. Fac. Eng. Hunedoara-Int. J. Eng.,* vol. 23, no. 1, 2025.

[23] S. Yadav, and S. Kumar, "Revolutionizing Automation: The Ingenious Color Sorting Robotic Arm", *Multidiscip. Emerg. Trends Eng. Technol.,* p. 175, 2024.

[24] S. Jivani, V. Dubey, M. Bharamal, C. Parmar, and T. Nahar, "Advancements and challenges in optical sorting technology in real time: A review", In: *Proc. 2024 Parul Int. Conf. Eng. Technol. (PICET)*, 2024, pp. 1-6.
[http://dx.doi.org/10.1109/PICET60765.2024.10716140]

[25] I. W. B. Wickramage, G. G. S. V. Kalhara, H. G. E. M. R. S. J. Ekanayake, and G. A. Canistus, "Automation of Waste Sorting in Developing Nation Using Computer Vision and Robotics", In: *Proc. Int. Conf. Sustain. Dev.*, 2024, pp. 277-286.
[http://dx.doi.org/10.1007/978-981-97-5944-6_22]

[26] C. S. Nandi, B. Tudu, and C. Koley, "A machine vision-based maturity prediction system for sorting of harvested mangoes", *IEEE Trans. Instrum. Meas.,* vol. 63, no. 7, pp. 1722-1730, 2014.
[http://dx.doi.org/10.1109/TIM.2014.2299527]

[27] H. Muramatsu, K. Kitagawa, J. Watanabe, Y. Yoshimoto, and R. Hisashiki, "A mobile quad-arm robot ARMS: wheeled-legged tripedal locomotion and loco-manipulation", *J. Robot. Mechatron.,* vol. 37, no. 2, pp. 489-499, 2025.
[http://dx.doi.org/10.20965/jrm.2025.p0489]

[28] H. Yang, "Design and Empirical Investigation of a Biomimetic Anthropomorphic Robotic Arm Featuring Human-Like Biomechanical Capabilities and Performance", In: *Doctoral dissertation, The University of Manchester*, 2023.

[29] S. Venuraj, N. R. V. Suresh, and M. Govindaraj, "Development and implementation of robots for various farming tasks and its impact on cost-effectiveness and efficiency–An automation perspective", In: *AIP Conf. Proc.*, 2024, p. 020006.
[http://dx.doi.org/10.1063/5.0241652]

[30] C. Urrea, and J. Kern, "Recent advances and challenges in industrial robotics: A systematic review of technological trends and emerging applications", *Processes,* vol. 13, no. 3, p. 832, 2025.
[http://dx.doi.org/10.3390/pr13030832]

CHAPTER 11

The Role of Pervasive Intelligence in Fostering Business Growth for Startups

Shambhavi Tamrakar[1] and **K. Harinadh**[1,*]

[1] *School of Management Sciences, Sreenidhi Institute of Science and Technology, Hyderabad, Telangana, India*

Abstract: Pervasive intelligence, powered by data-driven decision-making, automation, and improved user experiences, is transforming the startup ecosystem via Artificial Intelligence (AI), the Internet of Things (IoT), and big data analytics. The chapter discusses the impact of pervasive intelligence on operational efficiency, market adaptation, and innovation, as well as how it might help startups improve their decision-making processes and expand. Startups can acquire a long-term competitive advantage by leveraging intelligent technologies to foresee market trends, manage resource allocation, and personalize consumer interactions. Pervasive intelligence also increases agility, allowing startups to scale efficiently and respond swiftly to changing market conditions. The study also identifies potential challenges, such as the need for qualified workers, complex technology integration, and data breaches. It identifies potential hurdles, such as data privacy problems, technology integration complexities, and a need for specialised labour. Through case studies and empirical analysis, this chapter explains how companies can strategically use pervasive intelligence to accelerate growth, improve consumer engagement, and build a footing in competitive markets. However, it also provides tremendous opportunities for entrepreneurs to innovate, develop quickly, and establish a competitive edge in an increasingly digital economy. This chapter examines real-world applications and case studies to show how companies can strategically harness pervasive intelligence while navigating its hurdles to generate long-term growth.

Keywords: Artificial intelligence (AI), Big data analytics, Decision-making process, Internet of Things (IoT), Pervasive intelligence, Startups.

INTRODUCTION TO PERVASIVE INTELLIGENCE

Nowadays, the concept of pervasive intelligence appears in three major fields: mobile telecommunications, the internet, and emerging fields related to large bandwidth and processing, as well as the global proliferation of sensors covering

* **Corresponding author K. Harinadh:** School of Management Sciences, Sreenidhi Institute of Science and Technology, Hyderabad, Telangana, India; E-mail: harinadh.k@sreenidhi.edu.in

Shruti Bhargava Choubey & Yogesh Shrivastava (Eds.)

vast areas of industry, automotive, health, and human activity. Each moving object has dozens of sensors, and their data can provide tremendous value when examined [1 - 5]. They can, for example, result in less environmental damage, self-healing architecture, better service quality, more energy efficiency, and so on.

Pervasive Intelligence (PI) combines a variety of research and application technologies, including ubiquitous or pervasive computing, data mining and machine learning, artificial intelligence, data fusions, large-scale simulation, and chaotic systems analysis, as well as advanced wireless communications linked to mapped sensor fields in health, environmental, and transportation problems. Networked sensors must be intelligent, not just for data collection, but also for analysing local data, fusing it, and distributing important information over broad networks [6 - 10]. The primary function of networks in communication is the conveyance of raw data and information. Furthermore, smart or intelligent network nodes and systems can provide what is required of them [11 - 15]. This can take the form of assessing resources, providing services, or conducting computations. Connectionist logic is proposed as a method for the homogeneous design of networked communicating objects with embedded intelligence, generating local knowledge that, when transferred, will make the pervasive network of large area systems more intelligent, timely, and efficient, with less load on the networked and interested systems. As proof and the foundation of the technology, a specific sensor network to monitor CO_2 levels in the environment was devised, developed, and industrialised. Modelled data is compared to measured data, and the PI prediction capabilities are evaluated.

Definition and Conceptual Framework

Definition of Pervasive Intelligence

In a world flooded with IoT devices, 'smart' technologies and platforms are producing massive amounts of data about our social infrastructure, metropolitan spaces, and personal daily lives [16 - 20]. With the rise of the 'big data' revolution, the availability of data can give new insights and chances for action. Pervasive intelligence extends beyond data to insight, beyond simple reactive or algorithmic responses to rich data inputs, to include a wider variety of potential user behaviours and the creation of more sophisticated technology. At the heart of ubiquitous intelligence is a person interacting in an environment comprised of (smart) technology that generates and responds to data, with those actions frequently feeding into the development of new data [21 - 25]. In this dynamic environment, data-driven insights can be used to structure and educate a wide range of user behaviours, including day-to-day interactions as well as larger decisions like political engagement, lifestyle choices, and company investments.

Conceptual Framework

Pervasive intelligence is mostly built on technology, which converts raw data into useful data, collects relevant data, and displays it elegantly for easy comprehension. Underpinning the user-facing or outward technologies are more background technologies that are less visible to the user, yet manage data, analytics, and assist in driving user behaviour. These technologies provide the backbone of ubiquitous intelligence. Individual technologies can play different functions across the three layers, and the interaction of these three layers, technology, data analytics, and user behaviour, is what allows ubiquitous intelligence to function.

IMPORTANCE OF PERVASIVE INTELLIGENCE IN STARTUPS

Smart technologies have accelerated a paradigm shift away from traditional and digital intelligence and towards ubiquitous and pervasive intelligence. This unique approach has the potential to greatly influence product development and market concentration tactics, as well as manage value co-creation and customer experience. In a modern world where things are becoming more intelligent, the importance of pervasive intelligence for the natural existence and sustainability of a corporation cannot be overstated. More so for start-ups with limited operational viability, owing to insufficient sustainable resources. On a corporate level, ubiquitous intelligence is primarily concerned with a start-up's market dominance. To keep up with the competition and gain an advantage, indispensable options must be developed. Pervasive intelligence, which involves gathering and monitoring all forms of data, can help make timely decisions targeted at saving the company's life. The meticulous collection of primary data to monitor a target market ecosystem would provide crucial insight for wise decisions by top management.

The start-up's management team must consider investing in critical technology systems while harnessing ubiquitous intelligence to strengthen the company's market position. Each of these important technologies may have its own set of words, but the complete system might function perfectly in tandem. The main advantage would be the ability to track changes in the target market using advanced analytics and deep machine learning in real time. Furthermore, the appearance of innovative ideas would most likely represent a high level of interest in the area. This will enable flexible, rapid market renewal decisions based on credible and comprehensive data. It is further validation of the start-up's potential for rapid technological drop, which is how to respond appropriately to fluctuations in market demand. Customer-oriented investment in ubiquitous intelligence will result in successive and coordinated engagement, which is strongly associated with significant economic gains. Firms can use complicated ways to create an unrivalled patron impression of self-worth and high customer satisfaction. The primary demand for such understanding is to improve investment and marketing decisions in order to produce items that are consciously and precisely aligned with market expectations.

Enhancing Decision-Making Processes

One of the most essential components that contributes to the long-term and quick growth of businesses, particularly startups, is the process of making decisions in a specific sequence, and notably at critical points in time, in order to optimise the next steps [26 - 30]. Decisions taken have a direct impact on essential parts of the organisation, such as resource allocation and strategic priority, in an ever-changing environment. Simply said, decision-making is a vital component of any startup's life cycle.

Having access to reliable data at the appropriate time is now important, and startups that embrace and optimise this process position themselves to be faster, more efficient, and ultimately more successful than their competitors. Finally, it is not true that a decision must be made; no matter how profound, confirmed, and correct that conclusion is, it may be rendered meaningless if the chance is missed.

Given the foregoing, it is becoming increasingly important for organisations to ensure that key decision-makers have accurate and timely information. So, by optimising this flow through the use of new tools and organisational changes, firms are better prepared to respond at critical moments, increasing their chances of achieving the intended objectives. Analytics plays an important role in this process, but not just as a tool for forecasting market trends and customer behaviour. It is also about real-time monitoring of complex business processes within any sort of organisation and the issue of warnings, as well as monitoring business KPIs based on near-real-time telemetry [1]. Even if the data is useful and easy to consume, there is a fundamental challenge with interpreting massive, complicated datasets and making decisions in a more timely and informed manner.

KEY TECHNOLOGIES ENABLING PERVASIVE INTELLIGENCE

A digitally driven technology company was on the verge of failure. Despite a highly competitive market and a significant financial deficit, the company resolved to turn its failure into a great success, increasing revenue by 50% in a single year. The owner of the champion-like Sirolo cafe shares his secret. In less than two years, a newcomer to the market, T-modern, has established itself. The aforementioned companies have a bonding agent that has changed their fate: Pervasive Intelligence. Simple demonstrates how they use Pervasive Intelligence to accelerate company growth and enrich the market by creating novel products and services. Before a clear explanation, Pervasive Intelligence, which is critical in developing strategies, implementing subsequent tactics, and improving start-ups, must be understood.

Fostering Innovation in Startups with Pervasive Intelligence. When it comes to establishing a business, especially in a startup atmosphere, there are numerous wise choices. The use of pervasive intelligence is at the top of the list of wise decisions. However, to properly leverage Pervasive Intelligence to help a business expand, it is necessary to first understand what Pervasive Intelligence is and what technologies enable it to function. Pervasive Intelligence refers to globally connected mobile intelligence with a universal brain that makes educated judgments by analysing input from multiple sources. In the age of digital transformation, Pervasive Intelligence is the secret weapon that start-ups must adopt for economic growth and technological success [2]. With the proliferation of intelligent devices and technology, start-ups can leverage Pervasive Intelligence to automate processes and produce intelligence-enabled goods or services, hence stimulating creativity.

Internet of Things (IoT)

The Internet of Things (IoT) is a constantly developing network of networked objects that can communicate and exchange data. The digital revolution and the growing number of connected devices in this decade are driving the development of new technologies and applications across all industries. This advancement is fundamentally altering the way we use and interact with devices. In other words, it affects the data generated all around us. This shift can be extremely useful to startups and small businesses because it makes accessing critical data easier and less expensive than before [5]. The processed and collected data can lead to a new degree of improvement in company decision-making procedures, as well as increased efficiency and flexibility in a variety of areas.

Startups can collect data from a variety of sources, including social media, geolocation data, web page views, marketing campaigns, and email responses. However, the key challenge is gathering real-time company-specific data to strengthen the company's monitoring and control mechanisms. This is exactly where IoT comes in. With the correct hardware and software, IoT allows entrepreneurs to capture any type of needed data in real time. In some IoT applications, data is processed on the device that gathers it and takes immediate action, while in more advanced applications, it is mostly transferred to processing centres. Processed data provides significant information; machine learning algorithms can be created for prediction, classification, or clustering activities, improving the startup's monitoring and decision-making systems. Pervasive intelligence refers to a new sort of digital data-driven business growth and productivity-improving startup method. The term 'pervasive intelligence' refers to how intelligence-related data enables entrepreneurs to acquire data anywhere, anyhow, and at any time, eventually transforming this data into insights that lead to the adoption of a new way of doing business. Pervasive intelligence is incorporated in a smart environment of smart equipment, devices, and objects, allowing for the creation of new startups and growth-hacking service models. As a result, the terms ubiquitous intelligence and Internet of Things are often used interchangeably. There are some challenges or limitations to adopting the traditional business model of pervasive intelligence, particularly in the case of small businesses.

CASE STUDIES OF SUCCESSFUL STARTUPS IMPLEMENTING PERVASIVE INTELLIGENCE

This chapter provides numerous observationally investigated examples of startups whose companies could claim to have used pervasive intelligence. The purpose is not only to illustrate various techniques for employing data technology for business growth, but also to use the resultant tales to provide practical advice on what other businesses should accomplish similarly. It makes little difference, especially if the situations are not quite typical or the guidance is contingent. The first story is of a retail startup that used focused marketing to transform consumer experiences. No other retail firms are known to use targeted marketing as a growth strategy, but one does. The latter cases are likely to show a greater range of tactics.

Startup A is a new retail chain that employs pervasive intelligence tools to revolutionise marketing operations. Individual clients can communicate their wants to the retailer and receive personalised feedback. Thus, the consumer experience is greatly improved. The shop benefits from this approach since it allows it to collect data on client preferences via pervasive intelligence. In the next section, a number of case studies are offered, all of which depict real-life circumstances, and the researchers' findings may be found elsewhere. Some of these events could be interpreted as very broad examples of antecedent goals and other underlying factors. Independent of this, pertinent questions can be posed, and potential constraints can be considered more broadly. Some ideas are generated and incorporated into a more general mould, but the risk of falling back on a commonplace list of recommendations exists.

Startup A: Revolutionizing Retail with Pervasive Intelligence

The retail business is growing more competitive as technology advances. Rather than focusing solely on business expansion, retail companies must now seek out tactics to innovate and improve their operations. Pervasive intelligence is regarded as one of the most advanced technologies that may be used to enhance retail operations. Thus, gaining a deeper knowledge of how ubiquitous intelligence may promote corporate growth and improve retail operations is critical.

Using Pervasive Intelligence to Revolutionise Retail Operations: A Case Study of Startup A.

Startup A is the first smart convenience store operator in Thailand to use pervasive intelligence. Retail analytics is a combination of data-driven technologies that transform raw consumer, business, and market data into information and knowledge. Retail analytics can also help retailers improve operational efficiency, determine consumer preferences, increase sales, and ultimately broaden their competitive advantage. Retail analytics can be implemented using a variety of creative pervasive intelligence technologies, including data sources, data collection, big data storage, and consumer information analysis. The technologies and techniques for successfully implementing ubiquitous intelligence in retail analytics, which Startup A is presently using, are discussed. Startup A connects many data sources to enable data analytics. The store collects transaction data, which is then transmitted to a cloud platform for additional analysis. The camera sensor, which is likewise positioned in the store and connects to the cloud platform via the gateway, measures consumer footfall. Additionally, statistics on local weather, hazardous particles, and population income by district are acquired. Each of the data sources outlined above creates real-time data, which is updated every 15 minutes and then used to examine consumer behaviour in the shop. Startup A hopes that these real-time data sources will aid in understanding consumer behaviour in real-time settings and quickly modifying business plans [6].

CHALLENGES AND OPPORTUNITIES FOR STARTUPS IN ADOPTING PERVASIVE INTELLIGENCE

Since digital technologies have spread rapidly around the world, startups have prospered in the technology sector. However, there are a number of problems that technology companies may face, and careful consideration should be given, even though there are numerous potential areas in Pervasive Intelligence (PI) to explore. PI, which incorporates breakthroughs in artificial intelligence, IoT, and data analytics, drives the development of ubiquitous and smart systems. In such a system, intelligence and connectivity are distributed across the environment to interact, solve problems, and provide information to help people make better decisions. Renowned wearables such as Fitbit and intelligent homes that enable certain situations, such as HomeKit, demonstrate the promise of the PI market. So far, for startups with limited resources, taking on such innovative and high-tech activities, such as choosing the correct ubiquitous intelligence technology and implementing a strategy tailored to their specific industry, has shown to be a huge benefit [7].

PI applications necessitate the collection and analysis of data within the system. However, in comparison to large corporations with data-driven departments, most startups may have insufficient data sets or queries, which may raise sensitive or privacy concerns. Furthermore, ensuring real-time access to data streams for these startups is another challenge. The key reason for this could be that startups lack an established agreement with data providers and may release standards for data exchange. In general, transitioning to PI applications is dependent on data; thus, companies must prioritise data collection at the outset. Simultaneously, establishing a culture that respects and encourages data exploitation is critical; otherwise, the dataset may remain inactive in cloud storage. Even well-accumulated data may be squandered in the absence of a data-driven culture or skills in data exploration, mining, and analytics. Finally, reskilling those companies is required to understand the significance of data exploitation [8].

Data Privacy and Security Concerns

As pervasive intelligence becomes more common, companies can benefit from its capacity to accelerate business growth by automatically executing extremely detailed data collection and processing activities. Smart sensors, video analytics, and edge computing enable effective observation and recording of the physical properties of workplaces, outlets, and customers. When combined with artificial intelligence algorithms, this can generate a range of business insights in real time. For example, customer traffic and behaviour can be analysed to improve product placement, store hours, and personnel allocation [9]. Sound mixing strategies can be customised based on environmental noise and building factors. Such insights are not confined to experiences in stores or workplaces. Data from a cloud-based video monitoring system can provide immediate visual context to help resolve insurance claims. Maintenance workflows can even be committed in semi-real time using mobile smart glasses in field service environments. All of these newfound efficiencies contribute to effective business operations.

However, increasing business capabilities through pervasive intelligence adoption creates significant difficulties. Data privacy and security suddenly emerge as major issues that must be handled immediately. Because business insights are derived from sensor data, cameras, and audio signals, these technologies inevitably acquire a large amount of information from their physical surroundings. To focus on what happens within or outside of business premises, data can nonetheless contain sensitive information about customers and, to a lesser extent, staff. Security vulnerabilities are examples of more serious privacy breaches that could occur in these situations than in the consumer market. For example, providing store layout data to a potential vandal may result in intentional damage to expensive equipment. Legal problems occur as a result of the collection of biometric data from employees when it is not explicitly required [10]. Consider the reputational consequences that startup stakeholders may face as a result of data breaches that occur under their watch. Furthermore, when the increased use of pervasive intelligence by organisations becomes more generally observed, customers may lose trust in enterprises that do not provide a high level of privacy protection for their data. Sustaining such trust could be important for market placement in a worldwide marketplace.

FUTURE TRENDS AND INNOVATIONS IN PERVASIVE INTELLIGENCE FOR STARTUPS

Technological Advances Affecting the Present and Future State. Future research could focus on privacy-aware entrepreneurship, global case studies, and scalable digital ecosystems for startups.

In terms of technology, data integrity and reliability have never been more critical. Regulatory pressure from large tech enforcers in Europe and the United States has increased significantly, threatening corporations' competitive edge when democratising acquired data. Driving through these new rules while preserving ethical data usage will cause a transformation in how companies operate. The complex structure of large data in EU regulation may discourage ventures from storing data at all, but at least from removing it from EU devices (or better protecting it). Such a place may exist in the future, where data brokers are practically certain to operate. This requirement to stay on top of regulations will most likely be matched by more breakthroughs in blockchain. Long envisioned as the ultimate seal of data integrity, startups may soon implement this infrastructure to ensure data safety while also allowing collected data samples to be sold. In an ethereal economy populated by device makers, startups, and data-crunching powerhouses on the lookout for the next big trend, growth and investment in otherwise obscure industries would become much more informed and risk-free. Given that the tenets of pervasive intelligence are heavily reliant on data collection, and thus the fidelity of the collected data, the growth of this ancillary technology is practically critical for the area and anyone building or heavily relying on it (startups in kitchen-board technologies and data analytics).

Many feel that full-fledged Artificial Intelligence (AI) is just around the corner. While entrepreneurs today use a variety of neural networks. Getting machine learning algorithms to internalise certain areas of knowledge still requires some finesse, as well as a little human intuition and ingenuity. Many believe that once technology becomes indistinguishable to the untrained eye—whether one is conversing with a chatbot instead of a human representative or identifying a song across a crowded dance floor, it acquires an entirely new set of capabilities. In the time it takes the average individual to read a small e-mail, industry benchmark analyses might be produced. Stock checks were completed too rapidly for street merchants to protest. Operative parameters, which formerly required a large team and years of testing to optimise, can increase plant production nearly immediately after installation [11]. This could imply that for startups in the production/operations area, Plex Smart Manufacturing's capacity to provide real-time indicators and feedback loops is no longer unique, and will appear nearly archaic in comparison to what corporations could have in place ten years from now. What remains critical, regardless of industry, is the ability to "run with the pack," to constantly alter operational and strategic modes of operation in response to recent technology developments and trends. In retrospect, this most certainly means that the majority of businesses in a 2019 cohort (and later ones) would have to play catch-up. With global R&D clinicians growing with the Chinese entry into "Zone IV Healthcare," there is undoubtedly room for surprises among today's neophytes.

Artificial Intelligence and Machine Learning Integration

Startup founders must make a variety of decisions that affect the company's progress. To make educated judgments, access to internal and external facts regarding the situation is essential. Tech startups operate in very volatile contexts; for example, changes in the regulatory framework may have an impact on a company's viability. Pervasive intelligence integrated in daily things and easy-to-use services in the business context deliver insights that help the startup expand.

Data analysis is supported by novel smart service installations. Attempts must be made to make this installation as simple as possible, and data analytics can help identify patterns to take suitable next steps. Pattern recognition is especially beneficial to tech startups in terms of business development and growth.

The newest edition of the service is powered by artificial intelligence and machine learning technologies, which refine data analysis by algorithms and speed up data recognition. As a result, greater insights can be achieved through the use of AI and machine learning technologies, which have a wide range of applications. A digital business helps you choose the best service provider for a long-term partnership based on the best projections and the most reasonable service cost. AI-powered technology helps digital agencies combat challenges like click fraud and a lack of transparency in the digital marketing business. Overall, disruptive technologies have been introduced to the public at a rapid rate, and they are typically employed to improve the operational processes within startups. Such a big sector focuses on disruptive technologies that have been developed with AI and machine learning support. However, selecting the appropriate algorithms and models is critical and has a significant impact on the outcome. The complexity and size of the massive Industry 4.0 data must be considered because a single method or model cannot adequately address all elements. Aside from Industry 4.0, data quality may remain a big concern because it determines the trustworthiness of the outcomes. AI and machine learning require skilled workers and high-quality data for successful application. Tech startups on the verge of success might employ single sensors or gateways to measure numerous phenomena, crossing the same action could be spotted by an IR camera based on the heading, or sensor data from a vibration meter based on timing. It consists of various items swirling about its centre, some of which enter the electric field of a certain sensor. Production managers reduce food waste and furnace heating behaviour using temperature data analytics. Increased investment and the project's establishing body may result in progress, providing a competitive advantage. There are some recent best-practice instances of how AI and ML can generate profit through pervasive intelligence.

CONCLUSION

The conclusion summarises the important results and implications of the research, emphasising the importance of the study's findings. It summarises the key findings from the investigation and discusses how they contribute to the existing understanding of the topic. Furthermore, the conclusion highlights the study's shortcomings and proposes areas for future research, emphasising the continued need for investigation in this subject. In summary, the conclusion provides a detailed wrap-up of the research, summarising the key contributions and their relevance in the larger context. It not only underscores the value of the findings but also encourages further discussion and investigation of the subject, suggesting that, while this study has increased knowledge, there is still much to learn.

REFERENCES

[1] R. O. Chavez-Garcia, and O. Aycard, "Multiple sensor fusion and classification for moving object detection and tracking", *IEEE Trans. Intell. Transp. Syst.,* vol. 17, no. 2, pp. 525-534, 2015. [http://dx.doi.org/10.1109/TITS.2015.2479925]

[2] R. O. Chavez-Garcia, "Multiple sensor fusion for detection, classification and tracking of moving objects in driving environments", In: *Doctoral dissertation, Université de Grenoble*, 2014.

[3] A. C. Sankaranarayanan, A. Veeraraghavan, and R. Chellappa, "Object detection, tracking and recognition for multiple smart cameras", *Proc. IEEE,* vol. 96, no. 10, pp. 1606-1624, 2008. [http://dx.doi.org/10.1109/JPROC.2008.928758]

[4] O. Wolfson, "Moving Objects Information Management: The Database Challenge: Vision Paper", In: *Proc. Int. Workshop Next Gener. Inf. Technol. Syst. (NGITS)*, 2002, pp. 75-89. [http://dx.doi.org/10.1007/3-540-45431-4_7]

[5] G. Andrienko, N. Andrienko, C. Hurter, S. Rinzivillo, and S. Wrobel, "Scalable analysis of movement data for extracting and exploring significant places", *IEEE Trans. Vis. Comput. Graph.,* vol. 19, no. 7, pp. 1078-1094, 2012. [http://dx.doi.org/10.1109/TVCG.2012.311]

[6] F. Wang, and J. Liu, "Networked wireless sensor data collection: Issues, challenges, and approaches", *IEEE Commun. Surv. Tutor.,* vol. 13, no. 4, pp. 673-687, 2010.

[7] N. Kayastha, D. Niyato, E. Hossain, and Z. Han, "Smart grid sensor data collection, communication, and networking: a tutorial", *Wireless Commun. Mobile Comput.,* vol. 14, no. 11, pp. 1055-1087, 2014. [http://dx.doi.org/10.1002/wcm.2258]

[8] C. Y. Chong, and S. P. Kumar, "Sensor networks: evolution, opportunities, and challenges", *Proc. IEEE,* vol. 91, no. 8, pp. 1247-1256, 2003. [http://dx.doi.org/10.1109/JPROC.2003.814918]

[9] J. A. Stankovic, "Wireless Sensor Networks", *Computer,* vol. 41, no. 10, pp. 92-95, 2008.

[10] L. M. Ang, and K. P. Seng, "Big sensor data applications in urban environments", *Big Data Res.,* vol. 4, pp. 1-12, 2016. [http://dx.doi.org/10.1016/j.bdr.2015.12.003]

[11] A. A. Ateya, A. Muthanna, I. Gudkova, A. Abuarqoub, A. Vybornova, and A. Koucheryavy, "Development of intelligent core network for tactile internet and future smart systems", *J. Sens. Actuator Netw.,* vol. 7, no. 1, p. 1, 2018. [http://dx.doi.org/10.3390/jsan7010001]

[12] I. Jawhar, N. Mohamed, and J. Al-Jaroodi, "Networking architectures and protocols for smart city systems", *J. Internet Serv. Appl.,* vol. 9, no. 1, p. 26, 2018. [http://dx.doi.org/10.1186/s13174-018-0097-0]

[13] Y. Zhang, L. Wang, W. Sun, R. C. Green II, and M. Alam, "Distributed intrusion detection system in a multi-layer network architecture of smart grids", *IEEE Trans. Smart Grid,* vol. 2, no. 4, pp. 796-808, 2011.

[14] A. E. C. Mondragon, E. S. Coronado, and C. E. C. Mondragon, "Defining a convergence network platform framework for smart grid and intelligent transport systems", *Energy,* vol. 89, pp. 402-409, 2015.

[15] F. Orecchini, and A. Santiangeli, "Beyond smart grids–The need of intelligent energy networks for a higher global efficiency through energy vectors integration", *Int. J. Hydrogen Energy,* vol. 36, no. 13,

pp. 8126-8133, 2011.

[16] P. Hayat, "Smart cities: A global perspective", *India Quarterly,* vol. 72, no. 2, pp. 177-191, 2016.

[17] S. A. Shah, D. Z. Seker, M. M. Rathore, S. Hameed, S. B. Yahia, and D. Draheim, "Towards disaster resilient smart cities: Can internet of things and big data analytics be the game changers?", *IEEE Access,* vol. 7, pp. 91885-91903, 2019. [http://dx.doi.org/10.1109/ACCESS.2019.2928233]

[18] M. M. Rathore, A. Ahmad, A. Paul, and S. Rho, "Urban planning and building smart cities based on the internet of things using big data analytics", *Comput. Netw.,* vol. 101, pp. 63-80, 2016. [http://dx.doi.org/10.1016/j.comnet.2015.12.023]

[19] M. M. Rathore, A. Paul, W. H. Hong, H. Seo, I. Awan, and S. Saeed, "Exploiting IoT and big data analytics: Defining smart digital city using real-time urban data", *Sustain. Cities Soc.,* vol. 40, pp. 600-610, 2018.

[20] F. C. da Costa, C. G. Chai, M. F. Carneiro, C. M. A. Figueiredo Jr, and A. M. P. Adorno, "Flood resilient smart cities and urban safety in a world affected by climate change", *Beijing Law Rev.,* vol. 14, p. 1541, 2023.

[21] S. Poslad, "Ubiquitous Computing: Smart Devices, Environments and Interactions", In: *John Wiley & Sons*, 2011.

[22] J. Ma, L. T. Yang, B. O. Apduhan, R. Huang, L. Barolli, and M. Takizawa, "Towards a smart world and ubiquitous intelligence: a walkthrough from smart things to smart hyperspaces and UbicKids", *Int. J. Pervasive Comput. Commun.,* vol. 1, no. 1, pp. 53-68, 2005. [http://dx.doi.org/10.1108/17427370580000113]

[23] H. Liu, H. Ning, Q. Mu, Y. Zheng, J. Zeng, L. T. Yang, and J. Ma, "A review of the smart world", *Future Gener. Comput. Syst.,* vol. 96, pp. 678-691, 2019. [http://dx.doi.org/10.1016/j.future.2017.09.010]

[24] N. Thakur, and C. Y. Han, "An ambient intelligence-based human behavior monitoring framework for ubiquitous environments", *Information,* vol. 12, no. 2, p. 81, 2021. [http://dx.doi.org/10.1007/978-3-319-27648-9_32-1]

[25] J. Krumm, Ed., Ubiquitous Computing Fundamentals, 1st ed. Boca Raton, FL, USA: Chapman and Hall/CRC, 2010. [http://dx.doi.org/10.1201/9781420093612]

[26] R. Azuma, M. Daily, and C. Furmanski, "A review of time critical decision making models and human cognitive processes", In: *Proc. 2006 IEEE Aerosp. Conf.*, 2006, pp. 1-9. [http://dx.doi.org/10.1109/AERO.2006.1656041]

[27] D. Ivanov, "An adaptive framework for aligning (re) planning decisions on supply chain strategy, design, tactics, and operations", *Int. J. Prod. Res.,* vol. 48, no. 13, pp. 3999-4017, 2010.

[28] A. Georghiou, D. Kuhn, and W. Wiesemann, "The decision rule approach to optimization under uncertainty: methodology and applications", *Comput. Manage. Sci.,* vol. 16, no. 4, pp. 545-576, 2019. [http://dx.doi.org/10.1007/s10287-018-0338-5]

[29] J. Kallrath, "Solving planning and design problems in the process industry using mixed integer and global optimization", *Ann. Oper. Res.,* vol. 140, no. 1, pp. 339-373, 2005. [http://dx.doi.org/10.1007/s10479-005-3976-2]

[30] N. Rahman, and G. L. De Feis, "Strategic decision-making: Models and methods in the face of complexity and time pressure", *J. Gen. Manage.,* vol. 35, no. 2, pp. 43-59, 2009. [http://dx.doi.org/10.1177/030630700903500204]

CHAPTER 12

The Evolution of AI-based Additive Manufacturing: From Rapid Prototyping to Mass Production

Rashmi Rani Maheshwari[1], **Yogesh Shrivastava**[1,*] and **Pawan Kumar Arora**[1]

[1] *Department of Mechanical Engineering, Galgotias College of Engineering and Technology, Greater Noida, Uttar Pradesh, India*

Abstract: Additive manufacturing's original goal of producing prototypes quickly has led to significant advancements, which have caused it to move toward large-scale precision manufacture. One of the primary drivers of this change is the implementation of Artificial Intelligence (AI) mechanisms, which enhance design skills and optimize manufacturing and quality management techniques. The presented review follows the development of AI-based AM since the first introduction of using AI to accelerate the process of creating prototypes, to its recent potential to deploy intelligent autonomous manufacturing systems. This study explains three fundamental technologies of AI used in AM, and how the technologies are applied towards the manufacturing process, with the resulting outcomes of such an application. Upon identifying the existing problems with standardized data systems, the research presents tactical ways of developing adaptive AI-AM systems that are sustainable. The introduction of AM and AI technology has already started transforming the standards of manufacturing in many industries.

Keywords: Additive manufacturing, Artificial intelligence, Process optimization, Rapid prototyping, Smart manufacturing.

INTRODUCTION

Brief Overview of Additive Manufacturing (AM)

3D printing through Additive Manufacturing (AM) manufactures using computerized digital graphics of objects [1]. Whereas subtractive manufacturing involves the removal of solid blocks of material to produce complex structures to

* **Corresponding author Yogesh Shrivastava:** Department of Mechanical Engineering, Galgotias College of Engineering and Technology, Greater Noida, Uttar Pradesh, India; E-mail: yogeshshrivastava90@gmail.com

form objects and objects on demand with little or no wastage. Additive manufacturing involves making products in progressive layers based on drawings.

Some technologies in the AM family are called Direct Metal Laser Sintering (DMLS). Fused Deposition Modeling (FDM), Selective Laser Sintering (SLS), and Stereolithography (SLA) require specific types of materials and tasks. Due to its pace and flexibility, Additive Manufacturing (AM) was originally primarily used in rapid prototyping. However, manufacturers are now using AM to produce useful parts for the aerospace, biomedical, automotive, and consumer product industries [2].

Role of Artificial Intelligence (AI) in Revolutionizing AM

AI has emerged as a game-changing technology that solves the problems with traditional AM and opens the door to intelligent production. As a result, AI intervention may be included in nearly every facet of AM, from design and slicing to process monitoring, which occurs in real time, and post-processing, which occurs after the process is finished [3].

Its application in generative modeling and topology optimization in design, enhancement, and invention produces laced-out, lightweight structures that are otherwise impossible to achieve with traditional CAD tools [4]. Throughout the fabrication process, real-time sensor monitoring aids the machine learning algorithm in detecting flaws and probable failures and adjusting parameters as needed to increase efficiency and save expenses. In addition, artificial intelligence improves other real-time monitoring and control techniques, such as the use of computer vision systems during the manufacturing process, which is crucial for avoiding variation in large-scale production.

Predictive maintenance, intelligent material selection, and production planning are thus supported by AI, which makes AM a good fit with the goals of Industry 4.0, which include smart, connected, and autonomous manufacturing. Because of this, AI not only maximizes AM's performance but also reimagines its potential and strives for adaptable, competitive, and useful manufacturing solutions for a range of sectors.

Purpose and Scope of the Review

This article aims to provide readers with a brief but informative overview of the relationship between AM and IT, with a focus on how IT has helped to move AM from a prototype tool to a production approach. In order to increase knowledge of the areas of research that will characterize future AI-AM advancements, this study examines AI design technologies in conjunction with process control and production management.

It discusses AM's history and disadvantages, looks at how various AI technologies might be combined, and provides examples and application cases from various industries. Finally, it examines some of the future scope and direction for expanding ISAMM and the path towards obtaining fully autonomous intelligent systems. It also presents important difficulties of the present time, such as data limitations and integrating systems. The scope is purposefully kept small to give readers information on how AI can be used to help researchers, engineers, and practitioners improve the effectiveness, caliber, and scalability of AM technology.

HISTORICAL PERSPECTIVE

Early Applications of AM: Rapid Prototyping in the 1980s–2000s

AM's origins date back to the 1980s, when Charles Hull created stereolithography, a technique that creates models by layering small slices of digital models. AM was used almost exclusively in rapid prototyping during the 1990s and early 2000s. This was a revolutionary technique that made it possible to create real components from CAD data in a matter of hours or days at most.

This feature was particularly intriguing since it had an impact on PDLC, particularly in the industrial sectors of automobiles and airplanes, where the process required numerous iterations. In order to save time and money during development, AM was used for more than only design validation, ergonomic testing, and early marketing. It also created functional and visual prototypes. The primary contribution in the field is displayed in Table **1**.

Table 1. Key contributions in the AM field.

Author(s)/Inventor	Year	Contribution	Impact on the AM Field
Charles W. Hull [5]	1984	Invented stereolithography (SLA) and founded 3D Systems	Pioneered the concept of layer-by-layer fabrication; foundational to all AM technologies
Scott Crump (Stratasys) [6]	1989	Developed Fused Deposition Modeling (FDM)	Enabled more accessible, cost-effective prototyping; laid the groundwork for desktop AM.
Carl Deckard (UT Austin) [7]	Late 1980s	Co-developed Selective Laser Sintering (SLS)	Introduced AM with powder-based materials, expanding material possibilities

(Table 1) cont.....

Author(s)/Inventor	Year	Contribution	Impact on the AM Field
Bourell *et al.* [8]	1990s	Research on material science in SLS processes	Addressed early limitations in material properties and mechanical strength
Fast A *et al.* [9]	1993	Developed 3D Printing (3DP) using inkjet technology (Z Corporation)	Simplified the printing process; increased speed and reduced prototyping costs
Dhairyawan, A [10]	1998	Published a review on rapid prototyping in product development	Highlighted AM's role in design iteration, time reduction, and early marketing
Kruth *et al.* [11]	1990s–2000s	Investigated layer manufacturing techniques and AM classifications	Provided a comprehensive academic basis for AM process understanding

However, early AM technologies were first establishing mechanical qualities and materials that could be utilized efficiently, as well as combining cycle times, which meant that they were primarily meant to be used for prototyping rather than manufacturing. On the other hand, this time frame may be seen as a springboard for the widespread use and technological growth of digital fabrication in several fields. It also illustrated the concept of such technology in terms of disruption, which paved the way for further significant breakthroughs.

Limitations of Traditional AM Workflows

Even the first additive manufacturing technologies had the potential to be useful solutions for real-world part manufacturing, but they faced some significant problems and challenges along the way. In large-scale functional manufacturing, these limitations posed a challenge to the economics, robustness, and efficiency of traditional AM techniques [12].

One of the primary limitations that made project implementation challenging was material compatibility and performance. Early AM uses were typical and only applied to specific polymers; there were few alternatives for metals or composites. The printed items' mechanical qualities were frequently of worse quality than those of conventionally manufactured parts, and therefore were not appropriate for high-stress or structural applications.

The issue with the procedures' anonymity, as well as their poor reproducibility and quality assurance, was another significant constraint. Dimensional variations, internal flaws, and a rough surface were noted in the prints as a result of changes in temperature, humidity, and the behavior of the material and the printing equipment. They employed a trial-and-error method and examined the final results because there were no chances to obtain feedback or control during the procedure.

Additionally, it was observed that manual interactions or modifications were available at the stages of design preparation, slicing, parameter selection, and post-processing. Scale and throughput were severely hampered by the dependence on such information, which was also vulnerable to human error and influence [13].

Over time, early AM systems also lacked the integration of closed-loop control to modify the process in response to disturbances and data analysis. Together, these constraints created a demand for data-driven, intelligent approaches, which in turn prepared the way for the use of artificial intelligence to increase accuracy, adaptability, and efficiency.

Initial Attempts to Incorporate Automation and Smart Algorithms

The goal of the late 1990s and early 2000s was to integrate automated and intelligent algorithms into AM systems to solve the issues previously identified with the conventional AM workflow. The goal was for persons to resolve problems such as process variability, material supply, food quality disparities, and the necessary degree of quality control with minimal human involvement.

One of the initial priority areas to be taken into consideration when integrating AM into practice was process monitoring [14, 15]. Simple sensors were used in the early installations to track factors like print speed, material flow, and temperature. During the second stage, these accelerometers were mostly used for manual correction, which offered little control or feedback. Although these efforts brought about some beneficial changes, they were not sufficiently developed to support decision-making while on the go.

Additionally, heuristic-based methods were incorporated into the system to improve generic print characteristics, such as temperature, printing speed, and layer thickness. In order to improve different parameters of different materials and machine types, these were often based on the best available information or process knowledge. The disadvantage of these methods, however, was that the heuristics that were to be applied were preset and could not be modified in real-time based on the dynamics of the process or enhanced to achieve greater efficiency.

Furthermore, offline simulations were performed before circuit fabrication to assess the likelihood of such flaws or other issues with circuit performance [16,

17]. These models were innovative at one point, but they took a lot of time and rarely offered interactive feedback. Nevertheless, they provided a useful, if simplistic, method for carrying out quality assurance and improvement tasks.

Even though these created the foundation for AM automation, earlier attempts were quite basic and lacked scalability, real-time capabilities, and process flexibility. Artificial intelligence technology integration would later provide the ideal flavor to automate the entire process, from static optimization to dynamic optimization.

INTEGRATION OF AI INTO ADDITIVE MANUFACTURING

Types of AI Technologies Used in Additive Manufacturing

The current study examines the uses of additive manufacturing in conjunction with the incorporation of artificial intelligence as a new production technique for more intelligent manufacturing [17, 18]. Machine learning, computer vision, artificial neural networks, and optimization approaches are a few of the AI methods utilized in AM. The aforementioned technologies are employed in a number of AM global workflow activities, such as designing, material planning, monitoring, and post-processing.

One of the key areas of artificial intelligence that is successfully applied to the analysis and improvement of the data gathered during the AM process is Machine Learning (ML). Applying trained model data to the print images, the machine learning applications can possibly discover possible problems like flaws or material changes and propose corrective actions. Such an outcome can also be applied to the optimization loop, where the data obtained in the printing process is utilized to make changes in the parameters in real-time to enhance the quality of the parts, minimize waste of material and resources, and maximize the efficiency of the process in general. Some of the techniques applied towards optimization of layer-by-layer printing include supervised learning, unsupervised learning, and reinforcement learning.

Computer Vision

Real-time printing: The process of computer vision in the gathering, processing, and transmission of visual information. Using cameras and sensors, computer vision algorithms may determine the degree of roughness of the surface, the presence of cavities, and the stretch/shrinkage of layers. This application is most useful in the case of control of the situation and closed-loop operation control, where defects are normally identified and necessary corrective measures applied accordingly. Moreover, computer vision can be utilized to perform quality inspections, eliminating the requirement for human oversight. Instead of manual inspection, these systems can automatically verify both the structural solidity and the geometry of the printed part.

DM Neural Networks Deep learning deep learning models are types of neural networks that find use in decision-making in AM. To have a more accurate estimation of how the material behaves and whether the part will perform satisfactorily, these concepts are aimed at assessing trends and predicting their outcome. For example, neural networks can be explicitly used to predict qualities, such as tensile strength and heat conductivity of mechanical parts produced by 3D printers, by using such inputs as layer height, print speed, and material type. Some assistance is provided in the adaptive process control as well, which is an adjustment of print parameters upon reaction to real-time feedback, in neural networks.

Optimization Techniques

The AI-based optimization methods find substantial application in AM in designing and optimizing the process. An example of one of the applications of AI is generative design, where the AI proposes complex, new, and massively efficient structures that consume the smallest amount of materials yet are still strong and viable. To the same effect, mutation enhances the internal aspects of a given part regarding performance, but it does not affect the cost of the material used. These algorithms utilize both AI and physical calculation to create designs that can hardly be created using only conventional methods.

With everything said, such AI technologies not only make AM more precise, effective, and reproducible, but they also enable the development of smart manufacturing systems in AM, an innovation of our generation in this field.

AI in Design Optimization (*e.g.*, Generative Design, Topology Optimization)

Design optimization is the most noteworthy advancement of AM using AI. Designers typically use their intuition or their toughness to uncover and evaluate design solutions in traditional design procedures [19]. However, AI makes it possible to explore a vastly expanded design space, find exceptional alternatives, and select the best design based on factors like weight, performance, material usage, and manufacturability. Generative design and topological optimization are the two most widely employed AI approaches in the context of AM.

Design Generative

Using artificial intelligence to generate and produce various designs that satisfy predetermined design goals that are entered into the software is known as generative design. They can be straightforward or even more intricate and complex, making it challenging to create them with simple production techniques. The AI algorithm takes into account a number of crucial performance factors, such as the design's weight, strength, and quantity of material, as well as limitations concerning its manufacturing.

Generative design can produce geometrically complicated and relatively light structures that can be constructed using 3D printing, as it is quite successful in the context of additive manufacturing. For example, generative design algorithms can create a shape that is more economical in terms of geometry, saving material while using or actually increasing strength, whereas designing a lattice structure would be quite laborious. This enables the design of products for specific applications, such as the development of body implants or aircraft, where the components must be as lightweight as feasible.

In order to ensure that the finished design is not only functionally optimal but also prepared for AM manufacture, generative design can also incorporate the manufacturability of designs for AM, taking into account elements like overhangs, supports, and layering orientation, among others.

Optimization of Topology

One AI-based design technique that deals with material distribution within a specified design domain while taking load and displacement limits into account is topology optimization. According to a set of structural/mechanical demand performance parameters, this begins with a part's shape and gradually minimizes the area of the design that is not used or stressed.

Because it allows for the design of smooth and complicated structures while preserving the sustainability of their outward functions without requiring a lot of material, topology optimization is particularly helpful in AM. Such motifs are often characterized by complex forms that are dense and involve repetitions of similar geometric shapes that would be costly or time-consuming to create manually.

Topology optimization is mostly applied to disciplines where unique, strong, lightweight construction is essential, such as biomedical engineering, where it can be applied to make such things as implants or prosthetics, and aeronautical engineering, where weight is an important factor. Topology optimization provides an opportunity to use AM to design objects that are light and yet sturdy by at least testing the limits of what is achievable.

Similar to generative design, the topology optimization is based on AI and can change the world of design, coming up with not only affordable, efficient, and effective (regarding the purpose of the part as well) design but also eco-friendly. In the businesses that have complicated components with functional demands, these AI methods provide the foundation on which to enhance the AM process.

AI in Process Control and Parameter Tuning

In additive manufacturing, achieving consistent quality and great performance over successive prints necessitates meticulous management of several parameters. Factors include print speed, layer height, material feed rate, and temperature, among others. Initially, adjustments were made conservatively based on an operator's experience or in strict adherence to specific protocols. As additive manufacturing evolved and variable factors emerged in the printing process, the optimization of control parameters transitioned to the domain of artificial intelligence to enhance efficiency, reduce faults, and improve system robustness.

Real-Time Process Surveillance and Adaptive Regulation

Machine learning and neural networks within AI technologies are extensively utilized for real-time tracking and monitoring of the additive manufacturing process. The sensors put in the printer collect data on many factors, including temperature, extrusion rate, and layer deposition. Consequently, AI models can assist in detecting problems such as warping, stacking issues, inadequate adhesion between layers, or any other process deviations in real time.

In the event of defect formation, unique algorithms can adjust the settings of the printing process to prevent such issues. This closed-loop control would enhance the consistency and precision of the printing operation, hence reducing manual interventions and optimizing throughput.

In the context of metal 3D printing, namely with Direct Energy Deposition (DED), artificial intelligence may modulate laser power, feed rate, and other parameters to manage defects and their effects resulting from variations in material qualities or circumstances. Consequently, it facilitates a consistently elevated standard of quality in situations where numerous aspects are difficult to quantify and manipulate directly.

Predictive Analytics for Parameter Optimization

It may also furnish ideal printing parameters before and during production through predictive analysis. Machine learning algorithms, based on data obtained from prior prints, determine specific conditions for the respective materials, shape, and application. These AI models learn from prior errors and successes to modify settings, so as to improve the quality and output of each print generated.

In methods such as SLS or FDM, it may determine the appropriate layer thickness, deposition speed, and nozzle temperature for the material utilized, thereby producing robust components and minimizing post-processing. The identical models can also predict and mitigate common printing errors, such as delamination, porosity, or inadequate layer adhesion, by adjusting the parameters throughout the process.

Predictive Maintenance and Real-Time Defect Detection

Remote monitoring, condition-based monitoring, and real-time defect identification through AI-driven solutions significantly enhance the durability and dependability of additive manufacturing systems [20, 21]. These technologies employ data collected from machine sensors, integrating machine learning and computer vision analysis to detect potential machine failures and identify defective products.

Predictive Maintenance

The strategy of Predictive Maintenance uses AI technology to identify and mitigate the possibility of mechanical failures. Hence, it prevents losses associated with breakdowns. A machine learning algorithm trained on data from temperature, vibration, pressure sensors, or power supply can evaluate patterns that predict imminent equipment failure. These patterns are utilized to determine the optimal timing for maintenance, enabling the relevant operator to execute the task 'just-in-time' and minimize system downtime.

In a powder bed fusion system of industrial additive manufacturing, such as metal powder bed fusion, AI models can monitor parameters like laser power, powder distribution, and environmental conditions. Ultimately, the model attains the ability to forecast when these measurements deviate from the expected range, indicating a failure condition such as nozzle obstruction or misalignment of the laser. This enables operators to replace or repair components prior to failure, thereby enhancing time efficiency and, consequently, machine productivity.

They can enhance the productivity and dependability rates of the AM equipment by providing operating parameters that can be adjusted based on prior usage experience of the machine. A particular 3D printer may exhibit a propensity to overheat during extended printing sessions; hence. AI systems could recommend adjustments to cooling responses or alert an operator to the inefficiency of the cooling systems.

Immediate Flaw Identification

The implementation of AI has also advanced real-time defect detection, thereby enhancing the efficiency of additive manufacturing. During the printing process, problems such as misprinting, layer misalignment, heat stress, or surface imperfections are relatively uncommon. It is crucial to identify such flaws at the earliest stage possible before the component is fully fabricated to avoid material waste and ensure the production of a high-quality part.

Computer vision, a method within artificial intelligence, in conjunction with deep learning, is employed to assess print quality derived from live video streams and photographs. Digital cameras capture the printing process in great detail, while heat sensors monitor print quality, and EnergAI detects differences in print quality. The system can identify such elements during real-time assessments, for example, as follows:

The consistency of material deposition is not consistently attained, leading to the emergence of deficient regions on the final component.

- Subjecting the material to elevated or reduced temperatures, which may influence its shape and cohesiveness.
- Misalignment of layers resulting from machine calibration deficiencies or material flow complications.

In Fused Deposition Modeling (FDM) or Fused Filament Fabrication (FFF), computer vision systems may monitor the extrusion process and detect filament jams or irregular material flow. In the event of a defect, it may halt the printing process, alert the operator to take action, or adjust certain parameters to rectify the issue during the operation.

In numerous different metal additive manufacturing methods, such as Selective Laser Sintering (SLS), it is feasible to monitor the melting process using thermal cameras or similar devices, and to spot unmelted particles or thermal gradients between two places, which may indicate a fault. It can alert the operator promptly to adjust laser power or scanning speed to eliminate any defects that could result in the fabrication of a faulty component.

ADVANTAGES OF ARTIFICIAL INTELLIGENCE IN PREDICTIVE MAINTENANCE AND DEFECT IDENTIFICATION

The implementation of AI in various domains enhances operating efficiency, product quality, and reduces costs. The advantage of AI resides in its ability to forecast optimal maintenance intervals and identify issues promptly, hence reducing machine downtime and lowering production costs.

Similarly, artificial intelligence facilitates flaw identification, ensuring that no defects arise in a specific component, thereby eliminating the need for reprinting or post-processing. This aspect is most evident in areas such as aircraft, automotive, and particularly in medical equipment and devices, where the relative performance of various components is crucial.

TRANSITION FROM PROTOTYPING TO MASS PRODUCTION

How AI Addresses Scalability, Quality Control, and Repeatability

The evolution of Additive Manufacturing (AM) from a primarily prototyping and modeling tool to a method facilitating mass production is a significant subject concerning scalability, quality control, and repeatability, which are typically minimal in tooling and prototyping applications [22]. Nonetheless, AI enables AM to meet the requisite standards for extensive, large-scale, and ongoing production.

Scalability

A further difficulty related to additive manufacturing that determines the potential for scaling from conceptual models is scalability. Traditional additive manufacturing systems are designed for the production of prototypes or limited quantities; however, for mass production, it is essential to build systems capable of manufacturing huge volumes of identical components at reduced prices and with high precision.

AI addresses the scalability challenge by facilitating process automation and enabling real-time monitoring of the production line. Artificial Intelligence can instantaneously draw inferences from extensive datasets across various machines and adjust settings for the manufacture of different materials, geometries, or types of machines. In systems that incorporate multiple materials or print heads, artificial intelligence can function as a coordinator to manage these printers and optimize various controllable parameters, such as temperature, speed, and layer thickness, ensuring that prints produced by the different systems are consistent.

Furthermore, AI facilitates the integration of production sequencing and supply chain management, ensuring that subordinate components are built in an optimal order and that supply aligns with demand. This minimizes expensive wait times, enhances overall productivity and utilization, and enables production lines to expand and contract in a regulated manner that does not necessitate extensive human intervention.

Quality Assurance

The tendency to reduce variances is very strong in mass production, especially in the aerospace industry, automotive industry, and the manufacturing of medical devices. Advantages of using AI comprise real-time defect detection, predictive analysis, and closed-loop feedback systems that are meant to ensure production of high-quality parts.

Production issues like the misalignment of layers, inconsistency of material, or rough textures are impractical, despite the possibility of real-time monitoring of printing activity in the object using artificial intelligence vision and thermal sensors. When it detects a defect, the system can either change some of the configuration parameters on the fly (print speed or extrusion rate) or pause the process so that further waste and more working hours are not spent.

However, it cannot be argued that AI can utilise algorithms to detect certain conditions that can result in mistakes, to take preventative measures beforehand. As an example, we can predict certain imperfections in terms of quality achievement related to such factors as the presence of a high level of humidity or the wear out of the machinery used in the process.

Reproducibility

Repeatability has been found to be one of the key aspects of carrying out additive manufacturing in large-scale production. The customary techniques used in their manufacture include injection molding or CNC (computer numerical control) machining, such that production can be assured to be of high quality and with low tolerance of measurements. In order to compete in this category, AM must be able to manufacture each of the sections in such a way that the quality does not differ based on the wear and tear of the machine or the change in the environment, among other factors.

Through the ability to carry out advanced process control. AI assures that a process is carried out using the same sequences every time. Algorithms have the ability to examine a variety of features, such as material properties, AM hardware settings, and environmental factors, to make sure the system produces parts to fulfill the defined criteria. Using live data analysis of the historical prints, the AI systems are able to sense the slightest variations that stray away from the sub-optimal conditions, and hence, the AI systems can auto-adjust the parameters to suit the optimal standard.

Moreover, the ability of AI to predict changes in the functioning of machines or materials itself enhances the chances of making the most optimal choices in terms of printing cycles. For example, it can identify that a specific machine is deteriorating and subsequently adjust the printing parameters to ensure that future prints maintain quality standards.

Implementation of AI in Mass Production of Additive Manufacturing George Anesa "The Influence of Artificial Intelligence on the Progression of Additive Manufacturing Technology"

Regarding SC: AI facilitates scalability, quality assurance, and consistency, rendering additive manufacturing appropriate not merely as a prototype instrument but as a manufacturing solution. AI enables AM systems to eliminate human intervention in sophisticated decision-making by facilitating the process through software.

- Ensure quality control for several consecutive printings while maintaining the identification of flaws and their prompt rectification.
- Enhanced throughput by optimizing machine efficiency and reducing maintenance duration.
- Maintain production line needs and adapt to changes in machinery and the manufacturing environment.

These qualities enable additive manufacturing to fulfill mass production demands, hence broadening its applicability in businesses that would benefit from the fabrication of precision components or the manufacturing of short production runs that would otherwise be economically unfeasible.

ROLE OF AI IN SUPPLY CHAIN INTEGRATION AND SMART MANUFACTURING

The integration of AI in additive manufacturing also affects supply chain management and intelligent manufacturing. As additive manufacturing evolves from a prototyping technique to scale production, artificial intelligence significantly influences supply chain management, enhances flexibility, and optimizes manufacturing workflows [23]. Utilizing AI, a corporation can enhance product manufacturing processes through data-driven decision-making, automation implementation, and real-time modifications.

Artificial Intelligence in Supply Chain Integration

Substantial data indicate that this technology improves the applications of additive manufacturing and facilitates its efficient integration throughout the supply chain. Additive Manufacturing (AM) can entirely supplant the traditional supply chain paradigm, particularly in sectors that require spare parts or specialized components, owing to its capacity for on-demand and localized production.

Demand Prediction and Inventory Control

Utilizing AI-driven demand forecasting enhances the accuracy of projections regarding the demand for components and other materials by examining previous supply and sales events alongside external factors such as political instability and natural disasters. AI can estimate the demand for certain parts or materials required by manufacturers. This indicates a decrease in the creation of inferior or surplus items that fail to meet market demands, hence enhancing producers' preparedness for fluctuations in market trends.

The Supply Chain Optimization

Use of AI in supply chain management involves proper coordination of the supply chain by means of good integration of the supply chain suppliers, manufacturing unit, and the customers. Cognitive can be seen as a planner that evaluates different logistical information in order to identify the best transport relationships, lead time, and production schedule changes to meet the needs of the customer. Artificial intelligence can be applied in additive manufacturing to select the right materials, distributors, and suppliers, thus lowering the prices and speed of delivery.

Distributed supply networks and Decentralized Production

The use of AI in manufacturing permits that the process of making goods takes place at a global or regional level instead of the necessity to concentrate production capabilities in a certain place. It can be favorably used in any industry that requires high customization, like aerospace engineering, vehicle manufacturing, or medical equipment. Practically, it will be able to control the supply chain of several localized 3D printers, which will produce parts as soon as needed, eliminating transportation costs and time. This process is described as the on-demand manufacturing or the distributed manufacturing model, and this model enables the supply chain executives to become more flexible.

Artificial Intelligence in Intelligent Manufacturing

In this context, it may be asserted that AI is the fundamental facilitator of intelligent production inside additive manufacturing. Smart manufacturing is a production methodology that employs technologies such as artificial intelligence, machine learning, and the Internet of Things to establish a system capable of autonomously optimizing and improving its manufacturing processes. AI-integrated systems enhance Additive Manufacturing (AM) systems by enabling them to intelligently respond to alterations in the system or environment, detect abnormalities or outliers, and make or recommend educated decisions regarding the AM systems in real-time.

Self-Regulating Process Management

Automated control denotes that certain parameters within the process can be modified autonomously by the system, eliminating the necessity for human intervention. For example, in a metal additive manufacturing process such as Selective Laser Sintering, artificial intelligence may monitor parameters including powder dispersion, temperature, and laser power, among others. In the event of an issue such as overheating, the A.I. System can adjust the laser parameters to prevent the production of defective or substandard components.

Predictive Maintenance and System Health Surveillance

As previously mentioned, the application of AI in predictive maintenance is essential for ensuring the uninterrupted operation of production systems. This is accomplished by artificial intelligence, utilizing data collected from multiple sensors to forecast when components will be entirely degraded or necessitate repair or maintenance. This allows firms to do maintenance, proactively eliminate potential sources of operational downtime, and thereby reduce production delays.

The implementation of artificial intelligence will enable an organization to continuously monitor the condition of machinery and equipment, facilitating modifications or alerting operators to developments that may impact the production line or potentially halt it. This results in a reduction in machine failure rates, hence allowing additive manufacturing systems to maximize operational duration.

Real-Time Data Analysis and Decision-Making

Artificial intelligence directs data analysis for instantaneous decision-making in the industrial process without human intervention. It is especially beneficial for executing real-time modifications to the manufacturing process, printing profiles, standards, and the resources assigned for the entire production line. Real-time analyses enable manufacturing systems to be sensitive and adaptable to material qualities, environmental conditions, and the complexity of the components being produced, hence enhancing the versatility, precision, and efficiency of manufacturing processes.

Digital Twin Technology

It also includes the use of digital twins, definitive copies of physical production systems. The models simplify the operation of additive manufacturing machines, and they can be used to evaluate their response when subjected to certain conditions. Based on the information about actual machines and their digital twins, AI can detect challenges, bottlenecks, and other problems that can be optimized through operational processes. Physical and virtual systems will be closed so as to improve the predictive ability of the manufacturing processes and also provide decision support within the real physical system.

The Benefits of Artificial Intelligence in Supply Chain Management and Intelligent Manufacturing

Application of AI in smart manufacturing and supply chain is associated with several benefits, which include;

Increased Quality: With the use of AI, it is possible to constantly observe all the processes and implement the necessary changes that will result in an increased quality.

Lowered Lead Times: The application of inventory strategies, logistics services, and supply chain services enables the organization to have reduced overall lead times.

The efficiency in cost may also be improved by the efficient usage of raw materials and equipment, and by implementing the reductionist methods rather than using human hands.

Enhanced flexibility: The implementation of Artificial Intelligence, tailored to production demands or changes, thereby augments manufacturing flexibility.

Enhanced Product Quality: The monitoring capabilities facilitate the identification and rectification of problematic areas in real-time, hence improving the quality of the products manufactured by the machine.

Sustainability: Artificial intelligence optimizations reduce costs associated with resource scarcity, such as electricity, and mitigate environmental impacts throughout manufacturing processes.

AI possesses the transformative potential to enhance connectivity and efficiency in analytics systems inside production, fundamentally altering supply chain management and enabling more responsive, efficient, and flexible manufacturing delivery.

CHALLENGES AND LIMITATIONS

Despite the integration of AI in Additive Manufacturing (AM) and its potential to transform the AM process, numerous challenges and deficiencies remain that must be addressed to improve the application of AI in large-scale, commercial AM operations [24]. These challenges pertain to technological, operational, and organizational dimensions and are essential for the advancement of AI in additive manufacturing systems.

Data Integrity and Accessibility

One of the primary aspects to consider when adopting AI in additive manufacturing is the accessibility and quality of data. Although AM techniques necessitate substantial data for model training, the data acquired during AM operations are frequently limited, disrupted, or inconsistent.

Data Capture: Additive Manufacturing systems gather extensive process data, including temperature, material flow, and machine settings. Nonetheless, obtaining precise and current data from the connected sensors and cameras without interference or loss of frames and readings presents a hurdle. Deficient or inaccurate data adversely affects machine learning, as incorrect information undermines AI performance, resulting in suboptimal predictions and judgments.

Data Standardization: As previously discussed, the data formats and protocols for exchanging information across various AM systems and technologies lack standardization. The great diversity of machines, materials, and processes in additive manufacturing complicates the creation of a singular dataset for AI training. The integration of data from diverse sources necessitates standardization to prepare it for modeling.

Data and Security: The use of additive manufacturing for industrial applications leads to concerns regarding data privacy and security, as the majority of systems are interconnected with artificial intelligence. In recent years, securing against data breaches to mitigate content dangers while maintaining content accessibility for AI analysis has become essential.

Complexity of Integration

Implementing AI technology into existing additive manufacturing processes and systems is frequently challenging, time-consuming, and expensive. Certain previously deployed AM programs may lack the design to integrate an AI component and may not possess the requisite architecture to provide optimal AI applications.

Incompatibility with existing additive manufacturing machines, software platforms, and tools may provide challenges that necessitate upgrades or collaboration with third-party AI tools and systems. Integrating sensors, cameras, and AI algorithms into existing machinery can be expensive and must occur during periods of inactivity.

Engagement with Alternative Technologies: The integration of AI in additive manufacturing encompasses various technologies, including IoT, machine vision, big data, and cloud computing. A significant issue is ensuring the integration among them for information transfer and establishing a unified control system for their management.

Interpretability and Trust in Models

AI models, including deep learning and neural networks, are referred to as "black-box" models due to their operations being incomprehensible to humans. Although AI can generate very plausible predictions or optimize decisions, understanding the rationale behind the model's conclusions is unattainable.

Lack of Interpretability in AI Decision-Making: A significant problem of utilizing AI models is their inability to rationalize decisions, which poses a disadvantage, particularly in industries governed by laws related to compliance, safety, or quality. It indicates that for engineers and operators to accept the modifications introduced in the AM process by the AI system, they must comprehend the reasoning behind these changes to validate them.

Supplementary regulatory and certification obstacles: When a product is developed for use in sectors such as aircraft or healthcare, tight standards govern the manufacturing processes, necessitating that the firm obtain certification. This creates complications with certification requirements, since it necessitates that a corporation articulate in clear language the rationale behind decisions taken during the production process to demonstrate compliance with specific standards.

Financial and Resource Necessities

Adopting AI-based additive manufacturing systems, especially the ones that review a great amount of data and require powerful hardware to support their work, is expensive. One of the most significant challenges that SMEs face is that the high upfront costs of adopting AI can hinder their development, as they have few financial resources.

Considerable prestart-up capital is needed: The prestart-ups will be expensive, with the organizations having to invest in new sensors, good data gathering instruments, and AI growth tools. Moreover, the increased cost of highly qualified specialists, such as data scientists, engineers, and information technology professionals, increases the expenses.

Maintenance: Monitoring of Artificial Intelligence in production requires periodic inspection and correction to adapt to changing production environments, material characteristics, and manufacturing device conditions. Not only the costs of continued feeding and updating such systems, but also the costs of retraining the model, may prevent many manufacturers from using such models.

Scalability and Generalization

AI models yield significantly impressive outcomes, particularly when used in carefully regulated or planned contexts; nonetheless, they exhibit sensitivity to environmental fluctuations and emerging difficulties. In additive manufacturing, significant factors that can affect outcomes include material variances, machine performance, and environmental conditions; thus, the proliferation of AI systems for diverse and complex manufacturing applications presents a challenge.

Challenges of Generalization: A prevalent difficulty with AI models is their optimal performance being restricted to data derived from a single machine, material, or part shape. It should also be highlighted that further study on the generalization of AI across many types of AM technologies and conditions is necessary.

Restricted Efficiency in High-Volume Production: While AI can improve single-piece or low-volume additive manufacturing processes, scaling to the levels required for high-volume production poses significant challenges. Another critical aspect is that AI models and systems that excel in research settings, such as laboratories or pilot projects, may underperform in the rapid and high-volume context of mass production.

Labor Force and Competency Deficiencies

The incorporation of AI in additive manufacturing necessitates skilled personnel capable of designing, implementing, and maintaining these systems. Consequently, the proficiency for integrating AI into AM is constrained, resulting in a deficiency of demand for it.

Skill Gap: Presently, there is a deficiency of talent with the requisite skills for the implementation of additive manufacturing technologies and the utilization of artificial intelligence and machine learning. Employers may need to enhance staff education or collaborate with other organizations possessing these abilities to meet the demands for such competencies.

Humans versus Machines Cooperation: There are always human biases involved in any additive manufacturing, even in those performed by a computer. However, it needs people to perform certain tasks that require human cognition, like troubleshooting or calculations of the layer types and angles to be used. Integration of a working AI system with its human equivalent is required to improve the merits of AI in additive manufacturing.

FUTURE DIRECTIONS

Future research could explore autonomous AI-AM integration with Industry 4.0, 5G-enabled manufacturing, and biomedical applications.

The further development of Additive Manufacturing (AM) is going to make the abilities of Artificial Intelligence (AI) utilize many more possibilities and expand into previously unforeseen directions. The possible AI uses in additive manufacturing are associated with the optimisation of the process, the invention of new materials, additional customisation, and integration as a part of the Industry 4.0 system. Some potential areas are on the road to the AI revolution in additive manufacturing: autonomy, intelligent models, digital production environments, and sustainability.

Self and Self-Optimizing Systems

A self-optimizing manufacturing system is considered one of the most promising applications of artificial intelligence in additive manufacturing. Such systems would be implemented, with an automated component controlling the additive manufacturing process to optimize quality, speed, and other factors, continuously improving the final product quality, production rates, and other aspects.

The latest generation of additive manufacturing machines may be entirely autonomous with the implementation of artificial intelligence, which facilitates comprehensive control over operations such as material deposition, calibration, and inspection of the final product. They would possess the ability to select actions in a timely manner, utilizing sensor data, adjust parameters to ideal values, and rectify defects on the production line without operator participation.

Closed-Loop Systems: With the assistance of AI, a closed-loop control system is feasible, enabling machines to autonomously monitor and optimize their operational cycles iteratively. For example, AI could modify many parameters of layer deposition, the movement of the printer head, or laser settings based on real-time feedback during production.

Multi-Material and Hybrid Additive Manufacturing Utilizing Artificial Intelligence

Nevertheless, the integration of diverse materials and the simultaneous application of several processes in additive manufacturing are significantly increasing, particularly in the aerospace, automotive, and biomedical sectors, where there is a demand for geometric complexity and variety in material properties.

Hybrid and Multi-material Composites: Artificial Intelligence can be utilized to develop sophisticated material models to understand the behavior of hybrid and composite materials during processing. It may also be feasible to continuously ascertain an optimum material composition alongside machine learning algorithms to dictate the deposition procedure for the required characteristics of the final component.

Moreover, the integration of additive manufacturing with subtractive processes like turning and milling may be facilitated by the implementation of AI. AI would improve the global control mechanism between additive and subtractive processes to fabricate complex shapes of components and material composites.

Generative Design and Personalization

As advancements in AI-based generative design continue, new opportunities will rapidly emerge for mass customization and the production of lightweight structures through additive manufacturing. Automated generative design will assist engineers in creating lightweight component geometries that were previously challenging to achieve for various reasons.

Personalized Products: This domain presents an opportunity for AI to significantly assist AM in expanding by facilitating the production of mass customization. In the medical sector, it can be utilized to develop tailored prostheses or implants for individual patients. The integration of AI with additive manufacturing will enable the production of bespoke items with enhanced performance criteria as required.

Topology Optimization and Further Developments: Considering that topology optimization of materials for additive manufacturing is the prevailing method. Future advancements will incorporate more sophisticated AI algorithms that will account for several restrictions and material characteristics. This would lead to enhanced component efficiency with reduced material usage while maintaining adequate strength and performance standards.

AI-Enhanced Digital Manufacturing Ecosystems

The integration of AI into additive manufacturing will encompass not merely systems or components of production but the entirety of digital manufacturing systems. Such systems will encompass design and material acquisition, manufacture, inspection, and delivery.

Intelligent Manufacturing Networks: As additive manufacturing integrates with other manufacturing technologies, the notion of smart factory networks will encompass AI, enabling adaptive smart production networks. These factories will be able to adjust their operations in response to demand, supply, and production conditions to optimize resource utilization.

Real-Time Collaboration: It will enable designers, engineers, and operators involved in a project to work simultaneously, monitor, design, and exchange information irrespective of their geographical location. Self-service, cloud-based

AI solutions would enable manufacturers to leverage centralized resources for data and process analytics, modeling, and enhancement.

Integration with Industry 4.0

The advancement of AI within the automation of the industrial sector is closely linked to Industry 4.0, which emphasizes the digitization of this industry. AI will offer essential technological assistance for the realization of additive manufacturing systems within the framework of advancing Industry 4.0 systems.

Cyber-Physical Systems: AM systems are anticipated to evolve into cyber-physical systems. Wherein a physical asset and its computational model are synergistically interconnected, facilitating feedback control mechanisms between the physical and logical domains, contingent upon the level of connectedness. To mitigate this issue, AI will be utilized to manage the data flow, hence improving efficiency discrepancies among various manufacturing steps.

Intelligent Logistics and Supply Chain Integration: Artificial Intelligence will facilitate the seamless incorporation of Additive Manufacturing inside the supply chain *via* real-time production scheduling, automation of component delivery, and on-demand supply chain management. They will also assist in building localized or distributed manufacturing, hence reducing transportation costs for equipment.

SUSTAINABILITY AND ENVIRONMENTALLY CONSCIOUS PRACTICES

The sustainability of the organization and industry is increasingly becoming a vital component of production; AI is poised to enhance environmentally friendly and resource-efficient additive manufacturing.

Minimizing material waste: In this regard, the application of AI algorithms will result in the reduction of waste generated from part orientation, layer deposition, and other support structures. Consequently, the reduction in material consumption, which current additive manufacturing technologies aim to address, will enhance the efficiency and sustainability of the production process.

Energy Efficiency: By modifying the energy parameters related to the consumption of additive manufacturing based on environmental and production conditions. AI may enhance energy utilization efficiency. For example, AI could diminish the energy consumption of PBF machines by adjusting the laser power density upwards or the scan rate downwards, or vice versa, during the production process.

Improved Synergy Between AI and Human Operators

Despite the increasing integration of artificial intelligence in the additive manufacturing process, human operators will continue to play a significant role, particularly in high-precision applications. Future advancements are anticipated to enhance the interaction of computer-aided systems, leading to greater integration between artificial intelligence and the human brain.

AI-Enhanced Human Decision Making: This type of AI enables human operators to make decisions utilizing real-time information and recommendations from the system. For instance, AI can analyze data from sensors and recommend necessary adjustments to the process, while the ultimate choice remains with the operator.

Human Engagement with Advanced Mechatronics: Future AM systems will provide both direct and computed interfaces between the system and the user. This may include tools such as Augmented Reality (AR) or Virtual Reality (VR), allowing operators to engage directly with real-time data and effectively manage the Additive Manufacturing (AM) process.

CONCLUSION

The integration of AI in additive manufacturing represents a substantial advancement in the industry, evolving from a mere quick prototyping tool to a transformative production system. Initially utilized for enhanced design flexibility and subsequently for process optimization, quality assurance, and scalability, AI is a crucial tool for realizing the full potential of additive manufacturing.

Consequently, as the industry expands, AI will enhance additive manufacturing by improving personalization, efficiency, and sustainability in production to address diverse requirements and attain significant achievements in the manufacturing sector. Artificial intelligence in design optimization, maintenance, and process management will boost quality and production reliability while introducing novel materials and applications in multi-material printing, composite manufacturing, and hybrid manufacturing systems.

However, the integration of AI in AM is characterized by several hurdles, including data quality, system integration, model interpretability, and program costs. These obstacles, along with the scarcity of skills required for the supply and integration of human-AI partnerships, cannot be addressed only through collective efforts for a shared objective, primarily necessitating implementation by academia and industry. Nevertheless, the recent breakthroughs in AI technology are poised to resolve many of these issues, hence facilitating the development of more sophisticated AM systems that operate without human involvement.

The future holds greater promise for the integration of AI and AM. AI will be crucial in transforming paradigms for manufacturing conceptualization, design, and production by enhancing manufacturing environments for digital engineering and incorporating sustainable techniques and tests into product manufacturing processes. The incorporation of these technologies into the additive manufacturing platform will be pivotal to the Industry 4.0 Digital Twin idea, thereby facilitating the development of future smart, linked, and efficient production lines.

Ultimately, the amalgamation of AI with AM presents substantial prospects across all sectors of the global economy, facilitating innovative, cost-effective, and transformative manufacturing methodologies. AI has the potential to transform additive manufacturing from a prototype instrument to a manufacturing tool. As technologies advance, they will unveil new possibilities in manufacturing and the industrial revolution.

REFERENCES

[1] M. Manoj Prabhakar, A.K. Saravanan, A. Haiter Lenin, I. Jerin leno, K. Mayandi, and P. Sethu Ramalingam, "A short review on 3D printing methods, process parameters and materials", *Mater. Today Proc.,* vol. 45, pp. 6108-6114, 2021.
[http://dx.doi.org/10.1016/j.matpr.2020.10.225]

[2] A. Kafle, E. Luis, R. Silwal, H.M. Pan, P.L. Shrestha, and A.K. Bastola, "3D/4D printing of polymers: Fused deposition modelling (FDM), selective laser sintering (SLS), and stereolithography (SLA)", *Polymers (Basel),* vol. 13, no. 18, p. 3101, 2021.
[http://dx.doi.org/10.3390/polym13183101] [PMID: 34578002]

[3] Y. Wang, P. Zheng, T. Peng, H. Yang, and J. Zou, "Smart additive manufacturing: Current artificial intelligence-enabled methods and future perspectives", *Sci. China Technol. Sci.,* vol. 63, no. 9, pp. 1600-1611, 2020.
[http://dx.doi.org/10.1007/s11431-020-1581-2]

[4] H.Z. Hassan, and N.M. Saeed, "Advancements and applications of lightweight structures: a comprehensive review", *Discover Civil Engineering,* vol. 1, no. 1, p. 47, 2024.
[http://dx.doi.org/10.1007/s44290-024-00049-z]

[5] C.W. Hull, "The birth of 3D printing", *Res. Technol. Manag.,* vol. 58, no. 6, pp. 25-30, 2015.

[6] S.S. Crump, "Fused deposition modeling (FDM): Putting rapid back into prototyping", *Proc. 2nd Int. Conf. Rapid Prototyping,* pp. 354-357, 1991.

[7] C. R. Deckard, "*Selective laser sintering,*" U.S. Patent 4 863 538, Sep. 5, 1989.

[8] D.L. Bourell, "Perspectives on additive manufacturing", *Annu. Rev. Mater. Res.,* vol. 46, no. 1, pp. 1-18, 2016.
[http://dx.doi.org/10.1146/annurev-matsci-070115-031606]

[9] Z Corporation 3D Printing Technology: Fast, Affordable and Uniquely Versatile, *Z Corporation,* Burlington, MA, USA, White Paper, 2005. [Online]. Available: http://www.polynet.dk/rpt/zcorp3D_Printing.pdf

[10] A. Dhairyawan, *Rapid prototyping: A new beginning in product development.* Term Paper, 1997.

[11] J.P. Kruth, M.C. Leu, and T. Nakagawa, "Progress in additive manufacturing and rapid prototyping", *CIRP Ann.,* vol. 47, no. 2, pp. 525-540, 1998. [http://dx.doi.org/10.1016/S0007-8506(07)63240-5]

[12] S. Ford, and M. Despeisse, "Additive manufacturing and sustainability: an exploratory study of the advantages and challenges", *J. Clean. Prod.,* vol. 137, pp. 1573-1587, 2016. [http://dx.doi.org/10.1016/j.jclepro.2016.04.150]

[13] P. Mohan Pandey, N. Venkata Reddy, and S.G. Dhande, "Slicing procedures in layered manufacturing: a review", *Rapid Prototyping J.,* vol. 9, no. 5, pp. 274-288, 2003. [http://dx.doi.org/10.1108/13552540310502185]

[14] S.K. Everton, M. Hirsch, P. Stravroulakis, R.K. Leach, and A.T. Clare, "Review of in-situ process monitoring and in-situ metrology for metal additive manufacturing", *Mater. Des.,* vol. 95, pp. 431-445, 2016. [http://dx.doi.org/10.1016/j.matdes.2016.01.099]

[15] E. W. Reutzel, and A. R. Nassar, "A survey of sensing and control systems for machine and process monitoring of directed-energy, metal-based additive manufacturing", *Rapid Prototyping J.,* vol. 21, no. 2, pp. 159-167, 2015.

[16] Q. Fang, G. Xiong, M.C. Zhou, T.S. Tamir, C-B. Yan, H. Wu, Z. Shen, and F-Y. Wang, "Process monitoring, diagnosis and control of additive manufacturing", *IEEE Trans. Autom. Sci. Eng.,* vol. 21, no. 1, pp. 1041-1067, 2024. [http://dx.doi.org/10.1109/TASE.2022.3215258]

[17] L. Cheng, F. Tsung, and A. Wang, "A statistical transfer learning perspective for modeling shape deviations in additive manufacturing", *IEEE Robot. Autom. Lett.,* vol. 2, no. 4, pp. 1988-1993, 2017.

[18] M. Mehrpouya, A. Dehghanghadikolaei, B. Fotovvati, A. Vosooghnia, S.S. Emamian, and A. Gisario, "The potential of additive manufacturing in the smart factory industrial 4.0: A review", *Appl. Sci. (Basel),* vol. 9, no. 18, p. 3865, 2019. [http://dx.doi.org/10.3390/app9183865]

[19] L. Meng, W. Zhang, D. Quan, G. Shi, L. Tang, Y. Hou, P. Breitkopf, J. Zhu, and T. Gao, "From topology optimization design to additive manufacturing: Today's success and tomorrow's roadmap", *Arch. Comput. Methods Eng.,* vol. 27, no. 3, pp. 805-830, 2020. [http://dx.doi.org/10.1007/s11831-019-09331-1]

[20] K. H. Tan and N. Rao, "A Literature Survey on the role of Artificial intelligence in conditioning monitoring," *Authorea,* Nov. 07, 2022. Available from: https://doi.org/10.22541/au.166785465.56466533/v1

[21] G.S. Nastasi, "AI-based predictive maintenance techniques for bearings: Emerging research trends and engineering solutions", *Eng. Fail. Anal.,* vol. 156, 2024.

[22] Y. Ding, H. Lan, J. Hong, and D. Wu, "An integrated manufacturing system for rapid tooling based on rapid prototyping", *Robot. Comput.-Integr. Manuf.,* vol. 20, no. 4, pp. 281-288, 2004. [http://dx.doi.org/10.1016/j.rcim.2003.10.010]

[23] S. Sahoo, and C.Y. Lo, "Smart manufacturing powered by recent technological advancements: A review", *J. Manuf. Syst.,* vol. 64, pp. 236-250, 2022. [http://dx.doi.org/10.1016/j.jmsy.2022.06.008]

[24] D.J. Griffin, C.W. Coley, S.A. Frank, J.M. Hawkins, and K.F. Jensen, "Opportunities for machine learning and artificial intelligence to advance synthetic drug substance process development", *Org. Process Res. Dev.,* vol. 27, no. 11, pp. 1868-1879, 2023. [http://dx.doi.org/10.1021/acs.oprd.3c00229]

SUBJECT INDEX

A

B

C

Shruti Bhargava Choubey & Yogesh Shrivastava (Eds.)

D

E

F

G

O

P

Q

R

S

T

U

W

www.ingramcontent.com/pod-product-compliance
Ingram Content Group UK Ltd.
Pitfield, Milton Keynes, MK11 3LW, UK
UKHW060011051026
15591UKWH00002B/145
* 9 7 9 8 8 9 8 8 1 5 0 3 5 *